To Live Is to Resist

To Live Is to Resist

The Life of Antonio Gramsci

Jean-Yves Frétigné

Translated by Laura Marris

With a foreword by Nadia Urbinati

The University of Chicago Press

Chicago & London

The University of Chicago Press, Chicago 60637

The University of Chicago Press, Ltd., London

© 2021 by The University of Chicago

All rights reserved. No part of this book may be used or reproduced in
any manner whatsoever without written permission, except in the case of
brief quotations in critical articles and reviews. For more information, contact
the University of Chicago Press, 1427 E. 60th St., Chicago, IL 60637.

Published 2021

Printed in the United States of America

30 29 28 27 26 25 24 23 22 21   1 2 3 4 5

ISBN-13: 978-0-226-71909-2   (cloth)
ISBN-13: 978-0-226-71912-2   (e-book)
DOI: https://doi.org/10.7208/chicago/9780226719122.001.0001

Originally published in France as *Antonio Gramsci. Vivre, c'est résister* by
Jean-Yves FRÉTIGNÉ © Armand Colin, 2017, Malakoff. ARMAND COLIN
is a trademark of DUNOD Éditeur, 11, rue Paul Bert, 92240 Malakoff.

English language translation rights arranged through The French Publishers'
Agency.

Library of Congress Cataloging-in-Publication Data

Names: Frétigné, Jean-Yves, author. | Marris, Laura, 1987– translator.
Title: To live is to resist : the life of Antonio Gramsci / Jean-Yves Frétigné ;
    translated by Laura Marris ; with a foreword by Nadia Urbinati.
Other titles: Antonio Gramsci. English
Description: Chicago : The University of Chicago Press, 2021. |
    Includes bibliographical references and index.
Identifiers: LCCN 2021027260 | ISBN 9780226719092 (cloth) |
    ISBN 9780226719122 (ebook)
Subjects: LCSH: Gramsci, Antonio, 1891–1937. | Communists—Italy—Biography. |
    Philosophers—Italy—Biography. | Communism—Italy.
Classification: LCC HX289.7.G73 F7413 2021 | DDC 335.43092 [B]—dc23
LC record available at https://lccn.loc.gov/2021027260

À Isabelle, Rémi, Eugénie, Justine,
et Cordélia avec toute mon affection

Contents

Foreword

Nadia Urbinati

"To live is to resist"—Jean-Yves Frétigné could not have chosen a better title for his biography of Antonio Gramsci, which offers an excellent portrait of an extraordinary figure.

Gramsci's life cannot be understood and reconstructed without understanding and reconstructing the political history of the first half of the twentieth century. Indeed, his tragic life in many ways mirrored the failure of liberal regimes to manage their transformation into democratic societies. A victim of that failure, Gramsci sought to envision how self-government could function in a system made up of bourgeois and proletarians, thereby renouncing the aims of class abolition and socioeconomic uniformity. Gramsci understood that the Jacobin revolutionary moment had passed in the West as social differentiation and pluralism had taken solid root. His goal was to find out what kind of radical transformation a liberal order could bear without fully denying its historical heritage, the legal and political culture that predated the liberal and capitalist order. In Gramsci's historicist approach, unburdened by the determinism of the Second International socialists, there was ample room for the expression of a political will and for that will to adjust to specific contexts. In other words, a socialist transformation could not just be the mechanical outcome of social forces, but had to be devised, idealized, and envisioned by the party and the intellectuals so that social forces could become the political agents of their own transformation.

Gramsci had learned from the failed revolution in southern Italy that forcing revolutionary ideas onto a society with no attention to its historical specificity can ruin the potential for genuine change.

During Napoleon's campaign in Italy (1796), Jacobin forces in Naples revolted against the Bourbon king and proclaimed the Parthenopean Republic (January 1799), from the name of the ancient Greek colony, Parthenope, that gave birth to the city of Naples. The republic had no real domestic constituency and existed solely due to the power of the French Army; it was led by an enlightened aristocracy of men and women of culture, doctrinaire and idealist, who knew very little of the lower classes of their own country whose consent would be essential for the success of their enterprise. The process of "democratization" in southern Italy failed miserably under the attack of the Church, which mobilized the peasantry against the republic with the support of Russia, England, and Turkey. Vincenzo Cuoco's *Saggio storico sulla rivoluzione napoletana del 1799* [Historical Essay on the Neapolitan Revolution of 1799] offered a realist and critical account of that short-lived republic and indicated the cause of its failure precisely in the Jacobin abstractness of its elite of revolutionaries, totally detached from the people—right in theory, wrong in practice. Freeing people without forming their opinion meant preparing the terrain for the reactionary ideology of the restored Bourbon monarchy, whose harshly repressive politics would block the south's liberal transformation for decades to come—a preview of what the US provoked when it attempted to export democracy to Iraq in 2003.

Relying on Cuoco's theory of "passive revolution," Gramsci thought that a will that is *only* an instrumental vehicle for historical forces is mainly unpolitical, abstract, and in the end ineffectual. An heir of Italian humanism, whose main reference points resided in the early Renaissance, Gramsci envisaged a path to social transformation in politics that would rely neither on a subjective will nor on an objective social science. For him, as for Niccolò Machiavelli, political action was the most exquisite human artifact for knowing and acting, and, most important, for knowledge in the view of action. In this cultural environment, Gramsci developed his mind as a person, scholar, and political leader. Above all, he developed the most effective strategies for resisting captivity, which he suffered extensively.

Prison, the name of an extreme condition of reality that can never be fully emancipated from necessity, is the paradigm of political action as an art and science of liberation. Gramsci's entire life was essentially a representation of this paradigm. Indeed, no word can better express the nexus of Gramsci's personal and political life than "prison." His was a life of prisons, and prisons were the sources of his most seminal political categories—subalternity and hegemony.

Gramsci was a combatant, not only against Fascism, but also well before Fascism became a regime. He fought for moral and political autonomy his whole life, and he learned in his early youth that ideas are imperfect tools, which humans devise and refine in order to enlarge their capacity for self-government in an environment whose working logic is indifferent to the people's search for freedom and only indirectly subjectable to human goals. This was the lesson Gramsci learned from his beloved poet Giacomo Leopardi, and the philosopher he most admired, Machiavelli. It is not rhetorical to say that Gramsci's was a life of prisons, and that the search for autonomy was his permanent exercise for coping with and resisting them.

The first prison he found himself locked in was that of his own body and, more generally, of daily life in his native Sardinia. Other prisons would follow that had an impact on his will and action more directly: his experience as a poor university student in Turin, his life in the Fascist jail, and his gradual isolation from the communist movement, both international and Italian. The prison analogy fits the challenges he both was forced to and also chose to face, according to a mix of necessity and autonomy that marked his philosophy and conception of politics. Gramsci himself interpreted those various prisons as tests tempering his will, forcing him to inquire into reality in the proper ("effectual," Machiavelli would say) way. He embraced the Stoic maxim that one ought to decide what one ought to do based on knowledge of what one *can* do. This was the guideline he followed for transforming the conditions of captivity he suffered into practical opportunities for liberation—thinking effectually or politically was to him an exercise of intelligent resistance against a reality that did not admit of free choice but only of determinate choices. As we learn from Gramsci's writings and letters, knowing what it is possible for one to do entails understanding the conditions, social and otherwise, in which one is situated, so that what one does is necessarily what one *has* to do. Well before he encountered Marx's work, Gramsci made his prisons representatives of Spinozian philosophy, and we can situate his conception of social change within this immanent framework. One might stretch Gramsci's theory of a determinate will to action to include Machiavelli's famous dialectic of *fortuna* and *virtù*, which knows of no chance and no arbitrary free will either.

Gramsci's adopted maxim, "pessimism of reason, optimism of the will," makes this philosophy an effective answer to both idealist voluntarism and discomforting fatalism, the two lines of thought that guided (respectively) Italian maximalist socialists and Second International positivist socialists. Gramsci's life experience, personal and political, was akin to a training school of practical philosophy, one aimed at extracting the energies and passions capable of moving the will by posing the "right" questions and giving oneself the "right" objectives within an environment that was otherwise deaf to one's desires. This was the kind of normative realism, in a sense both radical and revolutionary, that informed his politics.

As we learn from this book, Gramsci was born on the periphery of a periphery. At the end of the nineteenth century, Italy was a periphery of Europe, and Gramsci was born in Sardinia, which was itself a periphery of Italy—geographically, politically, culturally, and economically. Sardinian people lived mostly as peasants and shepherds, with the exception of some working in the civil service and in the mining industry, which was perhaps the most important link to the industrial system of the continent. The state's most visible presence on the island consisted of a coercive and administrative force made up of a police apparatus and bureaucracy. Hierarchical power relations and subjection to the police dominated all social relations, and certainly agrarian work relations, which had for centuries been structurally based on domination by the landowners over semiservile peasants and their families.

As the fourth son of Francesco Gramsci, a clerk in the registrar's office at Ghilarza, Gramsci was brought up in poverty and hardship. As a child, he was constantly ill and withdrawn, and his anguish was compounded by physical deformity. Ghilarza was one of the first of his several prisons: he recalled in a letter to his wife the class structure of his village and the consequences he suffered as a brilliant child who was too poor to attend good schools. The psychological impact of this subjection, consolidated over several generations, translated into humiliation and fatalism, factors that paralyzed emancipatory action—individual and collective.

Gramsci's second prison was his body. He was born hunchbacked and almost a dwarf. When he was a child, his parents used to hang him several hours a day from the ceiling of their dark kitchen in order to stretch the limbs of his body. In the end, he remained as he was—a bright mind and stubborn will enchained in a body that was like a prison to him, keeping him from doing what a young person would desire and love to do. He had to fight all his life to monitor and control his body, to adjust his will to it, but in such a way as to govern it and not be fatally subjected to it. His body trained him to learn what he could and could not ask from his environment, how to resist a necessity imposed on his mind and will by a reality he did not create. The combination of necessity and freedom was akin to the first chapter in his self-made moral textbook. Domination by natural-seeming class subjection and domination by physical handicap—these were the prisons he consciously detected beginning in his youth. Necessity conditioned but did not negate his will: this was the first Spinozian lesson he derived from his early youth.

It was Gramsci's life on the periphery, though, that provided the starting point for his political and social thought: he gave that periphery a name, "the south." The south—southern Italy, which became for him the paradigm for all the "souths" in the world—implied not only a condition of subjection and domination but also an experience of resistance and a longing for liberation. The south was not made of industrial economy, structured classes, and a proletariat endowed with a consciousness of its emancipatory potentials. "Subalternity"—a term he coined—and subjection could be transformed into the conditions for emancipation by southern Italians and other people in other parts of the country and the world, yet on a different ground from Marx's class conflicts. The south was doubly subjected to domination according to Gramsci: it was dominated from inside (by landowners and wealthy masters, but also patriarchal relations within family) and from outside (by the north or the most industrial and advanced regions). The psychological structure of that domination was instrumental in its perpetuation, as it made people feel and think as if their station came about by pure chance and was, in this sense, "fatal" and "natural." Subaltern people were trained to acquiesce to their own domination so as to be deprived of their own will and autonomy of the mind, their desires and language. No rebellion but functional adaptation for survival: against that "natural" social life Gramsci wanted to understand what forces could be awakened and organized through politics. Knowing the social roots of what was deemed a natural condition was the starting point for understanding the political means that would allow for genuine change. Gramsci searched for an effective mode of emancipation from within these conditions of subalternity, and he began with popular culture and language.

Rebellion would not be enough. People in the south were constantly in rebellion and yet never emancipated, namely, capable of self-government. Emancipation would require the construction of an alternative set of political practices and social relations. Gramsci was convinced that since their subaltern position consisted in a social order that shaped their will and stripped it of its own goals, people in the south had to start the process of liberation from within—more or less as he did with himself in the attempt to emancipate his mind from his deformed body. Because his deformity was not something that an act of the will could change, it was useless to try to stretch his limbs. In fact, it was self-defeating. "Useless" rebellion would engender a sense of impotence and ultimately a fatalistic and depressing acquiescence to unwanted conditions. Likewise, it was useless for subaltern southerners to think that stretching their chains by boycotting and rebelling would be enough to break them. For Gramsci, subaltern people needed to understand the structural conditions of their domination; they had to denature them and could do so by understanding that their conditions persisted unchanged because of their own unintended contribution to them—their condition was thus not natural but fully artificial or social. Gramsci thought that this discovery would make transformation seem possible. And, on the contrary, he was convinced that instinctual and sudden rebellions against their masters and the police ended up only augmenting repression. cf. E. H.'s "primitive rebellion"

Gramsci's task in starting from the periphery (from any periphery) was understanding how to change a subjected society by changing the ethical and cultural habits of its subjected people. He thought that the solution to the problem of the stubborn fatalism of subalternity would derive from the understanding of the logic and strategy of domination from *within* and from seeing how principles of freedom and justice could be derived from popular culture, rather than imposed on dominated people from outside or above. This was the lesson he learned from Vincenzo Cuoco's historical analysis of the above-mentioned failure of the 1799 Neapolitan revolution. Imposing principles from outside that were just in theory had the effect of promoting a counterrevolution and justifying a popular reaction against those principles, prizing traditional values and a system of domination against liberal and republican freedom. cf. MAGA

Gramsci began reflecting on this logic of domination and failed emancipation when he moved to Turin as a university student. At the beginning of the twentieth century, Turin was the most industrial city of the country, the home of Fiat, the car industry. It attracted workers from many other cities and regions. Given the remarkable cultural pluralism of Italian regional traditions, history, and dialects, one might say that Turin was a melting pot of immigrants, in which any purpose of association and unity could come only from politics. Indeed, Turin was the place where Gramsci encountered politics. It was the home of organized unions, political parties (both right and left), cultural circles, journals, and magazines, and it was frequently the site of street demonstrations and clashes with the police or opposing political groups. Turin was a tumultuous and vibrant city, an experiment in political conflict and participatory democracy.

Gramsci moved to Turin to become a student in the university's department of literature and philosophy. Attracted by the study of linguistic diversity of Italian regions, he wanted to study dialects, folklore, and popular culture, topics that we would today group under the discipline of cultural anthropology but instead represented to him paths toward social and political transformation. Gramsci was not particularly happy with his life as a student, which was solitary and disconnected from the social life of the city. He felt like an immigrant, inhabiting a peripheral condition that resembled a sort of prison and against which he reacted through the art of politics, by becoming a political leader.

He lived in a tiny room in a building situated in one of the prettiest squares of Turin, Piazza Carlina. He would gather workers there from the automobile industry and hold frank and open dialogues with them on specific political and theoretical issues, such as liberty in relation to the working conditions in the factory and democracy in the workplace. Gramsci's Socratic method was meant to draw out ideas and judgments from the workers that university students generally derived from books. Gramsci wanted to form a worker aristocracy of teachers and leaders whose goal would be to lead their comrades to understand for themselves the reasons for their subjection and the potential for their emancipation. He was convinced that formation of a workers' aristocracy was the road toward emancipation: not imposing the truth, but leading people to recognize and grasp it within themselves.

Today, we would call this fostering autonomy. Gramsci defined the process as "hegemony": liberation from domination required people to change their ways of reading their conditions and thus also their system of values. "Hegemony" is originally a Greek word; it appeared in its current usage in Thucydides's account of the Peloponnesian War. Thucydides employed the term to describe the relation of domination imposed by Athens on its allies, city-states that were in theory equal partners. Today, this word is used mostly in international relations to denote relations of domination between a strong state and states that are in its orbit, although not occupied or conquered. "Hegemon" is the name of a dominator, and hegemony is a politics that aims at acquiring subjection through consensus and adhesion, without the use of explicit and direct coercive practices. Hegemony is the conquering of consented support by subjects that are at that point no longer passively dominated. As we read in Pericles's funeral oration, dramatized by Thucydides, the Athenians wanted to be the school of Hellas, not their imposing master. The United States was a hegemon in Western Europe for some decades after World War II, when its leadership was obtained not by mere use of force (although it did not abstain from toppling unfriendly governments), but by becoming a cultural "north star" and the inspiration for the political ideas and mentality of its subjects. For a country to be under the influence of the US meant that its people listened to American music, watched American television programs and movies, and used words and terms, and now also communication technology, that were part of the American popular culture and language.

Was there a hegemonic culture in Gramsci's time? Yes, there was: Gramsci had no doubt that his compatriots lived, like other Europeans and Americans, under the liberal and capitalist hegemony, and he thought this was detectable by paying attention to the language and the values people used and referred to in their ordinary life—what they read, what opinions they held, and even how they expressed their sentiments and emotions in their own private experience.

How to make people act as if they were their own masters—this is the goal of hegemony, which thus requires understanding the mechanisms of consensus and cooperation. A full-fledged liberal society relies upon this mechanism of obedience. Can this logic be adapted to a different social project, one that is based on the values that gratify not one class of people only but the entire community?

Gramsci used the word "hegemony" as the name of a project of emancipation through political culture, by liberating the subalterns' minds. We would need to have a true consciousness of ourselves—of the position we occupy in society but also of what means we have to react to the world in which we live—in order to understand what we can accomplish. According to Gramsci, subaltern people need to give themselves realistic expectations inspired by normative ideals. They should not give themselves goals that are unreachable or simply utopian, yet they should also not give themselves goals that are imposed on them by the ruling class and its pervading values.

This was the hard task of emancipation from subalternity. It was hard because people needed to give themselves appropriate objectives, so that they could achieve them with their own forces. Knowing what we are is essential to knowing what we can be and do: based on this immanent philosophy, Gramsci concluded that violent or direct revolution was out of place in the West, and hegemony would do the revolutionary job of subverting the system of domination. Writing in the age of a mass war, the First World War, he famously distinguished between war of maneuver and war of position. Thus, as a student, he was interested in understanding the ways human beings absorb meaning, form linguistic habits, communicate, and influence each other. Popular culture, dialect, mores, and folklore are, Gramsci thought, the repository of what socially situated human beings can do, of the meaning and symbols they use to make sense of what they do, and of how they relate to others. So the potential for emancipation—or its opposite, domination and the fatal acceptance of subjection—resides in popular culture.

For this reason, Gramsci strongly criticized "traditional intellectuals" or those sophisticated people who claimed the superiority of their status and culture based on their knowledge and competence.

These traditional intellectuals think of themselves as a privileged group and write for socially superior groups; they are not concerned with how culture can reflect and change the world, because they have no interest in changing people's mentality and in effect don't know anything about ordinary people's lives, their ways of thinking, loving, praying, and feeling. They don't want to. According to Gramsci, "traditional intellectuals" would obstruct or block emancipation, since they want to preserve distinct high and low cultures rather than create a broad (national) popular culture. Thus, Gramsci's challenge was that of reunifying intellectuals with ordinary men and women, high culture with popular culture. His project of hegemony depended on the achievement of this cooperation; it was an ideological enterprise.

In the eighteenth century, the Italian philosopher Giambattista Vico wrote in his *New Science* words that would have a profound impact on Gramsci, who quoted Vico to explain what he had in mind with respect to the true role of the intellectual. The kind of intellectual for whom Vico and Gramsci advocated corresponded to a new Solon, the chief of the democratic revolution in ancient Athens who led his fellow citizens to political freedom by teaching them that they were equal to the aristocrats. Solon was, as Vico wrote in the *New Science*, "the party leader of the plebeians." He wanted to change the political system of Athens from aristocratic to democratic, and to do so he first had to free the poor from their debts. Poor Athenians had become slaves to their creditors. Debts made them and their children enslaved, generation after generation. Solon, a poet, tried to give them the right words for their emancipation: he was a new kind of intellectual or, in Vico's words (which Gramsci adopted in his early essay "Socialism and Culture"), a "sage of vulgar wisdom" (*saggezza volgare*), speaking in ordinary rather than abstruse language ("vulgar" derives from the Latin *vulgus* which means "common people").

In ordinary language, wisdom entails superiority to the vulgar. But Solon's "vulgar wisdom" was able to overcome the power of the nobles and their domineering attitude. To retain their superior power in politics, the nobles wanted the people to believe that the nobles were of "divine origin" or superior, and that the "vulgar" people, the plebeians, should worship them and accept the condition of being dominated and acquiesce. Solon challenged the people to reflect and to realize that they were of the same human nature as the nobles and should, therefore, be made equal with them in civil and political rights. Gramsci's model of an intellectual was precisely that of the "sage of vulgar wisdom," one who could dialogue with subaltern people and make them understand that they need not accept their life status and subjection. Subversion of an existing sociopolitical system rather than mere rebellion renders the meaning of "hegemony" well.

This is paramount. People must *believe* that they are equal to their supposed superiors, because only then can they give themselves objectives to fight for. The role of ideology emerges here with particular force. The outcome of Solon's politics was truly revolutionary, because it was not simply a change in the rulers: transition to democracy transformed not only the subordinated class, but the entire Athenian society. The transformation was not simply in institutions—it was, more importantly, in that consciousness of being of the same flock, the same character, the same nature. This *belief* is what makes institutions meaningful, strong, and lasting, albeit imperfect and in permanent need of maintenance. *Believing* means a change in cultural attitude—this is what ideology does.

This is why Gramsci's philosophy of hegemony starts from the periphery. The periphery becomes a crucible of potential for new forms of life projects and new forms of emancipation, in and through a form of popular culture that is never fully permeated by so-called high culture. A life of difficulty, destitution, and solitude can be, like Gramsci's prisons (real and figurative), an opportunity for a kind of freedom that does not rely on abstract models imposed from the outside. Revolutions generally begin with an avant-garde, with just a few people. Not because those people are superior, but because they are perhaps more tenacious or because they are simply in a condition of deeper despair—the reasons are manifold. No liberation starts suddenly and for all people of the world together. The liberation process is gradual, diverse, and spoken in the language of ordinary people; it does not have a linear trajectory. Gramsci would say that people have to organize in such a way that their ideas can coalesce, meet, and cooperate. This is, for him, the meaning of operating politically, of creating an ideological web of shared meanings and purposes. Gramsci thought that organization was crucial, as social change needs to rely both on the conscious will and on determined action, on intellectual and cultural analysis and on political strategic activity. Organization requires first forming political parties: the party was, in Gramsci's mind, similar to Machiavelli's Prince—the party was like a "collective Prince" with the goal of emancipating institutions and society from principles that, like "foreign" agents, imposed their will to power on the people.

However, organization should not be confused with homogeneity, the notion that everyone should be uniform in thoughts and beliefs. Although he used Leninist language and had a strong view of the role of a vanguard leadership and strategy, and although he conceived of a hegemonic society as a "totality," Gramsci did not aim at homogeneity, nor did he think self-government entailed a docile community or a single-minded populace. He never repressed the spirit of rebelliousness that had accompanied him since his youth. Gramsci thought that spontaneous rebelliousness was a blessing, like a spark that can light a bonfire. He had felt as a child the instinct of rebellion, and it saved him from a life of passive acquiescence to misery. In Giuseppe Fiori's recounting, Gramsci asked, "What was it that stopped me from turning into a stuffed shirt?" answering, "The instinct of rebellion." He felt the same way when he lived in Sardinia, when he was fighting for the organization of the workers in Turin, and when he was in jail. His was a life of prisons, but never one of acceptance; he never fatalistically accepted his condition, and the spirit of rebellion was the blessing that saved him.

When he was sent to prison in 1926, he knew he would spend the rest of his life there. During those ten long years he lived in a small cell, and every day he forced himself to do the same things: Gramsci imposed a routine onto his life. Every morning, he woke up at the same time, exercised at the same time, fed a bird that visited him every day at the same time. He tried to eat at the same time, read at the same time. He created his own prison in order to resist the prison imposed from outside. He understood that, through this daily fight, he could avoid accepting his condition and capitulating to necessity. This is a lesson of rebellion conducted in an extreme condition of captivity.

For Gramsci, however, liberty did not stop at rebellion. Rebellion is the sparking sign that reveals something there, but it is not the end of the story of emancipation. Indeed, the process of emancipation has no end: it starts the moment one realizes that one is in the wrong place, doing the wrong thing, being treated the wrong way. This awareness helps the person realize that she can resist the impositions forced on her by those who tell her that this is her life and that she must adapt. Domination is victorious when the dominated person becomes the guardian of her obligations. Yet inside of that supposed prison she can also create, by herself, her own resistance. Just as Gramsci did when he depicted freedom not simply as a sparkling moment of rebellion, but as a condition that would last through time and especially in hard times.

Bologna, August 2020

PART I

From Sardinian Gramsci to National Gramsci

(1891–1915)

< 1 >

In Sardinia

(1891–1911)

A Poor Child from the Mezzogiorno

Gramsci: the root of this name most likely comes from the princi-
pality of Gramsh in southeastern Albania. After the death of the
Albanian hero Gjergj Kastrioti (1405–68), many of this region's inhabitants who were resistant to the Ottoman occupation and to Is-
lamization chose to go into exile, often putting down roots in southern Italy. These people, called Arbëreshë, formed communities that
were abundant in Campania, in Sicily, and particularly in Calabria.
In the province of Cosenza, at the foot of Mount Sparviere, prime
habitat for its namesake sparrow hawk, the little village of Plataci
welcomed Antonio Gramsci's ancestors, whose traces began there in
the eighteenth century.

This family, Italianized over several generations, threw in its lot
with the Kingdom of the Two Sicilies, where most men fought in the
army of the Bourbons. As a police colonel in the Neapolitan Army,
Gennaro Gramsci, Antonio's grandfather, kept his rank after Italian
unification, finishing out his career with a regiment of Carabinieri.
He moved to Gaeta with his wife, Teresa Gonzalez, the daughter of a
renowned lawyer, whose ancestors had arrived in Naples when southern Italy belonged to Spain. They had five children. Their daughter
married a rich landowner in Gaeta, and their four sons all pursued

high-ranking administrative careers. The oldest became an official at the Finance Ministry, the second oldest was an inspector of railroads, and the middle son became a career officer whose job would eventually include commanding the artillery depot at Ozieri in the province of Sassari. The youngest, Francesco, affectionately nicknamed Cicillo, started down the same path as his brothers, but the death of his father in 1873, coupled with his hope for independence, led him to abandon his legal studies at the University of Naples and take a civil-service exam, after which he was named the comptroller of the Ghilarza registry office in Sardinia.

In this little hamlet of three thousand people, between Macomer and Oristano, in the heart of a region known for the beauty of its cork oaks, Francesco met Giuseppina Marcias, the daughter of Antonio Marcias and Potenziana Corrias, a widow who already had two daughters from her first marriage. At seven years old, little Peppina (this was Giuseppina's nickname all her life) lost her mother, and five years later, her father also died, leaving his children under the guardianship of a relative who was a pharmacist in Oristano. The latter quickly exhausted the meager inheritance entrusted to him and was so mortified by his own conduct that he lost his mind. In her beautiful book *Le donne di Casa Gramsci*, Mimma Paulesu Quercioli, one of Antonio's nieces, tells us that to cure this man's fits of madness, they shaved his head in order to draw a cross on it, which was later traced with a knife to let out the "bad blood," a procedure that provoked the pharmacist to exclaim, amid his howls of pain: "I ruined the little Marcias children!"

Peppina certainly had the hardest lot, since unlike her two half sisters, Margherita and Grazia, she had no share of the inheritance that came from their mother's first marriage. And her brother Giorgio had emigrated to Algeria, establishing a stable situation for himself there. All the same, Peppina's poverty was eased by the solidarity and ties that existed in her small Sardinian community. Ties that allowed Grazia, her half sister, seven years older, to continue to help Peppina, thanks to inherited income that allowed her to live in relative comfort. Small, hunchbacked, and very religious, Grazia made sure that

Nino (as Antonio was called) was baptized by the Vicar General, Sebastiano Frau, rather than by the priest in Ales. Grazia never married, but became, along with Giuseppina, the bedrock of the family, the godmother or *nonna*, as they would say. Her home on the Corso Umberto in Ghilarza became the Gramscis' central household. Her death in 1912 was the end of an era for this family, which lost its guardian angel at the same moment Antonio left his native island for the University of Turin.

But back to 1883. Cicillo, who was twenty-three at the time, and Peppina, who was twenty-one (and born the same year as the Kingdom of Italy), fell in love and decided to get married, against the wishes of Teresa Gonzalez, who thought the couple was poorly matched. From a strictly social point of view, her opinion was generally unfounded. Though Francesco's family was undeniably more comfortable than Giuseppina's when it came to finances, this difference was less evident from their cultural backgrounds. Francesco had completed his advanced schooling, but Giuseppina had gone to school and could read and write Italian perfectly well. At the time, only one in thirty Sardinian women could read. Of the 2,200 residents that made up the town of Ghilarza, fewer than two hundred were literate. What's more, Peppina had a taste for books and for learning in general. Our two young lovers had much in common, since in the little Sardinian towns where they were likely to live (Sorgono, Ales, Ghilarza), the only social differences that counted were those between the elites and the peasants. Their level of education and Francesco's professional situation put them in the first category. The assertion that Antonio Gramsci was the son of poor peasants is therefore a pious legend that has hung on since it was first articulated by Palmiro Togliatti (1893–1964), the leader of the PCI, in the first commemorative article he devoted to Antonio Gramsci in 1937, the year Gramsci died. Gramsci's parents were elites, but small-time elites, at the mercy of fate.

And fate came knocking on August 9, 1898, the day Francesco was arrested by the *carabinieri*. In his capacity as a parliamentary elector and a relatively influential personality at the local level, he was no stranger to the political life of his province. At the end of the nineteenth century, the number of electors was limited, particularly in the Mezzogiorno, since the criteria for voting were based on census and population data that excluded poor people in general and anyone who didn't know how to read or write. This meant that in the 1897 legislative elections, only 2,120,000 Italians had the right to vote (roughly 6 percent), and only 550,000 of them were from the southern peninsula and the islands. If you combine this relatively low figure with the fact that the rates of participation among registered voters amounted to 60 percent on average, it is easy to deduce that the vast majority of the candidates resorted to clientelist practices, since the electoral competition was more about setting personalities against each other than about a confrontation between political platforms detailed by the parties, which were still in their earliest infancy. The PSI, the premiere political party of modern Italy, was created in 1893. By conviction or calculation, Francesco Gramsci decided to support Enrico Carboni Boy (1851–1925), an eminent law professor who had the misfortune in the 1897 elections of opposing Francesco Cocco Ortu (1840–1928) in his fief of Isili, which included the village of Ghilarza. As someone who had completed several appointments as Minister of Justice and Agriculture, Francesco Cocco Ortu was so important in Sardinian politics between the end of the nineteenth century and World War I that certain historians of Sardinia call the first fifteen years of the twentieth century the Coccortiana era.[1] Of course he won the election. After he was elected, Ortu quickly used his vast network of influence to create trouble for people who had supported his opponent. While Francesco was away on a visit to his brother who commanded the artillery station in Ozieri, an official examiner opened an investigation into his work. It revealed a few irregularities that easily could have been covered up or, at the very least, corrected, but they resulted in further investigation. Francesco was suspended from his job, and while he waited for the conclusions of the investigation, he withdrew to the house on Corso Umberto with his loved ones. After his arrest on August 9, 1898, he was imprisoned in Oristano, then in Cagliari. Francesco Gramsci stood trial on October 27, 1900. Even though the verdict revealed the triviality of the missing sums, Antonio's father was condemned to five years, eight months, and twenty-two days in prison, the minimum penalty for this type of offense in the penal code. He served his sentence at Gaeta.

At thirty-seven, Giuseppina found herself alone, with no income and seven children in her care, the eldest of whom, Gennaro, was only fourteen, while the youngest, Carlo, was still in diapers, not to mention Antonio, whose health was extremely fragile.[2]

Giuseppina became Mother Courage. With her Singer sewing machine, she devoted herself to several clothing endeavors, showing a real talent for fashioning men's shirts. To this source of income, she added what she could make from doing laundry for the veterinarian and the lieutenant in charge of Ghilarza's *carabinieri*. But these hard-won lire, earned through long hours of work, weren't enough to properly feed and clothe her seven children. Their meals invariably consisted of soup, beans, and cheese. It was a rare day when they might eat pasta, meat, or fish, and fruit was even more scarce. All too often, the children had only one meal a day. With the promise of a five-cent coin slipped under their pillow, the youngest family members, Mario, Teresina, and Carlo, would agree to skip the evening meal, sung to sleep by their mother's lullabies, dreaming of the good things they would buy with the five-cent piece. They never found the coin when they woke, since their mother always had to retrieve it. Conscious of their poverty and undeniably supportive of each other, they accepted the injustice done to them in favor of the group's survival. It is no wonder that these children would often imagine a treasure guarded by a gigantic fly, a story that had been told to them by a beggar woman. Out of charity, Giuseppina had given her a meal and a place to sleep as she passed through Ghilarza on her way to the abbey of San Palmiero to participate in the largest religious festival in that part of Sardinia.

If the Gramsci family managed to keep their spirits up during this period of extreme hardship, it was because of how well the family members supported each other. The girls helped their mother with her arduous daily tasks. The boys too. Young Antonio carried the laundry his mother had ironed to the next village. During one of these treks, he had a horrifying encounter that would mark him forever. But we'll come back to that. Antonio, too, had his share of sacrifices, since he had to interrupt his studies between the ages of eleven and thirteen to work beside his older brother Gennaro in the offices of Ghilarza's land surveyor, lifting enormous ledgers for ten hours straight, six days out of seven and Sunday mornings too, for a salary of nine lire, the equivalent of a kilo of bread a day. But how precious that kilo of bread was to the survival of his family! Another thing that helped the Gramscis was the fact that they lived in a little southern town where a harsh social structure was somewhat softened by a system of habits and customs that favored helping others, a system Antonio would miss when he moved to Cagliari.

Francesco's release, a few days before Easter in 1904, didn't immediately improve the household situation, since he was stigmatized as a former prisoner and had trouble finding a job. All the same, he managed to find modest employment at the tax office, and so he regained a certain elite status. As his reintegration into the reading groups of the little town shows, his fellow citizens were aware that he'd been the victim of an unmistakably biased court. As for Gennaro, he had finished his military service and was working as a foreman in an icecream factory in Cagliari. And Peppina had just come into a small inheritance. The horizon was finally clearing, but only so it could quickly darken once again. Wanting to get out of his situation as a poorly paid and unimportant employee, Francesco decided to invest the little nest egg his wife had inherited in raising chickens for fresh eggs and poultry to sell. Though it looked good on paper, the affair turned into a fiasco. Knowing nothing about poultry, Francesco was easy prey for unscrupulous sellers. Half his flock died and then the other half was stolen or sold for very low prices. To the Gramsci family, this failed enterprise became proof that their common sense was lacking. For a long time, Antonio blamed his father.

Suffering in Mind and Body

Until he was eighteen months old, Antonio (who was born in Ales on January 22, 1891 and baptized there seven days later) was in excellent health despite the food shortages he often had to endure. Then a blister appeared on his spine. The village doctor was baffled by the pathology and development of this puzzling symptom. Massages and compresses with iodine tincture did nothing to slow the tumor's growth. Francesco then decided to take his son to a doctor in Oristano, who sent him to a specialist in Gaeta. The latter prescribed new treatments based on a cruel gymnastic program to straighten the spine. Antonio's father had a sort of corset made for his son, which was dangled from a rafter in the ceiling. Poor little Antonio had to hang in it for hours. In vain. The child became more and more hunchbacked and continued to suffer great pain. At four, he collapsed in convulsions and had a terrible hemorrhage. He was diagnosed with epilepsy. For three days, convulsive episodes followed one after another, while the clueless doctor shook his head. In desperation, his mother, convinced her son was dying, made him a little white shroud and ordered a small coffin in the same color. Out of superstition, this coffin was kept in a corner of the house until 1912, the year Antonio left for Turin. The child survived. The family cried that it was a miracle and thanked *nonna* Grazia, who had brought him holy water. Giuseppina was convinced that Nino's physical ailments were from a bad fall he'd taken after being dropped by a young woman from the village who sometimes came to help with the household tasks. The girl denied it, and until her death she continued to deny that Antonio had slipped from her arms. It wasn't until much later, in 1933, after he collapsed in his cell and was examined by a doctor named Arcangeli, that the correct diagnosis was finally established. Antonio Gramsci hadn't been dropped as a baby and his convulsions weren't caused by epilepsy. He suffered from a rare form of spinal tuberculosis called Pott's disease. Subsequent analysis carried out through photographs validates this hypothesis, which Peppina would never learn, since she died on December 30, 1932.

Giacomo Leopardi (1798–1837), a great hunchback who was only four and a half feet tall, suffered his whole life from the same tuberculosis of the bone. Like the poet and philosopher from Recanati, Gramsci felt that his body was a prison and that only the force of his mind could free him. Though he was lucky to have a milder form of Pott's disease and was spared the ophthalmologic, digestive, and respiratory complications that were Leopardi's fate, Gramsci was never fortunate enough to possess an incredible library, in which the author of the *Canti* read so much he went blind.

As a small child gifted with a sharp intelligence, Antonio was pampered by his family so he could overcome his illness and continue his studies. Nino was allowed special treatment—every morning, he had an egg beaten with sugar and marsala wine, a small piece of white bread, and coffee, while his brothers and sisters had to content themselves with a slice of black bread and a sad, barley-based brew. Because of his illness, Antonio didn't start at the Sorgono school, which was run by nuns, until the autumn of 1898, when he was already seven and a half. Though his grades were excellent and he was always first in his class, he was forced to interrupt his studies for two years to help his brother in the surveyor's office. He studied just as hard on his own, sacrificing hours of sleep so he could learn the basics of Latin. His mother always managed to support him, patiently reading over her child's work. Later on, from prison, he remembered these late afternoons when Peppina would set aside her dressmaking tasks in order to correct one of his misspellings or tell him a story. For Gramsci, a staunch atheist, these moments of joy and goodness were "the only true paradise that exists,"[3] since these moments represented a harmonious transmission of knowledge between generations.

In 1905, through their sacrifices, Francesco and Giuseppina managed to send their Nino to secondary school about eleven miles from Ghilarza in Santu Lussurgiu, a small town several hours of travel away that might as well have been another world. He became a lodger at a local farm. This small village school, not run by the state, had five classes and only three instructors, none of whom had earned the official degree required to teach. Antonio very quickly realized how poor their lessons were—when they bothered to give them, that is! At the age of seventeen, in Oristano, he took the required exams to complete his secondary studies. Though he failed his first attempt with catastrophic grades, he passed on the second try, allowing him to enter, in fall 1908, a high school in Cagliari named for Giovanni Maria Dettori—a Sardinian intellectual born in 1773 who had been chair of moral theology in Turin before he was ousted. Though Antonio was a very serious student, his insufficient training soon became evident through his bad grades in math and science as well as through his ways of speaking and writing, which were still marked by Sardinian dialect. Ironically nicknamed "the physicist with a taste for Greek" by his physics teacher after handing in a fantastical homework assignment inspired by ancient theories, Antonio abandoned the scientific studies he had once planned to pursue. His childhood hobby of meticulously reproducing drawings, coupled with his talent for constructing little paper animals and model ships, which he would trade for a basket of apples or pears, reflected this penchant for engineering sciences. But with too many gaps in math, he chose to study Greek, turning to mainly philosophical and literary studies. He had the good fortune to meet Raffa Garzia (1877–1938), a teacher worthy of the name, who taught him to write well in Italian and initiated him into the local political scene. Finally encouraged, Antonio soon got rid of the Sardinian "flaws" in his Italian. He quickly proved to be such a brilliant student that a number of his compositions were read in class. Raffa Garzia, who directed *L'Unione Sarda*, one of the three principal daily newspapers on the island, was proud of the progress his student had made and got Gramsci his first press card on July 21, 1910. Five days later, under the initials G. A., Antonio published his first article, a twenty-five-line report on the elections in Ghilarza. In this piece, rich with the irony that would become one of the characteristics of his journalistic style, Gramsci tells his readers that the massive influx of *carabinieri* to suppress any outbursts caused the inhabitants of the little town to barricade themselves at home, forcing municipal authorities to go door to door to convince the electors to do their civic duty.

Despite this positive experience with journalistic apprenticeship, the years he spent first in Santu Lussurgiu and then in Cagliari, where he shared a room with his older brother Gennaro, mostly passed under the sign of sadness, bitterness, and poverty. With his small size, not quite five feet, Antonicheddu—"little Antonio," in Sardinian dialect—had neither time nor freedom to experience the youthful bohemia of the Sardinian capital. Even though the whole family would chip in to help him with money, including his older brother, who would set aside part of his wages to give him a few lire, and even though he worked to pay for his education by giving private lessons and sometimes taking on accounting work, Antonio's correspondence shows that he lived in extreme penury. His letters between 1908 and 1910, primarily addressed to his father, openly express Gramsci's frustration, while those to his mother are, on the contrary, reassuring. His need for money is virtually the sole, obsessive theme of these missives:

> That a father shouldn't think about his son when the son is in the city and has no means other than what comes from the family, to my way of thinking is a bit too much. I'm not in a village where you know enough people so that you can go on for a bit without having to pay straight away; here you're forced to pay on the spot, if not you don't survive even for a day. Great heavens, there are some things that have to be thought about![4]

Antonio was so perpetually late in paying his school fees that his high school principal threatened to prevent him from taking his end-of-year exams. In another letter, he declared that the state of his clothes was "threadbare and shiny,"[5] so much so that he didn't dare to participate in the field trip organized by his teachers, and he even skipped class for several days. All the same, his grades were satisfactory, even good, and in September 1911, he won a scholarship intended for deserving Sardinian high school students, allowing them to attend university in Turin.

Dressed in a new suit that his father had ordered for him from a tailor in Cagliari who succeeded in masking Antonio's deformity, and favored with an annual scholarship of 840 lire, a sum that seemed to all the Gramscis living in Ghilarza plenty to live well on—though they would quickly be disabused of this—Antonio left Sardinia for the "great and terrible world." How did he see his native island at the moment he prepared to leave it?

"Throw the Continentals Overboard!"

In 1926, shortly before he was arrested by the Fascist police, Gramsci wrote an important essay on the southern question (see chapter 6). Later, in his *Prison Notebooks*, he returned several times to the social, economic, and cultural conditions of the populations living in Italy's Mezzogiorno, and particularly in Sardinia. It's not the scrutiny of a seasoned and committed intellectual that interests us here, but rather the sentiments of this twenty-year-old young man at the moment he was leaving the region in which he'd always lived. He wasn't like the writer Gavino Ledda (born in 1938), the author of the bestselling *Padre Padrone: L'educazione di un pastore* [Padre Padrone: The Education of a Shepherd; 1975].[6] In the film version that the Taviani brothers took to the big screen, the protagonist urinates on the ground of his native land from the truck bringing him to the ship that will carry him to the continent. But Gramsci loved his native land. All the same, he thought it resembled a prison, with walls made of superstition and primitivism. Two of his memories support this reality—one provokes a smile, but the other is terrifying.

Aunt Grazia, whose generosity was so important to Giuseppina and her children, would say that the strength of her virtue came from a certain Donna Bisodia, who feared God and scrupulously respected the commandments. This Donna Bisodia, whose existence *nonna* Grazia firmly believed in, was nothing but an invention from the *Pater Noster* prayer, which has the words *Da nobis hodie* (Give us this day), a phrase twisted by her pronunciation into the made-up name "Donna Bisodia." The scene he witnessed at eight years old provides a much more traumatic example, and indeed, it haunted him all his life, returning to him in a 1933 letter. Here is the scene in his words:

> I used to know a family in a village near mine, father, mother and children; they were small landowners and they ran a tavern,

they were energetic people, especially the woman. I knew (I had heard) that besides the acknowledged and known children this woman had another son whom one never saw, about whom people spoke with sighs as a great misfortune for the mother, an idiot, a monster. . . . One Sunday morning, around ten o'clock, I was sent to this woman's house; I was supposed to deliver some crochet work and pick up some money. I found her as she was closing the door to her house, dressed in her best to go to attend the solemn mass; she carried a satchel under her arm. On seeing me, she hesitated a little, then she made up her mind. She asked me to accompany her to a certain place and said that when we returned, she would accept the work and hand me the money. She led me outside the village, into a small market garden cluttered with debris and chunks of broken plaster; in one corner, there was a shed used as a pig sty. . . . She opened the door and we immediately heard a bestial mewling; her son was in there, an eighteen-year-old youth with a very strong physique who could not stand up and so was always seated and hopped toward the door on his behind, as far as he was allowed by the chain that clasped his waist and was attached to a ring sunk into the wall. He was covered in filth, only his eyes blinked reddish, like those of a nocturnal animal. The mother poured the contents of her satchel into a stone trough, some chicken feed mixed with leftovers from the house's table and she filled another trough with water, then she locked up and we left.[7]

This terrible scene proved, in Gramsci's eyes, that the primitive character of the island's inhabitants was not synonymous with a sort of innocence, lost as it might have been, but rather meant that the inhabitants belonged to a forgotten era of world history in which reason was absent, or at least played an insufficient role. Why did this situation exist, and what could he do to improve it?

Answering these two tightly linked questions would have an impact on the early stages of Gramsci's cultural politics. All existing critical work about his oeuvre has acknowledged the role his native island played in his intellectual and political development. In a memorial speech given at Cagliari on April 27, 1947, ten years to the day after Antonio Gramsci's death, Palmiro Togliatti presented him as

> a great son of Sardinia. . . . From this island, Gramsci got his first impetus, the initial vocation of his life; what he had seen, observed, suffered in Sardinia became the fundamental element for elaborating his political thought, the decisive drive of his practical activism, leading the labor class and the Italian workers. Antonio Gramsci was a Sardinian, a Sardinian by birth, a Sardinian because he loved his land with an immense love; he loved it as it is, with its simple beauty, with its rough parts, its sufferings, the sufferings of the Sardinian people that he experienced, understood, and shared. The images of this land accompanied our unforgettable comrade until the last day of his life: tender childhood and schoolboy memories that we rediscover today in his letters, expressed in simple words, very nobly, far from all literary affectation and rhetorical artifice.[8]

Although these few remarks by the leader of the PCI (Partito Comunista Italiano, the Italian Communist Party) are themselves not exempt from the last two defects he mentions—we must understand that Togliatti's is a commemorative speech in which emotion plays a legitimate part—he rightly bears witness to Sardinia's influence on both the political and the emotional development of Antonio Gramsci. Togliatti would prove to be particularly sensitive to the emotional aspects of Gramsci's development, having lived in Sardinia himself when he was a high schooler in Sassari. The two young men were able to share impressions as Sardinians—one by birth, and the other by adoption—in exile at the University of Turin, where they met for the first time and became friends.

For Gramsci, Sardinia is the land of childhood. An arid, austere, and majestic countryside that the Sardinian writer and 1926 Nobel Prize winner Grazia Deledda (1871–1936) describes in her most famous novel, *Reeds in the Wind*, as a land whose beauty and purity contrast with the harshness of elemental human passions in the relations between men and women, fathers and sons. Isn't that what the young Sansoneddu ("little Samson," the affectionate nickname Antonio's playmates gave him because his hair was so abundant) felt with an absent father who, as he learned from these playmates, was absent because he had been imprisoned?

Antonio took long walks in the arid countryside around Ghilarza, and after reading *Robinson Crusoe*, he was never without a few seeds and sulfur matches in his pockets. Sardinia was his mysterious island, where he learned to notice the animals in the fields: the hare, the fox, the snake, the sparrow hawk, and his favorite, the hedgehog. For several months, he kept a whole family of hedgehogs in the Gramscis' garden. He recounted these experiences as charming little stories and fables in the letters he wrote to his two young sons, Delio and Giuliano. His political activism and then his imprisonment kept him from knowing his first son for more than a few months. He would never meet his second son (see chapter 5).

When he was very young, he realized his mysterious island was also a land where poverty reigned while wealth was concentrated within a narrow elite. In response, he liked to recall the story of the wandering monk and the bean, which went as follows. A beggar monk who owned only a bean entrusted it to a peasant. But the peasant's rooster devoured the legume, and to compensate for this loss, the monk left with the rooster. Our monk then entrusted the rooster to the good care of another woman so that he could go to church and perform his prayers, but the rooster was eaten by her pig. So the monk left with the pig, and in making his way like this, became master of the country, reigning over a mass of poor people whose meager belongings he had stolen. That was the image of Sardinia in the mind of this young child: a world that was divided between those who had to earn their bread to study and those who could frequent the school benches without having to lift heavy registers for the surveyor, such as the sons of Ghilarza's butcher, pharmacist, and cloth trader.

To the adolescent living in Cagliari, the image of Sardinia was that of his squalid, damp room, which he had no way of heating. As a middle schooler, and then as a high school student, Antonio began to formulate an answer to the questions raised above: why this poverty, and what could remedy it?

Though the Gramsci family respected the authority of the Kingdom, and Antonio's father carefully kept a portrait of King Victor Emmanuel III (1869–1947), a gift from his officer brother, in the best room of the house, Francesco and Giuseppina were not indifferent to the popular Risorgimento tradition embodied by the luminaries Giuseppe Mazzini (1805–72) and Giuseppe Garibaldi (1807–82). All the same, Francesco refused to let Socialist ideas into his house. However, he couldn't prevent his eldest son Gennaro from being won over by new ideas from the cohort of young European officials sent to Sardinia to revise the old land survey maps. Gennaro, who eventually became treasurer of the Cagliari Chamber of Labor, encouraged Antonio to frequent Socialist circles in that city.

By the end of the first decade of the twentieth century, the two brothers were pro-Socialist. They read *Avanti!*, the daily of the PSI (Partito Socialista Italiano, the Italian Socialist Party). Francesco hated this paper and would tear up any issues he could get his hands on. Antonio, with the help of his sister Teresina and the complicity of the postman, had to devise a strategy to steal the mail before it was brought to his father. However, it would be wrong to imagine that Socialist ideology had already given young Antonio a precise intellectual diagnosis of the problems of Sardinian poverty, since he experienced this poverty during his childhood and adolescence. Moreover, Socialism in Sardinia was still in its embryonic phase.

Before he left for Turin, Antonio Gramsci knew almost nothing about Karl Marx. As a high schooler, he was unaware of problems in political economy, preferring to throw himself into idealist philosophy. From age fifteen on, he made a habit of carefully saving newspaper clippings, filing the articles by Gaetano Salvemini and Benedetto Croce with extra special care. Even if this passion for the historian from Bari and the Neapolitan philosopher was shared by young people his age, it must have especially resonated with this young Sardinian, since his enthusiasm signified a desire to "deprovincialize"[9] himself and join with broader national and European culture as a result.

If liberating themselves from the habits and customs of Sardinia meant acknowledging the archaic nature of the mental and social structures of its people, it also paradoxically meant defending the island through a form of regionalist protest whose goals can be summed up in one uncompromising phrase: "Throw the Continentals Overboard!"

Characterized by a subtle mixture of local patriotism, resentment toward continental Europeans, and the will to free themselves from the central government, the Sardist movement sought to mobilize the discontented around demands for Sardinian autonomy. This political movement hoped to compete with special legislation enacted in July 1907 to develop a vast policy for irrigation and the general modernization of Sardinian economic structures. Similar policies had been attempted, but this legislation extended the experiment for the first time to the entire region, thanks to the support of Francesco Cocco Ortu, a faithful collaborator and close supporter of the principal Italian political leader of the moment, Giovanni Giolitti (1842–1928), who served several terms as prime minister during the first fifteen years of the twentieth century. If the majority of the liberal Sardinian political class agreed with this policy, certain intellectuals—particularly those with a democratic sensibility—denounced this maneuver by the central government for failing to confront the real problems in their native land. These problems were exemplified by two tragic episodes: the miners' rebellion in Buggerru, Iglesiente, in September 1904, and the popular riots across several parts of the island in May 1906. Here and elsewhere in Italy, the authorities responded with "the lead cure": four deaths in 1904, and fourteen in 1906, not to mention hundreds of wounded. The theory that islanders were being exploited by the state was reinforced by the way mainland officers sent to repress demonstrating workers and bandits behaved—as if they were colonial troops attempting to "civilize the natives." In this vein, Colonel Giulio Bechi (1870–1917), a young officer from Florence, compared the 1899 operations he oversaw against a particularly active group of bandits in the Nuoro region to a big-game hunt—like the wild boar hunts that were a Sardinian specialty. Though the book Bechi wrote under the pseudonym "Miles" wasn't entirely devoid of irony and his account of the Sardinian people conveyed both scorn and fascination, the book was very poorly received by the island's intelligentsia. After reading it carefully and recognizing the complex nature of its underlying ideology, Gramsci didn't hesitate to roundly condemn *Caccia Grossa. Scene e figure del banditismo sardo* [Big Game: Scenes and Characters of Sardinian Banditry]. Gramsci penned this unequivocal judgment: "The book instead shows how Bechi took the opportunity to make mediocre literature out of serious, tragic events in our national history."[10] Bechi had in fact participated in the events of May 14 and 15, 1899, in which not only men, but whole families—including old people, women, and children—were unjustly arrested. Though it aroused indignation from some quarters of public opinion and resulted in a legal fiasco, this behavior led to a conception of Sardinians as subhuman, belonging to an inferior race. And hadn't Bechi himself displayed a white man's paternalism toward Sardinian women, whose virtues he praised? This racist attitude had a whole literature behind it that was once considered erudite, in the tradition of Cesare Lombroso's arguments in forensic anthropology, describing this island as if it were inhabited by an archaic population, marked by atavism and corruption, still incapable of adapting to the modern standards of life in a nation-state. Until World War I, such a hermeneutic managed to erase the positive image that Giuseppe Manno (1786–1868) gave his native island in *Storia della Sardegna* [History of Sardinia, 1825–27], in which this politician and senior Piedmont official wrote a detailed tribute to Sardinian language and culture in response to a German travelogue full of clichés about the island and its inhabitants. Though his message—that Sardinia resembled not an isolated territory so much as a place that had always progressed through its permanent contact with other civilizations—was taken up by the Sardinian intelligentsia, eager to defend the autonomy of the island within the Italian realm, this argument suffered a sudden eclipse in Italy when positivist conceptions took hold.

Seventeen years before the "Sardinian Saint Bartholomew's Day," the members of the French Anthropological Society gathered on April 20, 1882, in their rooms on the rue de l'École de médicine, for a session devoted to the anthropology and ethnology of the Sardinian peoples. The challenge, no less, was to find out whether or not these peoples were intelligent. Most of those assembled didn't think so. This idea of a childish people, made up of lazy shepherds suffering from various physical and moral flaws, took hold in Italian thought after the publication of "Paesaggi e profili di Sardegna" [Landscapes and Profiles from Sardinia, 1869], an essay by the famous Doctor Paolo Mantegazza (1831–1910), who had participated in the first of three rigorous investigations by the Italian government to take stock of the social and economic situation in Sardinia. But it was mainly at the end of the 1880s, after the rupture in trading between France and Italy, which created a rise in banditry, that the island was thought of as a place where delinquency reigned. "Sardinia is a desert of criminality with a few oases of honesty," was the definition the young anthropologist Alfredo Niceforo (1876–1960) proposed in his 1897 best-seller *La delinquenza in Sardegna* [Delinquency in Sardinia], which made him famous at the tender age of twenty-one. In this book, which was the result of a field study commissioned by the Italian Geographical Society and the Roman Society of Anthropology, Niceforo "proved" that a special race existed in the center of Sardinia—the area in which banditry was most rampant—a race characterized by a tendency toward delinquent behavior that spread throughout the rest of Sardinia, turning the island into a hotbed of criminality. The book was prefaced by Enrico Ferri (1856–1929), the co-founder, with Lombroso, of the Italian School of Criminology, and very wisely criticized by Napoleone Colajanni (1847–1921), an internationally renowned sociologist and the principal opponent of Lombrosian[11] theories. *La delinquenza in Sardegna* put forward an argument that dovetailed perfectly with the spirit of scientific discourse in an era marked by racist ideas that swayed a large portion of the public, even among Socialist workers and intellectuals (at the time, Lombroso, Ferri, and Niceforo all shared the Socialist sensibility).

But in the heart of the PSI, the Sardinian miners' strike in Buggerru made people aware of the limits of these racist interpretations surrounding the southern question and of the modernity of the social question in the Mezzogiorno (the southern half of Italy). This realization had begun ten years earlier with the League of Sicilian Workers—a vast movement to occupy lands, with reverberations large enough to influence discussion among the European Socialists gathered in London for the Fourth Congress of the Second International. The oppression of the Buggerru miners was the occasion for the first general workers' strike in Italy, called out of solidarity on September 16, 1904. Though this strike was carried out by the decisive action of the radical unionist wing of the PSI, led at the time by Arturo Labriola (not to be confused with philosopher Antonio Labriola),[12] it created a shift in strategy for the PSI leadership, which had been more inclined to favor an alliance with the southern bourgeois progressives than to make connections with the manual laborers from the Mezzogiorno. These *braccianti* (field hands) were thought to be too backward to have a political or unionist bent. Chaotically, a link began to form between the Sardinian question and the social question that intrigued young Antonio, who recognized himself in this ideology that was both Sardist and populist—populist because it was influenced by socialism, and Sardist because it was militantly in favor of Sardinians living out their own destiny without depending on others. This first political stance, which he would abandon as he dialectically surpassed it, nonetheless played a decisive role in his political education and his development as an activist. Before Piero Gobetti (1901–26), who was one of the most brilliant young intellectuals of his generation and knew Antonio in Turin, died in Paris at twenty-six of injuries sustained from Fascist beatings, he deftly summarized the relationship between Gramsci and his native island. To Gobetti, this relationship was strained by Antonio's desire to "replace the diseased inheritance of Sardinian anachronism with a chill, inexorable drive toward the modernity of the citizen."[13]

As he left his native island to become a student in Turin, Antonio Gramsci expanded his consciousness to become an Italian citizen and a militant Socialist.

< **2** >

A Poor Student in Turin
(1911–1915)

"I Never Laughed, Just as I Never Wept"

After spending the summer of 1911 on vacation with his family in Ghilarza, the young university student spent a few weeks at the home of one of his uncles in Oristano, where he gave private lessons to one of his younger cousins. With a sharp knack for pedagogy, he translated Latin and Greek phrases into Sardinian dialect for him. But this tutoring took much of the time and energy he wished to spend preparing for the written exams in the competition to win a Carlo Alberto scholarship. This scholarship was for poor Sardinian students who had received a high average on their baccalaureate exams (as Antonio had when he scored an 8/10 on each portion and even a 9/10 in Italian composition), so they could study at the University of Turin.

Then he began his journey north by boat. After stopping for a night in Pisa, where he saw his uncles, in particular Zaccaria Delogu, an army captain about to leave to fight in Libya, Antonio finished his train trip in a second-class carriage—a luxury afforded by the university, which had paid part of the ticket in advance. Toward the middle of October, he arrived in the Piedmont capital to take the exams that began on October 18. On October 27, 1911, he climbed the hundred steps to the University of Turin's majestic entrance. He and

Palmiro Togliatti, who was also aiming for the scholarship, congratulated themselves on passing the written parts of the exams and wondered what questions the professors of philosophy and Italian literature would ask them during the orals. The two young men who would soon be called to a common destiny had not yet become friends. Later, during a lecture at the University of Turin in 1949, Togliatti would reflect back on these two youngsters worried about passing their exams. Of the twenty-six eligible students hoping to enter the faculty of law or of letters, fifteen would be eliminated during the orals. Of the seven who triumphed during the entrance exams, Palmiro came in second, and Antonio was fifth.

On November 16, 1911, the two students registered at the faculty of letters. Palmiro quickly switched to studying law, and, exactly four years later, under the supervision of Luigi Einaudi (1874–1961), he obtained the *Laurea*, his master's degree, a precious item that in Italy grants the enviable title of *Dottore*, a title that Antonio was forced to relinquish. This sacrifice was not due to any intellectual failings or a dissipated way of life, and least of all to a lack of interest in his studies. Far from it. Gramsci was a student whose seriousness and intelligence were recognized by all his professors and fellow students. He lived an ascetic life and had an all-consuming passion for his studies, spending most of his time reading more and more, diligently frequenting the university library, and when his physical energy didn't desert him, taking all the classes he could possibly attend, going so far as to attend private lessons with his philosophy professor, Annibale Pastore. The reason for his failure had a name: material and physical poverty.

The letters Gramsci wrote between the autumn of 1911 and the end of 1913 support this idea, and they are undoubtedly among the saddest he ever wrote. There was not a single letter in which he did not beg his parents to send him money. Of the hundred lire he had in his pocket when he left Ghilarza, forty-five had been spent on the trip, and the fifty-five that remained were not enough to pay for his lodging and his food in Turin, especially since the exams lasted for two weeks. In a bitter, angry tone, Antonio narrates, item by item, how he tried to survive—for it was truly a matter of survival. The provision of a monthly scholarship of seventy lire—and not eighty as he constantly reminded his parents—wasn't enough to live decently in the Piedmont capital. Unaccustomed to the hectic life of a big city, he wanted to live in a neighborhood close to the university so he wouldn't have to take a long route on foot through a city he considered sad, cold, and dangerous, with its many tramways and vehicles. After he entered the school on November 16, 1911, he lived first on Corso Firenze on the banks of the River Dora, which joined the Po in Turin. Then he lived for a time on Via San Massimo, a few steps from the room inhabited by Angelo Tasca (1892–1960), one of his few friends before he became a companion in political struggle. Finally, on the advice of the concierge at the school, he rented a little room on the top floor of an apartment building at number 15 on the Piazza Carlina, still not far from the university. This was a small room, more like a garret, so lacking in comforts or heat that he had to pace back and forth in order to avoid freezing during the long Turin winter. Though this place, through the irony of history, has become the site of a luxury hotel, it was nonetheless his home for nine whole years. In a letter to his father dated December 20, 1911, he writes, with biting irony, that he wishes his whole family a happy end-of-year holidays, and he reminds them of their distinct luck in not having to walk continuously so their feet don't freeze! This grim attic room was nonetheless a shelter for the young student who had spent months searching for a rent he could afford with his meager resources. For a time, he had seriously worried that he wouldn't be able to pay his daily living expenses in Turin and that he would be hauled back to Sardinia for not paying his debts, cuffs on his wrists, between two policemen. One can imagine the fright such a thought would provoke for his father, who had experienced the humiliation of arrest. Antonio knew it, and this carefully formulated threat in a letter was also a way of conveying his exasperation with his loved ones and their inability, particularly on his father's part, to understand the dramatic character of his material situation and, as a consequence, his physical and mental state. He strongly criticized his father for his negligence: the latter did, in fact, twice mistake the address when he wrote to Antonio to send him only some of the documents he desperately needed to complete his registration at the university and get his scholarship. But the most serious criticism he leveled at his family was their lack of generosity, their ungratefulness, their lack of love that translated into the absence of financial support—Gramsci irregularly received twenty lire each month. Though it is true that those twenty lire, combined with the seventy that made up his scholarship, amounted to a sum that was largely insufficient for his food, clothing, and suitable lodging in Turin (his rent went up to twenty-five lire a month), his criticisms of his family were unfair. Since his return from prison, his father had only a menial job at the land registry in Ghilarza, with an undeniably low salary. Moreover, his brother Gennaro, who worked at an ice-cream factory in Cagliari, regularly set aside part of his wages to send to his brother. Antonio knew it, but nonetheless condemned this "negligence and this indifference" in his family, who found themselves branded with an interesting phrase, which he would later use in the political sphere: "their Mohammedan equanimity."[1]

He ate little and badly. A plate of pasta and an egg cost almost a lira, so he mostly contented himself with a little *panino* that was less than an ounce, costing him five cents, and a glass of milk that cost twice as much, as he scrupulously noted. The only *trattoria* he frequented, to dine there frugally for two lire, had clients who were so poor that the glasses, forks, and knives were chained to the table so that they wouldn't be stolen! His clothes were poorly suited to a northern city and so worn and threadbare that he had to save at least five lire a month to maintain them. For months on end, he asked for a real coat, though we don't know if he ever got one. With his long, disorderly hair, his badly groomed beard, his thin coat, and the long scarf his mother had knitted for him, Gramsci was not a bohemian student frequenting "rowdy cafés with sparkling lights" but instead, like Jules Vallès's hero, he belonged to the category of "those who, nourished on Greek and Latin, have died of starvation."[2] Gramsci was a student living in poverty, looking sadly into the windows of bookstores displaying works he couldn't afford, even after skimping on everything and saving the few cents he made from giving private lessons to students his professors had introduced him to—when these professors weren't lending him a few lire so he could eat. Sometimes, as if to defy this poverty, he would buy a supply of books. Already in his time in middle school in Santu Lussurgiu, his mother had scolded him for selling the cheeses she gave him to improve his ordinary meals so that he could buy himself books to satisfy his insatiable appetite for reading.

From this somber picture, it is easy to imagine that his physical condition, already weakened by sickness, deteriorated rapidly toward collapse.

A determined worker who marshaled all his efforts to acquire a solid academic mastery, Gramsci successfully passed his first exams. Returning from his vacation in Sardinia, where he took baths at Bosa Marina to ease his pain, he performed brilliantly on three exams: geography, on November 4, 1912, with the highest grade (30/30), then Greek and Latin grammar (27/30) on the 11th of the same month, and especially on the linguistics exam, where he received, once again, the highest grade and the congratulations of the jury. However, though he continued to attend class and take, along with Togliatti, the economics lessons given by the law faculty under Luigi Einaudi, he didn't sit for a single exam during the 1912–13 academic year. Nonetheless, his scholarship stipulated three requirements: going to class, passing all exams, and earning at least a 27/30. From winter 1912 on, Gramsci fell gravely ill. He suffered from daily bouts of dizziness and experienced frequent mood swings and increasing memory loss, to the point that he sometimes had difficulty speaking without searching for words or stammering. He found himself caught in a vicious cycle: to keep his scholarship, he had to redouble his efforts, but in redoubling his efforts, he sank deeper and deeper into physical and mental despair. At first, his scholarship was only suspended for four months before being restored to him after a doctor named Allasia diagnosed him with "periodic nervous crises which prevent him from pursuing his studies with proper alacrity."[3]

Through many difficulties, Antonio succeeded in passing four exams in 1914 and again in the spring of 1915. Though he hadn't given up on the idea of earning his degree in linguistics or in philosophy, his two favorite subjects, he never seriously returned to his university studies after autumn of that year. However, in 1917 his literature professor, Umberto Cosmo (1868–1944), invited him to write an essay about Machiavelli, and in 1918 the philologist Gustavo Balsamo-Crivelli (1891–1929) entrusted him with the publication of an anthology of writings by Alessandro Manzoni about the Italian language—two works that never saw the light of day but that make for interesting developments in the *Prison Notebooks*. Antonio's fundamentally fragile health, his nutritional deficiencies, his suffering linked to a climate that was particularly harsh for a southerner (winter in Cagliari was like spring in Turin), and, finally, his dogged engagement with his studies got the better of not only his body but also his mind, as Doctor Allasia's grim diagnosis shows. Further evidence comes from Antonio's extremely dramatic recurring dream of a giant spider sucking his brains, a dream that haunted him for a long time, and that he evokes in a March 1924 letter to his companion Julia. Could this nightmare have been a result of the opium cure he received for a time to calm his exhausted nerves?

This physical and psychological fragility was the cause as much as the consequence of his great solitude. With the exception of a few conversations with his professors and fellow students, Gramsci's life was solitary. Becoming increasingly cut off from his family through both geographical distance and a spiritual barrier (he replied less and to his mother's letters), he didn't participate in any form of political or recreational socializing in the student world. His only pleasures were smoking and reading. Despite the respect his teachers had for him, especially his literature professor, Umberto Cosmo, who helped him find private lessons, Antonio didn't enter into any bourgeois circles in Turin and still knew nothing of the world of workers. His conversations were intellectual in nature. His only distractions came from his mind, with the exception of a few solitary walks under the arcades of that great northern city, most often in the neighborhood of bookstores or bird-sellers, where he looked sadly at the canaries and goldfinches in their cages. Like these fragile, exiled creatures, whose delicate and profound sadness was so magnificently captured by the Dutch painter Carel Fabritius, Antonio felt like a prisoner, exiled within himself. He turned inward, withdrawing into himself, becoming a tower with neither doors nor windows. "I have lived everything for the mind and nothing for the heart. . . . Inside and out, I have become more like a bear than a man. It has been for me as if other people did not exist and I was a wolf in its lair. . . . Perhaps in two years [1911–13] I never laughed, just as I never wept,"[4] he wrote to his sister Grazietta in 1916, offering pertinent analysis of his psychological situation.

Antonio nonetheless succeeded in overcoming this crisis by turning to political engagement, and more generally, toward life itself. This first took place through a change in his assessment of Turin, which he started to see as the future city of the proletariat, to use the title of a unique special issue that he edited in February 1917 for the Socialist Youth Federation in Turin (see chapter 3). He no longer saw it as the old capital of the Savoy monarchy, with its topiaried streets, its vast barracks, and its palaces whose elegance was both sober and severe. All the same, for the rest of his life, he was grateful to this bourgeois Turin because of the serious, rigorous university education he received—a culture that had known how to transform him, in his own words, from a "triple or quadruple provincial"[5] into an Italian citizen of the world.

At the School of Liberalism

The young Sardinian who arrived at the University of Turin didn't study as a means to an interesting job and a good social situation but rather as a way of forging his own personality and understanding his rights and duties as an Italian at the beginning of the twentieth century. Though Antonio certainly never claimed any affinity with Mazzini, his approach to existence mirrored the one put forward by the great champion of Italian unification, whose best-selling political treatise was titled *On the Duties of Man* (*Dei doveri dell'uomo*). His professors at the University of Turin knew how to respond to this expectation, especially the four who played a decisive role in this aspect of his education.

The first was Matteo Bartoli. Born in Istria in 1873, Bartoli earned his doctorate at the University of Vienna. When Gramsci first took his courses before becoming his favorite student, Bartoli had been teaching in Turin for four years. He specialized in glottology, a term created by Graziadio Isaia Ascoli (1829–1907) to indicate a form of linguistics that was no longer reduced to the comparative history of classical dead languages, focusing instead on Sanskrit, Persian, or even the language of the Goths. Ascoli advanced the major idea that languages were rooted in history and that they therefore had to be studied from a diachronic perspective. Understanding the roots of a language through the layers of time and the variety of places counted much more than studying morphology of the palate and the vocal organ, as the neogrammarians thought. Ascoli's importance owed much to his journal *Archivio Glottologico Italiano*, which he founded in 1872. This journal allowed Italy on the one hand to catch up after being late to the scientific field of modern linguistics, and on the other hand to contest the idea attributed to Manzoni and even more to his so-called disciples that Italian should be constructed artificially with Florentine as its base, neglecting the numerous dialects. From his first essay, published in German in 1906 on the neo-Latin dialects that had since become extinct in Dalmatia, Bartoli laid the foundations of his method on establishing the chronology of linguistic facts in order to determine the different linguistic areas, an undertaking that resulted in the publication, just after his death in 1946, of a linguistic atlas of Italy, whose scientific authority is praised to this day. Since he was very much interested in Sardinian dialect, about which he had published an essay at the turn of the century, he was aware of the fact that Antonio Gramsci was one of his rare students at the University of Turin who spoke it fluently. And so Matteo Bartoli frequently asked him for information about a word or an expression. In order to answer as seriously as possible, Antonio asked his family, and particularly his younger sister Teresina, about the vocabulary used in Ghilarza to indicate this or that activity, tool, or custom. As he put it in a letter to his mother:

> Please ask Teresina to put together a list for me of all the terms she can think of for bread making, from when bread is taken to the miller's to when it is eaten (and if she can she should also include the names of all the parts of the "mola" [millstone]) and then list the words referring to *weaving*; if she wants she should send me her drawing of a Sardinian loom, done as well as she can, just so as to have an idea, and the name of the part next to the part itself; the list that I wrote down during the vacation is very incomplete; she should do this as thoroughly as she possibly can, then I'll see if there's something missing and write to her.[6]

This letter reflects Gramsci's rigor and his desire to satisfy his professor to the best of his abilities. His excellent grades in linguistics and the importance of this relationship explain why Gramsci didn't definitively renounce earning his doctorate in this discipline until 1918. This was much to the chagrin of Bartoli, who had great hopes of Antonio's becoming his disciple and "the archangel destined to put to definitive rout the neogrammarians,"[7] as Gramsci wrote, entertainingly, to his sister-in-law in March 1927. Though he broke off his studies, he never forgot the importance of linguistics. He dealt with this theme in several of his articles written during World War I. In this same vein, he set out a polemic in the columns of *Avanti!*, the main daily of the PSI, against Esperanto, a language that was put forward for a time by his comrades in arms, whom he accused of acting like Manzoni, who claimed to artificially model the Italian language on what was spoken in Tuscany. Recent essays have made the case that he was very attentive to the debate around this discipline in the Soviet Union, a debate whose principles and implications would have been difficult for him to understand without his solid background in this material.[8] Beyond his academic interest, this marked preference for glottology can be explained by the spirit of investigation and precision this exacting philological discipline required. On an even deeper level, his adherence to Bartoli's methodology confirmed and clarified a vision of the world defined by a historicist approach to knowledge.

This last reason allows us to understand the role Umberto Cosmo played in Antonio's spiritual development. A disciple of Francesco De Sanctis (1817–83) and, like him, influenced by Romanticism and his reading of Hegel, Umberto Cosmo made his mentor's idea his own, by which ideals, feelings, political conceptions, but also science itself can only be understood through their relation to life, to reality. Born in 1868, Cosmo studied at Padua, then taught in different high schools throughout the Italian peninsula, including the Dettori high school in Cagliari. In 1911, he became a professor of literature in the faculty of letters at the University of Turin. While Bartoli and Cosmo shared the same intellectual reasoning founded on the historical method, which Cosmo applied to his interpretation of Dante, becoming an eminent specialist, the relationship between Antonio and Umberto Cosmo was even closer and friendlier. Aware of the extreme pecuniary distress of his student, Cosmo arranged for him to give private lessons to young pupils and didn't hesitate to loan him money personally at times. What's more, the two men shared the same Socialist ideal: Cosmo was a member of the PSI from 1895 on, and he played an important role in organizing the public sector employees, who were not allowed to unionize at the time, into one association. The collaboration between the two men reached its height in 1914 when they campaigned together for Gaetano Salvemini (1873–1957) in the by-elections organized in the fourth electoral college of Turin (see below). Much more up-to-date about the Sardinian reality than many Italians in the north, the professor joined his student in his fight to abolish the protectionist regime, put in place in 1887, whose first victim was the Italian south. Even though, once he became a Communist, Gramsci harshly critiqued his former professor, who was tending toward a moderate form of liberalism, the two men always maintained a profound respect for one another, which was apparent in a letter Gramsci wrote to his sister-in-law Tatiana on

February 23, 1931. The arrival of Cosmo's book *La Vita di Dante* in his cell reminded him of the amusing and moving memories of their reunion in Berlin in May 1922. While Cosmo was carrying out the duties of secretary to the Italian ambassador in Germany, Gramsci, passing through the German capital on his way to Moscow, decided to pay him a visit:

> When in 1922 the solemn doorman of the embassy deigned to telephone Cosmo in his diplomatic office that a certain Gramsci wished to be received, his ceremonial soul was thunderstruck when Cosmo descended the stairs at a run and flung himself at me, inundating me with tears and beard, saying again and again: "You understand why! You understand why!" He was in the throes of an emotion that astounded me, but made me understand how much distress I must have caused him in 1920 and what his friendship for his students meant to him.[9]

Gramsci was not as close with Annibale Pastore—not to be confused with Ottavio Pastore (1887–1965), one of the major Socialist journalists—or with Luigi Einaudi as he was with Matteo Bartoli and even more with Umberto Cosmo. All the same, their influence on him bears mentioning. Annibale Pastore (1868–1956) was considered one of the most prominent Italian epistemologists of the twentieth century. In a 1951 article in *Avanti!* he described Gramsci as one of his disciples, recalling that he had given him private lessons. Cross-referencing several sources, we can confirm only that Gramsci took his courses during the 1914–15 academic year, courses devoted to the notion of historical causality and to the concept of *homo faber*, according to which human beings master techniques and apply their intelligence to fabricating new tools. According to the philosopher's comments, the young man showed a marked interest in the problem of transforming ideas into practice: "He [Gramsci] wanted to know how thoughts bring about action (the technique of spiritual propaganda), how thought makes the hands move, and how and why one can act through ideas."[10] We can measure how important this line of questioning would prove for Gramsci's future trajectory.

The last professor who had an influence on Gramsci was Luigi Einaudi (1874–1961). This young economist had been a professor of economics and finance for nine years when Gramsci arrived in Turin, and he would become a major politician after the fall of Fascism, to the extent that he was considered one of the fathers of the Italian Republic and became its president from 1948 to 1955. Einaudi was the favored disciple of Salvatore Cognetti de Martiis (1844–1901), who, in 1893, had founded the Laboratory of Political Economy in Turin, a real incubator for prestigious Italian economists. For Gramsci, who took some of his courses with Togliatti, Einaudi was a professor with an international reputation and a renowned journalist who wrote regularly for the two great liberal dailies of Italy, *La Stampa*, published in Turin, and *Il Corriere della Sera*, from Milan, someone who represented coherent and consequential liberalism, particularly the need to develop unionist relationships between workers and management. In this way, Gramsci was strongly influenced by liberalism, which he didn't confine to just the economic sector, indicated in Italy by the term *liberismo*,[11] but which also had a moral and political implication that created an ideology with "a universal meaning that transcended class limits,"[12] as he wrote in an August 19, 1916 article in *Il Grido del Popolo* (The Cry of the People, or *GDP*), the newspaper founded by Turin Socialists in 1892. The lessons and writings of Einaudi were one of Gramsci's preferred ways to grasp the logic of capitalism's development, with its lines of force but also its contradictions.

Hovering above these four professors were the figures Benedetto Croce (1866–1952), Giovanni Gentile (1875–1944), and Gaetano Salvemini. These three were already the main intellectual references for Antonio when he was in Cagliari, and they became even more prominent for him in Turin. In many essays on Gramsci, the pious veil of oblivion is cast over the face of Gentile. However, before he espoused Fascism, Gentile was one of the prominent thinkers for the younger generation (as much as Croce, if not more)—and he remained so at the beginning of the 1920s, far beyond the circle of Fascist supporters. In a 1918 article for *GDP*, Gramsci still wrote that he was "the Italian philosopher who has produced more than any other in the field of thought in the past few years."[13] From the notes Gramsci took as he read—a habit that had begun in Ghilarza, while he was still an adolescent, and which he kept up all his life—it emerges that he had read the major works Gentile published at the time. In addition, as he took courses with Annibale Pastore, he studied Gentile's *Sommario di pedagogia* (1911–12),[14] which Pastore used extensively in his class. Gramsci was therefore familiar with actualist philosophy, an absolute form of idealism according to which it is impossible to conceive that reality would not be the creation of activities of thought, of the thinking mind (*pensiero pensante*). It is no wonder Gramsci was seduced by this conception of humans and the world, which was a response, at least as a theory of knowledge, to his preoccupation with understanding the mechanisms that allowed an idea to become action. It is also not surprising that, in an article in *Avanti!* in June 1916, Gramsci criticized the fact that Gentile was not selected for a philosophy professorship in Turin in 1914 because of opposition from "a cabal of colleagues close to the clergy."

From Croce, the young student retained precisely this fundamental idea, that modernity meant the abandonment of all positive religion, whether it was based on divine revelation or on mythology. In Gramsci's eyes, the two major figures of Italian idealism in his time were first and foremost Hegelian intellectuals who represented the values of Risorgimento liberalism, against clericalism in the service of the moral and political status quo. Hegel's victory over the *Syllabus of Errors*, the catalog of eighty errors accompanying the *Quanta Cura* encyclical issued by Pope Pius IX to the bishops on December 8, 1864, to categorically condemn modernism, signified the triumph of the modern spirit, which was no other than an acknowledgment that humans, endowed with a historical conscience, have the possibility to act on history in order to transform it. Gramsci saw himself in this leftist reading of Hegel[15] as a bearer of modern liberalism, which was the foundation of all Italian liberalism, from the brothers Silvio and Bertrando Spaventa up through Croce and Gentile, and which Gramsci took to the heart of his own unique Marxism.

Why, in the five years preceding World War I, did Gramsci look at modernity from the side of liberalism and neo-idealist philosophy rather than from the Socialist culture of that era and from the works of Marx, which Gramsci knew only secondhand, filtered through the interpretations offered by Croce and Gentile? Why was Gramsci not yet able to integrate Engels's celebrated analysis, according to which "the proletariat is the heir of classical German philosophy"? Antonio, the "triple or quadruple provincial," who had come up to Turin from his little Sardinian village, was grateful early on to the Italian Idealist philosophers for having been able to transform him into an Italian citizen and, furthermore, into a citizen of the world in touch with the most advanced philosophy—Hegel's—whose tradition he continued to defend, since his Marxism was rooted in Hegelianism. By contrast, the Socialist ideology of the early twentieth century seemed at best to be a generous but hollow discourse, and at worst to be a fabric of clichés tinged with anti-southern racism, a position he rejected with fierce disgust as a young Sardinian, and as the Sardinian he remained all his life. Like many of the young people of his generation, he took aim at positivism for dismissing philosophy outright, in the name of a narrow conception of science reduced to the experimental method that uncritically favored facts over any kind of systematic thought—and, by extension, dismissed the fields of knowledge and action that are history, aesthetics, ethics, and politics. And yet, unlike some of his contemporaries, he was still faithful to Croce's intellectual rigor, and his rejection of dry, dulling positivism didn't degenerate into irrationalism, into tainted idealism, into a refusal to live his life by the rules of moral conscience, confounding truth and error in the same cult of intuition, of action for its own sake, of exaltation of a limitless freedom, of the value of interiority as a glorification of the superhuman, all manifestations of a poorly assimilated "spiritual unrest"[16] that would be unleashed during World War I as the laudatory delirium of violence propagated by the futurist poet Filippo Tommaso Marinetti and his followers. But he did participate in the Crocean polemic refusing to consider historical processes as natural, refuting the view that was expressed, in several ways, as a stigmatization of southerners based on stereotypes that were explicitly or implicitly racist. Just as he respected Croce and Gentile during World War I for not descending into anti-German hysteria, he also condemned the absurdity of conceiving of the German people as a superior, elected race, or, by contrast, as barbaric and reprobate (see chapter 3). Later, in his *Prison Notebooks*, Gramsci rehabilitated positivist intellectuals like Napoleone Colajanni (1847–1921), an excellent representative of progressive positivist culture, showing, with a factual basis, the ineptitude of racist theories about the inferiority of southerners.

Gramsci's first three political engagements (the defense of free trade, the campaign for Salvemini's candidature in Turin, and finally, the rejection of the PSI's passive neutrality in the face of the Italian government's entrance into the war) reflected the intellectual progress he made during his time in Turin. These engagements also communicated the need for a coherent liberalism and the need to reject all naturalist economic determinism that denied humans' creative capacity to shape history.

Defense of Free Trade and of the Interests of the Mezzogiorno

When Gramsci arrived in Turin, the city was in the last days of the Turin International World's Fair, celebrating the fiftieth anniversary of the Kingdom of Italy. There was no better way to signal the changing times in Italy, even if Giovanni Giolitti (1842–1928), who had dominated political life from the beginning of the century, was still in power. In March 1911, he entered his fourth term. After the troubles at the end of the nineteenth century that had called the Italian liberal political regime into question, first Luigi Zanardelli, then Giovanni Giolitti had allowed a young Italian state not only to anchor itself in liberalism but also to modernize economically, industrializing and absorbing a large part of its debt. This modernization was helped by the protectionist measures enacted in 1887, an unhappy but undoubtedly necessary choice, which created a virulent trade war with France—the largest trade war of the nineteenth century— whose cost was massively subsidized by the southern Italian regions. By deciding to involve Italy, in September 1911, in the war against the Ottoman Empire to conquer Libya, the Italian political class was not only responding to a politics of prestige and to the need to shore up its economic undertakings, but it also wanted to erase the shame of Adwa, where the Italian armies had been defeated by the Ethiopian troops under Menelik II on March 1, 1896. Giolitti also satisfied the cries for revenge from groups of Italian nationalists who, for the first time in Italian history, occupied the streets and successfully imposed a hawkish political stance on the Italian government, which until then had appeased the Great Powers through a politics of neutrality, and had finally, and grudgingly, been admitted into the inner circle. Faced with this choice of entering into war with the Ottomans to satisfy the small but noisy nationalist minority, the trajectory of Giolittism, which until then had been thought to resemble that of progressive liberalism, seemed to crumble, or at least to get sidetracked. The prime minister's determination to establish universal suffrage for all men in the next legislative elections of October 1913 did not compensate for this new political direction. In fact, Giolitti had, until then, decided to form an objective alliance with the PSI, at least with its reformist wing, which had long dominated the fate of the party and especially that of its parliamentary contingent, which expanded election by election. Facing fears of a possible Socialist victory, Giolitti decided to align himself with the Catholics, i.e., the other political family capable of guiding the masses. Following the common political mechanism of *quid pro quo*, a coalition was formed between the Catholics and the liberals, a coalition crowned by the Gentiloni pact (1913)[17] that basically lifted the *non expedit* imposed by Pius IX in 1874 when his papacy forbade the faithful from participating in elections organized by the Italian state, which it accused of despoiling the Patrimony of Saint Peter. As *L'Osservatore Romano* emphasized, the massive numbers of Catholics who participated in the first elections following universal suffrage turned out to be decisive in garnering a liberal conservative majority in the Chamber, preventing the Socialists from becoming arbiters of the political game.

In this way, Gramsci's true political awakening as a student took place during a time when Italy was shifting to the right, concluding, in March 1914, with the arrival of Prime Minister Antonio Salandra (1853–1931), a leader of the conservatives who were swayed by the siren song of nationalism. Antonio's first Socialist steps were quite timid, and so he didn't participate in any of the numerous workers' protests against the war in Libya, but these small steps already displayed a deep, personal intellectual ambition, the same one he had pursued in reading the neo-idealist philosophers and in taking private lessons with Annibale Pastore. How was it possible for an intellectual to spread his ideas to the masses and have them transformed into action by the people? For Gramsci, that question was not theoretical, but entirely existential. In providing himself with an education, wasn't he looking to forge a character that would embrace the national and universal and allow him to escape from physical and mental isolation?

Through his brother Gennaro, the treasurer and member of the executive committee of the Chamber of Labor in Cagliari, he was familiar with early indications of the sociability of Socialist politics. But such a politics remained fragile. In Turin, he was mainly preoccupied, for a long time, with passing his exams and resisting the physical and psychological suffering that assailed him. In October 1913, Antonio's first concrete engagement was to sign a petition to abolish protectionism. This petition was proposed by the Group of Action and Anti-protectionist Propaganda founded by two young Sardinian intellectuals born in Nuoro, Attilio Deffenu and Nicolò Fancello, who accused the Italian ruling class of scorning the interests of southern populations to enrich the bourgeoisie and Italy's northern proletariat. Gramsci's second confirmed engagement was his membership in the cultural group for Socialist students created by Angelo Tasca in March 1914, whose first significant action was to organize a dinner to celebrate small-scale industrialist and economist Edoardo Giretti (1864–1940) and his twenty-five-year battle against protectionism. This free-market (*liberista*) and southern-leaning theme was heralded by Gaetano Salvemini. The historian was even better known as one of the principal opponents of Giolitti, whom he criticized not only for sacrificing the economy of the Mezzogiorno, but also for his political immoralism, which rested on his shameless practice of cronyism that made him the *Ministro della mala-vita* (Minister of the Underworld).[18] Salvemini, an anti-Giolittian, laissez-faire defender of the Italian south, determined opponent of the war in Libya, had everything it took to please Antonio Gramsci, who considered him, along with Croce and Gentile, to be one of the thinkers who had the greatest influence on his intellectual development. So it was not surprising that Gramsci was a fervent supporter of Salvemini's candidacy for the seat representing the working-class neighborhood of Borgo San Paolo in Turin, left vacant by the death of its previous holder, the worker Pilade Gay, longtime president of the Turin Chamber of Labor.

The Turin Section of the PSI was searching for a candidate to face Felice Panié, the conservative candidate, and Giuseppe Bevione, supported by the nationalists (since, in his capacity as special correspondent[19] for *La Stampa*, he had enthusiastically covered the Italian campaign in Libya). The Socialist Youth Federation, which then included Angelo Tasca, Gramsci, Togliatti, and Umberto Terracini, ardently supported the initiative by the new secretary of the section, Ottavio Pastore, to endorse Salvemini's candidacy, since he had just been beaten in the legislative elections in the Electoral College of Melfi, where he ran on a free-market, anti-Giolittian platform as a representative for the interests of the Apulian peasants. His failure, due, in large part, to governmental maneuvers, scandalized a large portion of Italian Socialist youth, especially students from Turin, avid readers of *L'Unità*, the newspaper founded by Salvemini.[20] The latter declined this invitation, personally relayed by Ottavio Pastore, who had specifically made the journey to Florence, where the historian was teaching at the university. In the end, the Socialist candidate was the reformist Mario Bonetto, who had succeeded Pilade Gay at the head of the Chamber of Labor in Turin after winning the internal primary against Benito Mussolini (1883–1945), who was at the time the charismatic representative of the intransigent wing of the PSI. Mussolini and Salvemini immediately came to Turin to oppose Bevione, who defeated Bonetto by a handful of votes (67). When 83 ballots, all in favor of the Socialist candidate, were canceled for obscure reasons, Bevione was elected on June 28, 1914, the day a pistol shot fired in Sarajevo would change the history of Europe.

Gramsci's support for electing "a deputy for the Apulian peasants"[21] in Turin anticipated his 1926 essay "Some Aspects of the Southern Question," written just before his arrest by the Fascists, in which he argued for a revolution in Italy founded on an alliance between the northern proletariat and the peasants in the south—the only alliance strong enough to topple the hegemonic bloc made up by the coalition between the industrialists from the Po Valley and the major landowners of the Mezzogiorno.

First Encounter with the Proletariat

Though Gramsci's universe tended to be confined to the university, he still lived in one of the largest and most modern cities in Italy, and in 1912 he began to grasp the dynamics of the political and union battles that played out there. During the war with Libya, Turin had been seized by daily demonstrations for and against this colonial "adventure," as it was called. Gramsci noted that the opposition to the war was almost unanimous among the workers, while the student youth was deeply divided on this question. On May 1, 1912, more than 30,000 demonstrators, mainly workers, parodied the song "A Tripoli," composed in 1911 to celebrate Italian colonialism. The song that began with the line "Sai dove s'annida più florido il suol?" [Do you know where the land is most fertile?] became "Do you know where the land is most sterile?" while the refrain "Tripoli bel suol d'amore" [Tripoli, beautiful land of love] became "Tripoli bel suol del dolore!" [Tripoli, beautiful land of sorrow]. While some of the Socialist leaders such as Bissolati and Bonomi were excluded from the PSI[22] for their support of the Italian colonialist enterprise, the leadership of the party, then headed by Filippo Turati and Claudio Treves, succeeded in preserving the autonomy of the PSI by condemning Giolitti's foreign policy without breaking with him on social reforms. Nonetheless, the old leaders of the PSU (Partito Socialista Unitario, the Unitary Socialist Party) could not prevent the fact that many branches of their party, including those in Turin, became radicalized by the idea of "war against war."

The history of Socialism in Turin, which unfolded alongside the transformation of the city, whose population grew from three hundred thousand inhabitants at the end of the nineteenth century to more than five hundred thousand in 1921, is a history punctuated by the always latent and sometimes violent conflict between reformists and revolutionaries. Initially, the "socialism of professors" dominated, whose key figures were the doctor Cesare Lombroso (1835–1909), the founder of criminal anthropology, the writer Edmondo De Amicis (1846–1908), author of *Cuore*, a best-selling children's book (1886), and the poet and literary critic Arturo Graf (1848–1913). Breaking with the well-meaning, devout Turin establishment, these professors put forward a sentimental, humanitarian, and generous socialism, which, by ignoring Marxism, revealed itself to be ultimately incapable of producing a serious analysis of capitalism. All the same, it raised awareness about the deplorable living conditions of manual laborers. For its part, the world of small-time artisans and workers developed a whole network of organizations for solidarity, the most important of which was the Chamber of Labor founded in 1865.

Though Fiat had only sixty workers in 1899, the Giolittian era was one of exponential growth of the modern proletariat, which would transform this city at the foot of the Alps into the city of the automobile and a laboratory for political and union experiments. In 1911, when Gramsci arrived in Turin, Fiat was producing three thousand cars and had begun to make the first airplanes in 80,000-square-foot factories that employed 3,320 highly qualified workers. It is more generally estimated that, at the start of the twentieth century, 100,000 of the 350,000 inhabitants of Turin worked in industry, of whom three-quarters were true factory workers, performing their duties in units of production greater than twenty-five employees. Through these circumstances, Turin was a laboratory for testing relations between those who represented labor and those who represented their bosses. After the second general strike in March 1906, an agreement was reached between the workers and the automobile manufacturers, an agreement whose twentieth article established representation by putting five workers on the board of each factory for the first time in Italian labor history. In response, the Industrial League emerged in September of the same year, led by the Franco-Italian Luigi Craponne. It was the first organization of employers in Italy, which became, three years later in May 1910, the Confederazione Italiana dell'Industria (Confindustria), which exists to this day. Though this 1906 agreement didn't withstand the crash of 1907, which hit the automotive sector especially hard, these double beginnings made Turin the most modern capitalist city in Italy.

Turin is still a political laboratory. For a long time, the Turin elites resisted Giolittism, the liberal progressive ideology jointly supported by the daily newspaper *La Stampa* and by reformist Socialists. Contrary to this marriage of convenience, an intransigent socialism developed whose two features were, on the one hand, fighting to establish *commissioni interne* (internal commissions, or shop committees) within the factories and, on the other, resorting to general strike as a weapon for advocacy (the first general strike in Turin took place in 1902). Socialism therefore found itself torn between a reformist tendency, which advocated for a pacifist socialism that respected the laws of history, and another revolutionary tendency that advocated for proactive measures and demanded the revolutionary syndicalism then spearheaded by Arturo Labriola (1873–1959). Caught between adventurous extremism and a withdrawal into simple collective bargaining, Turin socialism (and Italian socialism more generally) displayed great weaknesses, but that didn't prevent it from acting. And so, in 1912, the Turin Socialists held a large general strike, which collapsed after a sixty-five-day struggle. After such a resistance, this failure didn't curb the Turin workers' determination, since they launched a new general strike one year later, almost to the day. Thanks to their resistance funds, the solidarity of workers from other Italian cities, and the money they received from foreign metallurgical organizations, for three months (93 days exactly) the Turin workers resisted Luigi Craponne's attempts at intimidation. Two months into the strike, he responded with force, laying off large numbers and making the false calculation that the more workers were unemployed, the less effective their solidarity would be. With the help of *La Stampa*, Giolitti endeavored to keep the situation from degenerating further. With his consummate political skill, he attacked Craponne personally in the daily *La Tribuna*, accusing him of being "a foreigner [Craponne was French] stirring up agitation in our country."[23] Craponne was forced to resign as president of the Industrial League, which then abandoned its strategy of direct confrontation. The workers had won. But their victory was Pyrrhic, since the wage gains were modest, while in terms of worker's representation within the factories, the unionized workers had to content themselves with a compromise that nonetheless had a strong symbolic importance: the establishment of an arbitration commission, presided over by the mayor of Turin, including four seats for the Federation of Metallurgical Workers and Employees (FIOM). This group had been founded in Livorno in 1901 and participated in the creation of the General Confederation of Labor (CGL) in 1906.

The two major workers' strikes of 1912–13 made Turin the center of Italian capitalism and turned its proletariat into "the spiritual leaders of the masses of Italian workers," using the same terms that Gramsci employed a little bit later to describe this period immediately preceding World War I.[24] Though he wasn't directly involved in the workers' demonstrations or in protests against Italian colonialism, this memory of Togliatti's could have been Gramsci's own:

> In 1912 and 1913, at certain hours of the morning when we would abandon our courses and leave the university to follow the streets of arcades that brought us toward the Po, we would meet groups of men who were different from us, following the same route. A whole crowd would be moving toward the banks of the river, where at the

time, the meetings for striking workers would take place. . . . And we would go there, us too, accompanying these men; we would listen to their speeches; we would speak with them; we took an interest in their struggle.[25]

Gramsci was even more aware of this atmosphere of political and social combat, for he had begun to regularly frequent the Socialist youth in Turin, after meeting them through his classmate Angelo Tasca, the friend who certainly contributed the most to his early political development. The son of a Socialist railway man, Tasca, who was exactly the same age as Gramsci, became an organizer within the ranks of the PSI at his father's urging and helped to found the Socialist Youth Federation in Turin at the end of 1909. In that role, he established himself as one of the important Socialist figures at the National Congress of the Socialist Youth Federation that took place in 1912. Of the four musketeers who made up the ranks of *L'Ordine Nuovo* (see chapter 4), Tasca and Umberto Terracini were the most precocious militants. Terracini, who was four years younger than Gramsci and the son of an engineer from Genoa, joined the Socialist Youth Federation at sixteen years old. For their part, Gramsci and Togliatti were slower to get centrally involved, not joining the movement until 1914. Gramsci, who had already come into contact with Socialist ideology during his days in Cagliari, was primed to absorb the special atmosphere of the prewar years. Even in Ghilarza, where the social structure was a far cry from Turin's, he was quickly captivated by political intrigue. In fact, in his little Sardinian village, where he took a break with his family in October 1913, he was attentive to the profound changes that had followed the adoption of universal suffrage. He saw the peasants who went to the office to vote with their pockets sewn shut, since they feared the *carabinieri* would slip knives into their clothes to try to get them arrested so they couldn't perform their duty as voters. From this seemingly laughable behavior, he took note of a greater maturity on the part of the Italian people.

Despite his physical and psychological difficulties, Gramsci began to be intellectually prepared to understand the world around him. Like Terracini, Togliatti, and Tasca, who were all students—the first two in the faculty of law, the last in that of letters[26]—he was equipped with the frame of mind he acquired from the intellectual rigor of his professors, an intellectual rigor that was sorely lacking, as he saw it, in the previous generation of Socialists. In the eyes of these young students, Filippo Turati (born in 1857), Camillo Prampolini (born in 1895), and even Claudio Treves (born in 1869), director of *Critica Sociale*,[27] were wrong on three counts. This previous generation had the triple defect of being influenced by positivism, of never having seriously studied the economic and social conditions of the Italian proletariat, abandoning this task to the liberal intellectuals, and, finally, of trusting too much in a gradualist evolution of capitalism leading naturally to socialism.

Without formulating it as precisely as he would in his *Prison Notebooks*, Gramsci condemned the preceding generation of Socialists for diluting Marxism and for subjecting it to the hurdles of Herbert Spencer's philosophy, which was quite fashionable from 1870 to 1880, instead of tying it back to Hegel's thought as did Antonio Labriola (1843–1904), an isolated genius who was little known within the political culture of the first Italian and European Socialists. This absence of serious scholarship translated politically into a lack of serious studies of a sociological nature and manifested in an excessive faith in the progress of socialism through reforms alone, which explains the objective alliance between Turati and Giolitti. Trained in another intellectual environment under the auspices of neo-idealism, our four musketeers couldn't accept that interpretation of history, which they saw as a sign of weakness. And so they advocated, first and foremost, for an intellectual leap among Socialists through a strengthening of their culture. This idea earned them the name *culturisti*, which was given to them during the polemic between Tasca and Amadeo Bordiga at the National Congress of the Socialist Youth Federation in Bologna in September 1912. Amadeo Bordiga (1889–1970), whose importance we will return to in subsequent chapters, theorized that people exist as Socialist, or rather are born Socialist, by virtue of the class they belong to, experiencing solidarity innately rather than learning it through education, which always has a bourgeois framework. In response to this reasoning, Tasca claimed that Socialists should not skimp on a solid education, even if it would be somewhat bourgeois. Perhaps even more than his future companions in the struggle, who came from backgrounds that were a bit more sociologically elevated than his own, Gramsci experienced this need for spiritual elevation to gain a holistic conception of the world and existence as the only way, or perhaps the best way, of "deprovincializing" himself.

This *Weltanschauung* (the recourse to German here is to invoke Hegel and his Italian readers, Croce and Gentile foremost among them) came to the young student through the interpenetration of thought and action. Along these lines, Tasca's argument before the young Socialists gathered at the congress on August 30, 1912, could have been Gramsci's own:

> The positivists wondered, how would future society be? This question amounted, in their minds, to the following: what thing will give us the future society? And they contrive reigns of infinite justice and infinite beauty. We, the young people of the new generation, openly antipositivist, ask ourselves instead: what will we bring to the future society? What will we be able to create? We wish only for what we are capable of accomplishing and we ask our culture to accompany us in this effort to express our society for ourselves. The Socialist revolution will not take off as the inevitable result of the actual state of things. Neither will it take off through determinism, but by an effort of the will. The ethical element in building the revolution is indispensable, fundamental.[28]

First Article, First Polemic

It was in this ideological context that Antonio Gramsci made his first public statement. While the elections of 1913 (the first for universal men's suffrage) marked a relative increase in the number of votes for Socialism, this rise was then curtailed by the electoral mechanism when it came to the number of seats,[29] and the tensions between nationalists and Socialists, which were already running quite high around the colonial question, escalated in the immediate prewar period. At Ancona, on June 7, 1914, an antimilitarist gathering took a dramatic turn when riflemen fired on the crowd that was trying to reach the center of town. Three of the demonstrators were killed. The old anarchist leader Errico Malatesta (1853–1932) called for an insurrection; he was among the organizers, along with other representatives from leftist groups, including Mussolini, who was then the leader of the revolutionary wing of the PSI. For a week, the Adriatic city was overtaken by a thousand outraged people. Though this episode, passed down through history as the "Red Week" (*Settimana rossa*), led to nothing concrete, it unleashed a call for strikes across most of Italy. In Turin, skirmishes took place in the center of the city, at the edge of a demonstration Gramsci participated in. After war was declared, the leadership of the PSI found itself isolated and bewildered when their German, French, and English comrades decided to support their respective governments. Nonetheless, though it was shaken for a time by the German army's invasion of Belgium, the PSI's doctrine remained a neutral one, summed up a year later with the phrase: "Né aderire, né sabotare" (neither adhere nor sabotage). It was in this context that the "Mussolini bomb" exploded, as Tasca called it in an article for the *GDP* on October 24, 1914.

On October 6, 1914, in a letter addressed to the *Giornale d'Italia*, the daily founded by the nationalist conservatives Sidney Sonnino and Antonio Salandra, who were then presiding over the fate of Italy (Salandra was prime minister beginning in March 1914, and Sonnino was on the point of becoming his minister of foreign affairs), Mussolini made a distinction between Socialist revolutionary opposition to an Italian war against France and the simply "ideal and legal" opposition to a declaration of war between Italy and Austria. Twelve days later, on October 18, 1914, in an editorial in *Avanti!* where he was still the editor-in-chief, he "decided to cross the Rubicon"[30] by writing a long article, whose title alone articulates an agenda: "Dalla neutralità assoluta alla neutralità relativa ed operante" [From Absolute Neutrality to Relative and Operative Neutrality]. On October 20, Mussolini resigned from *Avanti!*. On November 15, he published, thanks to secret funds arriving from Paris, *Il Popolo d'Italia*. On November 24, he was forced out of the PSI. Then his transformation from Socialist to Fascist began. This transformation is not what interests us here, but rather the formidable echo these articles produced.

It was truly a bombshell, for Mussolini had been one of the most important leaders of the PSI, one who had been the long-standing frontrunner of the maximalist (or intransigent) group that had been at the head of the party since the Reggio Emilia conference in July 1912. At the center of student youth but also a worker, Mussolini enjoyed real popularity, buoyed by his talents as a journalist and as a peerless orator: the *GDP* had chronicled in hyperbolic terms the meeting he had led in the Chamber of Labor in Turin on January 11, 1913. The words of the editor-in-chief of *Avanti!* always produced debates and polemics, requiring each militant to clarify his position on an increasingly likely war involving the Kingdom of Italy. The whole spectrum of positions emerged, ranging from Claudio Treves, who was ready to accept that Italy would go to war to defend itself, to Amadeo Bordiga, who was resolutely hostile to any form of war, no matter the circumstances. We are particularly interested here in the reaction of the *culturisti*, the Socialist students in Turin, to Mussolini's argument, since, for them, neutrality took on a "reactionary" dimension, placing the PSI in a subordinate position relative to the ruling class, and thus negating the national dimension of socialism.

Though we don't know Togliatti's position at the time, we know he had read Gramsci's forthcoming article and seemed to have agreed with it before it was published. We also know that Tasca was not convinced by Mussolini's idea that absolute neutrality would represent a negation of the concept of nation, since for Tasca, the Socialist education of the future nation did not include defending the actual backward nation of the bourgeoisie. The Italian proletariat also showed great wisdom, considering the war a harmful myth. Gramsci's position was different from the one expressed by his friend Angelo in an article in the *GDP* on October 24, 1914. In the pages of the same newspaper, Antonio published, on October 31, 1914, his first real political article: "Neutralità attiva ed operante" [Active and Operative Neutrality]. Until then, he had written only brief snippets under the pseudonym Alfa Gamma for the private *Corriere Universitario* and was unknown in the Socialist universe. But after "Active and Operative Neutrality" came out, he wouldn't remain unknown for long.

Though he agreed with Tasca about distinguishing the emerging Socialist nation from the bourgeois nation already in place, he opposed those who upheld neutrality at all costs by putting forward three linked arguments that followed one after the other: (1) absolute neutrality was a good slogan, but it was already too late, since it was obvious that Italy would enter the war and they must therefore act with this certainty in mind; (2) absolute neutrality signified a fatalistic waiting in the face of events, while history must be made from creation; and last, (3) the PSI should not jump on the bandwagon of the bourgeoisie, but rather make it understand that this war, which the bourgeoisie hadn't known how to stop, was the sign of its failure, and as a consequence, indicated the pressing need to change society. Therefore, they must give up the slogan of absolute neutrality and turn toward active and effective neutrality. We agree with the following analysis from Angelo D'Orsi, for whom this article signifies the necessity to move away from the idea "of war against war [to that of] a war within the war."[31] Aware of the actions of the Turin proletariat since 1912, Gramsci gathered that the former had acquired a national consciousness and that, from then on, it should assert itself as a protagonist of history, since it was no longer a political minority. This concern for initiative over and against "over-ingenuous contemplation and Buddhist renunciation of our obligations"—these last words of his article took up, significantly, words similar to those he had used to protest the resigned attitude of his parents toward his material difficulties—was the central element of his conception of the world. Also, though he didn't give Mussolini a free pass, he appreciated "realistic concretism" that he set against the "doctrinaire formalism" of the PSI leadership, for he was primarily concerned that Socialists should seize this occasion to free themselves from Giolittism. This argument, as original as it was fragile—how could he deny, as Tasca rightly pointed out, that the logic of war pushed people toward national unity—revealed an ideological limit, which didn't include the notion of an imperialist war that Lenin was in the course of developing. This first ideological position of Gramsci's was much more in line with the reasoning of Salvemini, who considered the war a possible factor in the cohesion of the Italian nation, as opposed to the Leninist idea that war could set off a revolution.

Though it is interesting to note that unionist Turin Socialists, then led by the metalworker Emilio Colombino, remained radically opposed to a war that concerned only arms dealers, it is also important to realize that none of the young *culturisti* surrendered to the siren call of Fascism. All the same, Gramsci was considered by many of his companions at the time to be a supporter of interventionism, a position that provoked a leftist critique from Bordiga and a commendation from the right wing of the PSI, which saw Gramsci as a patriotic figure. Though this article was not propaganda and though the position it took was subtle, this accusation of Mussolinism and interventionism weighed heavily on the shoulders of the Sardinian student, who was not yet hardened by political combat, forcing him to isolate himself for almost a year as if to "atone for his mistake."[32] This reputation as an interventionist Mussolinophile stuck to him for a long time. And so, seven years later, after the founding of the Partito Communista d'Italia (henceforth PCdI),[33] some militant Communists demanded the expulsion of comrade Gramsci the interventionist, who had been ready to write for *Il Popolo d'Italia*—though no document corroborates this last criticism.

Antonio didn't pick up his pen again until October 31, 1915. By then, he was a journalist compensated by the Turin editorial staff of *Avanti!*. Italy had entered the war some six months earlier. He had emerged from poverty and had overcome, for a time, the psychological crisis that had caused him so much pain. The Sardinian student was no longer a provincial but rather a professional revolutionary who would make Turin into the Petrograd of the Italian proletarian revolution and into the city where "Antonio" became Gramsci. From his years as a poor student in Turin, he preserved, as he wrote in an article in *Avanti!* on December 29, 1916, the idea that knowledge is not the mere accumulation of facts but rather "the ardent flame of a new life . . . an act of liberation." These words—which evoke those of Charles Péguy in *Notre Jeunesse* (1910), a book that Gramsci much admired—made him into a wartime intellectual who was more attentive to the great ideological issues of his time than to party politics. The young Sardinian who became the Turin student searching for meaning in his life developed into a national figure by transforming himself into a militant professional revolutionary.

PART II

From National Gramsci to Internationalist Gramsci

(1915–1922)

< **3** >

A Socialist Journalist, Marginal and Original
(1915–1919)

Sotto la Mole

Thanks to the few letters he wrote to his sisters, we have a few facts about Antonio Gramsci's private life between the autumn of 1914 and the winter of 1915–16, facts that bear witness to his turmoil. Though he didn't finally renounce the idea of earning his *Laurea* until the end of World War I, his confusion was deep during this period. He left his university studies, cut himself off from his family, continued to experience financial difficulties, and backed away from the political fight he had barely begun in the autumn of 1914. Gramsci took a year, almost to the day, to overcome the political and psychological crisis that followed the publication of his first political article. In *I primi dieci anni del PCI* (The First Ten Years of the PCI, 1953),[1] Angelo Tasca reports that Gramsci "was very hard on himself, as if his attitude in 1914–15 had not been a marginal incident but, rather, something that related to a more general error that had its own logic and that he had to cast off afterwards."[2]

The contrast between the distraught, young ex-student and the journalist writing nearly an article a day in 1916 is quite striking. Exempted from military service owing to his physical deformity, Gramsci did not experience the trial by fire that his political allies had to go through along with his brothers by blood (Carlo, as an officer, and

Gennaro and Mario as petty officers). After he refused a position running the elementary school in Oulx, a small town in the high Susa valley, he was employed by the Turin-based Socialist newspaper *Il Grido del Popolo* (*GDP*), and two months later, he began writing for the newly established Turin edition of *Avanti!*, the PSI daily headquartered in Milan. Long before he was a militant Socialist and revolutionary Communist leader, Gramsci was a journalist. Under the pseudonym Alfa Gamma, he published his second article in the *GDP* on November 13, 1915, on the Tenth Congress of Spanish Socialists.

For several years, most of his life became concentrated in the little office on the top floor of an apartment building (which has since disappeared) in Corso Siccardi, a building that sheltered every kind of organization within the Turin Socialist world: cooperatives, *case del popolo* (proletarian community centers), chambers of labor, unions, not to mention a theater and a popular restaurant. The three offices allocated to the *GDP* journalists, who were also working for the Piedmont Section of *Avanti!*, were shared by Gramsci and Giuseppe Bianchi. Bianchi, a former typesetting worker, became the first director of a Socialist newspaper to compete for the job and get paid, and he was responsible for both the *GDP* and the Turin Section of *Avanti!*. After he left for the front, he was succeeded by Maria Giudice, a school principal, the mother of eight children born from a common-law marriage. She took over the direction of the *GDP*, and Ottavio Pastore handled the Turin edition of *Avanti!*. Despite his impressive output, Gramsci remained a little-known journalist until 1919, as evidenced by the frequent misspellings of his name in the major newspapers of the peninsula: in July 1918, *La Stampa* still called him "Granichi," while the *Gazzetta del Popolo* referred to him, in the same period, as "Granci." Why was he unknown? The first reason is that he rarely signed his articles, preferring to use only his initials or his pseudonym Alfa Gamma. It is important to see this choice not as timidity or false modesty, but rather as the refusal of all forms of self-esteem. For the Socialist intellectual he was, the individual was supposed to give precedence to the ideas. The other reason was the marginal position he and his arguments occupied within the center of the Italian Socialist movement. Outside of his work as a journalist, Gramsci played no role in the leadership of the PSI until 1917, and the position he subsequently took was very modest up until his experience with *L'Ordine Nuovo* (see chapter 4). As a result, his name never appeared in the assembly minutes of the Turin Section of the PSI. Until the Russian Revolution, with the exception of a speech advocating for Turin Socialists to be provided with their own daily newspaper, he didn't participate in the life of Socialist organizing in his adopted city. Likewise, he devoted very few articles to the internal questions of this political family, though he had belonged to the party since 1914. All the same, he identified with the intransigent group that had dominated the fate of the PSI since 1912, both at the national level and in Turin. With the exception of a few speeches on the French Revolution, the Paris Commune, or even about works of art, pronounced in a clear, precise voice that was somewhat professorial but without a real orator's talent (hence their weak echo), Gramsci concentrated fully on his journalistic work, which he took seriously. Though his work with the *GDP* was unpaid, he received one hundred lire a month for his work on the Piedmont edition of *Avanti!*. This salary may have constrained him to a parsimonious life, but it did provide him with independence. Still more important, by putting an end to his morbid solitude and allowing him to open up to sociability, his daily activities as a journalist had the cathartic effect of liberating him from his torments. Each day, after climbing to the top floor of the Siccardi Palace, he often saw newspaper employees and members of the Socialist Youth Federation, who occupied the office next to his, and whose conversation he particularly enjoyed. His new duties also led him to go to the theater and the movies often, and though he didn't make friends in artistic circles, he still had a social life, in particular among the Sardinian community who had remained in Turin.

Until 1917, Gramsci wrote the vast majority of his articles for a newspaper column called *Sotto la Mole*. Created by Giuseppe Bianchi, this column, whose title was a reference to the Mole Antonelliana,[3] was intended to chronicle Turin's realities, capturing daily life as closely as possible, but charged with political meaning. The word *mole*, which means burden as well as dome, appeared as a metaphor for the condition of workers weighed down by capitalist oppression. Gramsci first wrote almost half of the articles that appeared in this column, then began to write nearly all of them after Giuseppe Bianchi left for the army on May 1, 1916. These texts quickly captured the attention of his contemporaries, and eventually the attention of critics, especially since some of the themes he sketched out in these articles were developed more deeply in his *Prison Notebooks*. As early as the 1920s, Umberto Cosmo wanted to publish an anthology of the articles Gramsci had written for the *GDP* and the Turin Section of *Avanti!*. Without being opposed in principle, Gramsci didn't follow up, both out of a refusal to put himself forward and out of concern that he might not have the opportunity to proofread these writings carefully while being so completely absorbed in political action.

Throughout his entire life, Gramsci was a journalist who treated his work with the highest degree of seriousness. Those who saw him often in his little office in Corso Siccardi described him with pockets stuffed with manuscripts, never writing a whole piece at once, bent over his worktable in the midst of rewriting and correcting his text carefully to find the most appropriate phrase that would strike the reader while keeping the censor's scissors at bay. It is significant that Gramsci actually wrote his first articles during World War I, under the rule of "Lady Scissors." Several critics have emphasized that he was one of the first Italian journalists to make use of the pamphlet as a weapon. He did it with sure talent, to the point of being compared to Karl Kraus (1874–1936), the celebrated Austrian writer and satirist, every new issue of whose magazine *Die Fackel* (the torch) was anticipated with angst and delight by all the Viennese intelligentsia. Like Kraus, Gramsci cared about linguistic purity, and he refused all stylistic compromises, including those employed to reach a larger or more working-class audience.

At the time, the Sardinian intellectual defined himself as a journalist of Elzevirs, the name of the typeface traditionally used for the culture pages. That had been Gramsci's plan since he had arrived in

Turin: to spread a new conception of life, a new culture, so to speak, breaking with the present one whose pitfalls and inconsistencies he aimed to demonstrate, for example by criticizing false morality, misplaced patriotism, or hypocrisy of customs. Gramsci was especially fearsome in this role when he wrote reviews of cinema and theater. He pitilessly denounced the provincial character of Turin theater, where the public would applaud much more warmly for a piece when they knew the author. In the Piedmontese capital, even the dialect theater, which often served as a cultural alternative to that of the bourgeoisie, was marred by bad taste and ridicule. His take on the actors was no less harsh. The established reputation of the comic Giuseppe Sichel (1849–1924), with his particular physique—he was very tall and very thin—didn't prevent Gramsci from concluding that his work revealed "the mediocrity, the banality, and the vulgarity of the farce" (*GDP*, September 23, 1916). As for the diva Lyda Borelli (1884–1959), *prima donna* among *prime donne* and considered an heir to Eleonora Duse, Gramsci thought she represented a sensuality that "remains and will remain the major preoccupation of our society, of established society, of society that does not work or cannot work" (*GDP*, September 4, 1918). It would be a mistake to interpret this commentary as some kind of prudishness on his part. Of course, Gramsci was, in his personal behavior, the opposite of the bourgeois portrayed in literature (i.e., married but regularly visiting brothels and maintaining a mistress). As it happens, we would know nothing about his love life at the time if it weren't for a few indirect documents that lead us to suspect a possible romantic relationship with Pia Carena, stenographer for the Turin editorial staff of *Avanti!*. But it's not important to dwell on it. Rejecting the traditional conception of the bourgeois couple, in which the woman occupies an inferior legal and social position, he advocated for equality between the sexes by turning to an interpretation that grew directly out of Gentile's actualism as it was applied to teaching,[4] a meeting of the minds between student and teacher:

Another standard, whereby woman and man are no longer just muscles, nerves, and skin, but are essentially spirit; whereby the family is no longer just an economic institution, but is above all *a moral world in process, completed by the intimate fusion of two souls which find in each other what each individually lacks. . . .* The standards of high and petty bourgeoisie rebel, they cannot comprehend a world of this kind.[5]

The public's vulgar taste for sensuality on the stage was even more flagrant in cinema, an artform in which Turin was ahead of the rest of Italy, and one that Gramsci disdained, since it reflected the privileging of bodies over the mind, expressed decadent bourgeois morals, and flattered the instincts of the herd. Still strongly influenced by neo-idealism of the Crocean and Gentilian variety, Gramsci deplored that, in silent films, movements prevailed over words. The journalist of Elzevirs once again criticized mainstream films and theater productions, organized by film trusts or the theater guild, for wanting merely to entertain people with purely recreational spectacles of great mediocrity. Such a reading of artistic life explains why Gramsci was one of the first theater critics to praise the works of Luigi Pirandello (1867–1936), whom he presented as an *ardito* of theater (*GDP*, September 24, 1917)[6] who understood how to "deprovincialize" the Italian public and undermine the foundations of so-called established morals. In several articles devoted to theatrical and fictional works by the Sicilian playwright, Gramsci anticipated the interpretation of Adriano Tilgher (1887–1941), Pirandello's most celebrated critic, who noted that humor was central for the author of *Il fu Mattia Pascal* [The Late Mattia Pascal], who blended comedy with melancholy, drawing on the discrepancy between what is expected and what actually appears.

In his column *Sotto la Mole*, what interested Gramsci the journalist was to denounce, with polemical verve, all the *Stenterelli* (named for Stenterello, a character from the commedia dell'arte representing the vain, chatty blowhard) and to call for Italians to forge a real character for themselves. This wish was very much an extension of his idealist legacy: it was the Hegelian Francesco De Sanctis, one of the primary influences on Croce and Gentile, who called for destroying the old Italian type represented by Francesco Guicciardini, who was certainly cultivated but cut off from the ethical-political debates of his time, in favor of the new Italian, aware of his patriotic duties, whom Machiavelli called for. The key word in Gramsci's prose in these years was "character." Italians needed to arm themselves with a true character so that they could undertake their own moral and intellectual reform, delivering themselves from Catholicism, which represented an obsolete stage of history, to prepare for a new Socialist society, which would also be a new civilization. Highly aware of the success the magazine *La Voce* was having with the young population (this magazine was established in 1908 by Giuseppe Prezzolini [1882–1982] and Giovanni Papini [1881–1956], whose goal was the politico-social and cultural renewal of Italy, which they criticized for being trapped in Giolittism), Gramsci planned to create a weekly that would be for Socialists what *La Voce* was for the bourgeoisie: a breath of new ideas to revive a tired world. As with the journalists at *La Voce*, Gramsci first thought of putting in place a group of intellectuals whose education was solid, conceived of as a kind of military staff who could form future soldiers for socialism. Alongside the partisan and syndical organizations, whose importance and function Gramsci supported, there should also be a "a cultural organization . . . the third organ" (*GDP*, December 18, 1917). The latter could not be in any way compared to the people's universities, which were "neither a university, nor populist. Their directors are amateurs in matters of cultural organization. What causes them to act is a mild and insipid spirit of charity, not a live and fecund desire to contribute to the spiritual raising of the multitude" (*GDP*, January 11, 1916). Words worthy of "the petty bourgeois aristocratism . . . spread widely among intellectuals who are poor but proud to belong to the aristocracy of the intelligentsia thanks to their cultural baggage"?[7] Perhaps. But it seems more interesting to emphasize that Gramsci's articles for the column *Sotto la Mole* were aligned with his cultural positions, and they reflected his desire to define himself as a "creator of culture."[8]

The crowning step in this agenda was the February 1917 publication of the unique issue of *La Città Futura*. In this little four-page leaflet that came out on February 11, 1917, all the articles (none of which were signed) were penned by Gramsci, with the exception of three reprints of essays by Benedetto Croce, Gaetano Salvemini, and Armando Carlini (1878–1959), a neo-idealist philosopher close to Gentile. As the advertisements in the *GDP* and *Avanti!* tell us, this single issue was published by and for the Socialist Youth Federation in Turin in order to "educate and create young militant Socialists." Though some of the articles were reprinted in *L'Ordine Nuovo*, *La Città Futura* was still deeply marked by Gramsci's idealist education, harnessed in service of Socialism, for advancing a new vision of the world while dismantling the old order from the ground up. This old order's flaw was "common sense—blockheaded common sense" that "preaches that an egg today is better than a chicken tomorrow. And common sense is a terrible subjugator of spirits."[9] In this way "Socialists must not replace order with order. They must bring about order in itself. The juridical norm that they want to establish is the *possibility of the complete realization of one's human personality for every citizen.* With the realization of this norm, all established privileges collapse. It leads to maximum freedom with a minimum of constraints."[10]

The Gramscian ideas and vocabulary, in service of his cultural and metapolitical fight, clashed with the conceptions of the reformist old guard who had regrouped behind *Critica Sociale*, whose principal associates, Claudio Treves, Filippo Turati, and Giuseppe-Emanuele Modigliani (1872–1947—the older brother of the painter Amedeo), form the essential library of militant socialism. This library also included several essays on the French Revolution and the novels of Victor Hugo (which Gramsci had never liked), not to mention Karl Marx's *Das Kapital*, in an abridged version edited by Carlo Cafiero (1844–92), which had the great merit of being the first general presentation of the German thinker's work for the Italian public.

But Gramsci's line of argument was not much more popular among the younger, intransigent generation, which won an early victory in the spring of 1914 by placing Ottavio Pastore at the head of the executive committee of the Turin Section of Socialists. In fact, some of the intransigents had been scalded by the painful experience of Mussolinism, and Gramsci couldn't shake their suspicions that he had been a proponent of interventionism. This suspicion was ultimately reinforced by Togliatti's position, since after war was declared, he decided to resign from the PSI to volunteer as a medic with the Chasseurs Alpins—forcing him to rejoin the PSI in 1919. In this way, an ideological distance seemed to persist between Gramsci and the majority of militant Socialists, including the youngest. Of the three other musketeers, only Umberto Terracini openly defended the Gramscian approach at the congress of the Socialist Youth Federation in July 1916. After the latter's arrest in September of that same year for distributing pacifist tracts and his conscription to the front as a simple infantryman, Gramsci was the only one who hadn't put on a military uniform. Without circulation among the PSI at the national or even the local level, his arguments were not widely read, as the very low distribution of *La Città Futura* shows. He was forced to give up, at least temporarily, the idea of publishing a new Socialist magazine carrying his conception of the world, which was still strongly influenced, as he himself would later recognize, by the neo-idealism of Croce and Gentile, a philosophy that was incompatible with the essential political culture of the vast majority of Italian Socialists.

Italy and World War I, Analyzed by Gramsci the Journalist

After the failure of *La Città Futura*, a transformation took place in Gramsci's activities, leading him to write fewer and fewer chronicles of daily life and culture in Turin and more and more frequently about national and international political events. Until 1918, it was rare for Gramsci's articles to focus on subjects outside of Turin. This rarity makes them all the more interesting. They can be grouped into four themes:[11] an analysis of the Italian bourgeoisie, reflections on the war, remarks about socialism, and, last, texts about the Bolshevik Revolution in Russia and the one hoped for in Italy.[12] Studying these texts demonstrates the prevalence of his neo-idealist background and the paucity of his knowledge about Marxism, at least until 1918. The early influence of Antonio Labriola on Gramsci's thought—the philosopher's name wasn't mentioned by the Sardinian thinker for the first time until a January 29, 1918 article—is an invention we primarily owe to Palmiro Togliatti, but one that doesn't correspond to reality.

Gramsci delivered a harsh critique of Giolittian Italy. The central idea he developed was that Italy was only a counterfeiter of capitalism. This idea, repeated over and over, is elaborated from different angles. The first is through praising England. In his own way, Gramsci participated in the Anglophilia that had been prevalent among liberal elites in Italy since Cavour, whose character he celebrated, presenting him as the opposite of Giolitti. Since Gramsci proved to be incapable of grasping the positive modern transformations Giolittism had brought, it isn't surprising that he supported England, which he presented as a country that hadn't been marked by Catholic education's superficial and dismal view of the world. He also presented England, on the other hand, as a country known for liberalism and free trade, the triumph of the Spencerian model of unregulated competition within a state reduced to its simple administrative functions. In creating this tableau, he seems to have forgotten that the country of Herbert Henry Asquith and Lloyd George was an imperialist power. As we will see later, the notion of imperialism was long absent from Gramsci's political culture, but it was theorized by Lenin (though not until 1916) and by John A. Hobson in 1902.

Conversely, his analysis of the evolution of the Italian bourgeoisie came to be more relevant, since this group had proved to be incapable not only of creating a new economic order, but also of imposing itself as the dominant political class without the mediation of the state. This pathological development had repercussions for public authorities, making the Italian state into a "Punchinello [state] in which no one is in charge because an infinitude of irresponsible people are in charge."[13] More seriously, the Gentiloni pact (see chapter 1) advanced by Giolitti reduced the state to a "genuine theocracy"[14] and annihilated all efforts by Cavour and his disciples from the historical right (*Destra storica*) who had tried to subordinate religious authority within a secular state. As a counterpoint to this virulent critique of his country, the *GDP* journalist celebrated Turin's modernity as a forward-looking city "because it was not very Italian,"[15] but rather completely devoted to work, a blueprint for the city of the future, in which capitalist antagonism had already taken place between those who owned the means of production and the proletariat. Though he rejected any mechanical transition from capitalism to socialism (which, in his view, the reformist Socialists mistakenly supported), before the October 1917 revolution Gramsci still thought that a country's modernity depended on the actualization of capitalism, as a precursor to establishing socialism. Yet this development was blocked by Giolittism: "Giolitti, practically, has always meant protective tariffs, state centralization with bureaucratic tyranny, the corruption of parliament, favors granted to the clergy, to the privileged classes, shots fired in the streets against demonstrators, and shadowy electoral schemes."[16]

Gramsci's anti-Giolittism can be further explained by the pernicious role this statesman's seductive political strategy played within the reformist wing of the PSI, to the point that there was an objective alliance between the Giolittian liberals and the reformist Socialists. World War I actually reinforced this alliance, for Giolitti remained the uncontested leader of the neutral bourgeoisie that the nationalists hated. This fact was verified by the speech he gave at Cuneo on August 13, 1917, in which he argued that the accentuation of social dramas caused by the conflict must be solved through establishing greater social justice after the war. Gramsci interpreted this analysis as akin to exonerating the Italian bourgeoisie from its responsibilities, all the while continuing to seduce the reformist Socialists, who had been temporarily swept under the rug but never abandoned, even after the Gentiloni pact.

The second theme of national and international consequence that Gramsci developed was the war. The latter was never analyzed from a military perspective and barely from a geopolitical one. Instead, it was grasped through the lens of the culturalist and neo-idealist hermeneutics that had become Gramsci's specialty. In this way, following Croce and Gentile, the *GDP* journalist refused to conceive of the war as a conflict between civilizations and, consequently, to justify it in the name of abstract ideas and values, for example, as an opposition between the fully mechanized Germanic *Kultur* and the Latin *civiltà* focused on spiritual refinement. He categorically rejected any naturalist views of culture as the product of a national spirit. Science and truth had no borders, and the rigorous, serious mind existed just as much in the Entente powers as they did among the Dual Alliance. All the same, Gramsci concentrated his critiques on anti-Germanic texts like those written by Vittorio Cian (1862–1951), a vehement nationalist, the founder of the Turin anti-German league, and a professor of Italian literature in that city since 1913, who obtained the removal of Umberto Cosmo from the university on the charge that he would espouse anti-Italian arguments there. For Cosmo's former student, Cian belonged to "the scholarly and literary demi-monde," to use Croce's lethal phrase.[17] Gramsci also shared the Neapolitan philosopher's negative view of the French republic—which we will come back to—and his refusal to let himself be overcome by feelings, always keeping a cool head. Along these lines, the violation of Belgium's neutrality and the violence committed there must not turn Socialists away from their opposition to the war.

All the same, it is important to avoid exaggerating the commonalities between Croce and Gramsci. For Croce, founder of the journal *La Critica*, the conflict in progress not only proved that the internationalist ideas Socialism conveyed were weak but also demonstrated that war remained an inevitable factor between states and that one therefore had to defend one's country while continuing to preserve the educational realm from ideological impurities. Ultimately, by joining patriotism with a concern for protecting the universality of the discipline, Croce didn't propose to be above the battle, as he judged this attitude to be part of a Masonic, cosmopolitan, abstract mindset. Gramsci took the opposite position, praising

Romain Rolland, whom he thought of as a universalist intellectual par excellence. He meant to make the French writer's position known by translating his articles for the *GDP* and by delivering a speech, on August 25, 1916, to support Rolland's masterpiece *Above the Battle* on the occasion of its Italian translation.

But at the time, Gramsci still saw France as the land of Jacobinism and Freemasonry, the country of abstract humanitarianism, founded on the outmoded ideas of natural law and universal justice, and he preferred to praise Anglo-Saxon seriousness. He applauded the intelligence of Woodrow Wilson's plan for the League of Nations, which rejected "the old conception, that one could call Latin, the conception according to Victor Hugo, humanitarian, Masonic . . . anti-historical, tenderly constructed with the mortar of tears and the stones of sighs."[18] Instead, the league wanted to establish itself through free trade, the only way of preventing the war, as the writings of Edoardo Giretti demonstrated, writings that were celebrated by the culturists (see chapter 2) and by Norman Angell in his book *The Great Illusion* (1909). At the time, this position shows an astonishing shortsightedness on the part of the Sardinian thinker, who imagined capitalism as nothing but an economic integration between countries thanks to economic exchange, and not as a clash between their rival military expansionisms. At the same time, Gramsci never veered toward Wilsonianism, which enticed so much of the reformist Socialist family and so many Italian progressives, since for him, that would amount to confusing bourgeois internationalism with Socialist internationalism. As he saw it, the development of bourgeois internationalism must be encouraged only to the extent that it served, in some minimal way, a Socialist agenda.

His interpretation of postwar geopolitics proved to be much more stimulating, since he theorized that a new hierarchy among powers had been put in place, transforming the world "into a trust in the hands of a few dozen banks, ship captains, and Anglo-Saxon industrials," in which Italy "has become a market of colonial exploitation, a sphere of influence, a dominion, a land of surrender, everything except an independent and sovereign State."[19] As he expanded his horizon toward political questions of a national and international order, Gramsci began to take on duties in the heart of the PSI.

The First Steps toward Militant Engagement

The Turin context explains why Antonio Gramsci assumed his first political responsibility. As a stronghold of Giolittian neutralism, perceived as the city of loafers giving themselves over to the pleasures of the theater and the cinema, Turin was still the citadel of intransigent Socialists. In July 1914, the latter took over the leadership of the Turin Section of the PSI, outstripping by a few votes the list of those who supported reconciliation with the government, led by Bruno Buozzi (1881–1944), the prestigious leader of the FIOM, who was ready to participate in the committees for mobilization that were put in place by the authorities to accelerate industrial production in exchange for wage increases for workers and the maintenance of a minimum of contractual function. The intransigent Socialists consolidated their hold after decisions made at the Zimmerwald Conference (September 1915) and Kienthal Conference (April 1916). The maximalism[20] of young Socialists earned them (somewhat redundantly) the moniker of "rigid intransigents" or more simply *rigidi*. Though Gramsci was absent from these PSI debates between 1914 and 1916, he was, on this ideological line, openly internationalist and intransigent. Otherwise it would be difficult to understand why Giacinto Menotti Serrati (1874–1926), chosen as the director of *Avanti!* after Mussolini's expulsion from the PSI, would have accepted a collaborator whose conceptions were opposed to his own.

From spring 1917 on, the idea of bringing the war to an immediate conclusion was a recurring theme in Socialist propaganda. The first, confused echoes of the February Revolution in Russia encouraged Socialist Italians, particularly intransigent ones, to raise their voices, with the *rigidi* foremost among them. Popular anger, accumulated in the face of daily difficulties, and in particular, in the face of problems linked to diet and the cost of living,[21] would transform into a riot.

These were problems that Gramsci had constantly criticized, attacking the pernicious role played by middlemen like "Monssu Botegari" ("Mister Shopkeeper").

Everything began on August 21, 1917, when the bakeries had closed due to a lack of flour rations. On August 22, there was no bread anywhere in the city of Turin, and several shops selling food were plundered. Aware of the gravity of the situation, the authorities responded by mobilizing troops but also by requisitioning flour, allowing most of the bakeries to reopen starting the next day. But the protest, while remaining spontaneous (i.e., not decided or overseen by the PSI or by the CGL), continued to take on a more political character, as the slogan "do it the Russian way" proves. In the workers' neighborhoods such as Borgo San Paolo, the Barriera di Nizza, and the Barriera di Milano, barricades went up, streetcars were burned, and confrontations between the crowds and the soldiers became particularly violent, even if there were a few halting attempts at fraternizing between the troops and the demonstrators. On the evening of August 24, the workers lost the battle. It still took several days for the factories to reopen. These riots, which were the most significant a country at war had experienced outside of Russia, concluded with the deaths of some fifty demonstrators and three infantrymen, not to mention the two hundred and fifty wounded, who were mainly workers. They also resulted in the arrest of 822 militant Socialists, who were imprisoned until their trial, which opened in August 1918 and concluded the following year with the acquittal of all the defendants. The imprisonment of the Socialist leaders of the Turin Section forced the PSI to draw from its reservoir of militants. The need was even greater because the Turin Section had less room to maneuver in autumn 1917, not only because Turin was declared a war zone on September 16, but also because of the disaster at Caporetto (October 24 to November 12, 1917), the worst defeat the Italian army suffered, with the deaths of thirty thousand men and the surrender of three hundred thousand soldiers, clearing the road to Venice for the Austrian and German troops placed under the command of Otto von Below. Even though the enemy offensive was stopped at

Monte Grappa, it was no longer the right moment for a head-on confrontation with the Italian authorities. In addition to these external difficulties, there were the usual polemics between the reformist wing and the intransigent wing of the PSI. Through their spokesman Claudio Treves in an article in *Critica Sociale* in September 1917, the reformists criticized the futile unrest in Turin, judging the exaltation of elites expected to drive history as harmful and contrary to the lesson of Marxism, attracting reproach from the *GDP*, who scolded the lead thinker of *Critica Sociale* for his detached, cold view of the revolutionary spirit of the masses. In the midst of the wave of emotion and fear unleashed by the rout at Caporetto, the most important reformist Socialists like Turati, Treves, or even Rinaldo Rigola (1868–1954), the first secretary of the CGL, who remained at the head of that union until the end of the war, called for defending the sacred soil of the fatherland. Such a position drove the maximalists to organize a counteroffensive, whose first step was to quiet their differences. So they decided to meet with the utmost secrecy, without, however, escaping the surveillance of the police, at the house of Mario Trozzi, a Florentine lawyer who was the *Avanti!* correspondent for that city. Gramsci observed this encounter, which took place on November 17–19, 1917. In fact, after the wave of consecutive arrests during the riots of August 1917, the leadership committee of the Turin Section had been greatly reduced and had to rebuild. Antonio Gramsci joined it at the end of summer 1917. This meeting was dominated by the two most important figures on the revolutionary side of the PSI at the time: Costantino Lazzari (1857–1927), the national secretary of the PSI, elected after the maximalist victory at the Reggio Emilia conference in 1912, and Giacinto Menotti Serrati, the director of *Avanti!*. Despite the legend that Gramsci negotiated with the Sardinian soldiers of the famous Sassari brigade[22] and led them to fraternize with the crowd, Gramsci played no role in the August 1917 riots (the brigade wasn't even in Turin at the time). During this meeting in Florence, which served as a small-scale conference for the PSI, Gramsci maintained a very reserved position. This attitude can perhaps be explained by his shyness and by his desire to remain withdrawn, but even more by his marginal role in political action in a strict sense. In fact, Gramsci's main fight was still essentially cultural in nature. He devoted all his energy to transforming the *GDP*, where he became the de facto editor-in-chief after the August 1917 arrest of Maria Giudice, so as to transform it, in his own words, from "a local weekly into a review of Socialist political culture developed in accordance with the doctrines and the tactics of revolutionary Socialism."[23]

It is interesting to note that at the end of 1917, Gramsci tried to establish a cultural organization intended to prepare the proletariat intellectually for the revolution. This small club, which had only a handful of young members, automatically fell apart after a few of them joined the army. The discussions were organized around a book, with each person offering his analysis. Gramsci followed a pedagogical model that was openly Gentilian, going so far as to write to Giuseppe Lombardo Radice (1879–1938), one of Gentile's main disciples in the educational sector, to find out if his method conformed to the spirit of Gentilian actualism. In response, he received a good thrashing from his correspondent, who replied that, after Caporetto, the priority was fighting to defend the sacred ground of the fatherland, which was in danger, not organizing pedagogical speeches. As this epistolary exchange shows, Gramsci remained tied to the neo-idealist intellectual world that had shaped his education. As a result, he was profoundly isolated within the Socialist world. Neither the PSI nor the trade union organizations were interested in his plan to create a cultural association. The metapolitical positions he took were attacked by the reformists and ignored by the maximalists, who were little disposed, if not hostile, to culturalist arguments that seemed cut off from organizational plans and concrete ideologies. The latter group were upset that Gramsci had begun by criticizing their populist vein, which, according to him, maintained the people in their minority position. It is also significant that he interpreted the failure of the workers' rebellion in August 1917 as proof that the workers did not yet have a true character. Finally, we must remember that Gramsci's isolation was still due to his noxious reputation as an interventionist. This whole cluster of reasons meant that Gramsci played no role at the meeting in Florence in November 1917. No comments from him are mentioned in the minutes of the meeting recorded by Giovanni Germanetto (1885–1959), a militant Socialist and barber by trade, who would become a leader of the International Red Aid (MOPR) and make a name for himself by publishing, first in Russian and then in French, *Memoirs of a Barber: The Autobiography of an Italian Revolutionist* (1931), a best-seller translated into twenty-three languages that explains the inner mechanisms of the Italian Communist family and the Communist International.

During the meeting in Florence, the whole debate revolved around the disagreement between the Serrati-Lazzari group, which intended to remain faithful to the strategy developed at the start of the war, "Né aderire, né sabotare," and the strategy of Amadeo Bordiga, who supported the idea that the proletariat should revolt to seize power. Though he judged that the proletariat wasn't yet ready, since it lacked character, Gramsci's position was likely quite close to Bordiga's at the time. In fact, as he explained to Germanetto during the return trip from Florence to Turin: "In the struggle that awaits us, the PSI will not be able to do anything if it remains what it is at the moment. What has happened in Russia indicates the route to take. *Avanti!* exalts the revolution, but the revolution is not at all as our leaders imagine it."[24]

Gramsci and Bordiga shared the idea that from then on the revolution was possible, and that the failure of the Turin riots in August 1917 didn't mean the end of their hopes for change, far from it. But Gramsci left this argument to the charismatic Neapolitan leader of the intransigent wing of the PSI, which the latter had consistently championed since 1910. After distinguishing himself in 1912, when he triumphed over the culturalist arguments Tasca asserted at the fourth conference of the Socialist Youth Federation in September of that year (see chapter 2), Bordiga enjoyed a growing audience among Italian Socialist youth. In 1914, as the head of the Neapolitan Section of the PSI, he adopted an uncompromising antiwar position. An unparalleled propagandist and organizer, he defended a

Marxist conception of the party as an active minority. As director of *L'Avanguardia* in 1917, he was one of the first Socialist thinkers to welcome the Russian Revolution with enthusiasm.

These few biographical elements illustrate the differences in strategy and, to a greater extent, in temperament between the Neapolitan and the Sardinian. While Bordiga established himself as a political leader of the first order within the intransigent majority of the PSI, Gramsci remained a journalist, defending original but marginal arguments. And so it wasn't surprising that Gramsci wasn't elected as a member of the Interim Committee of the Turin Section of the PSI during the party's restructuring in January 1918. Until the middle of 1919, Gramsci didn't play any role in politics, not even at the Turin level, while Bordiga established himself as a Socialist figure on the international stage. Further proof of Gramsci's marginality comes from the fact that his name continued to be improperly spelled in reports to the prefect of Turin: Granci in one place, Gransci in another, or even Granisci! But he would emerge from this anonymity by publishing a front-page article in the national edition of *Avanti!* on December 24, 1917, an article that would make an immediate sensation: "The Revolution against 'Capital.'"

Italian Socialism and the Bolshevik Revolution

Until the October Revolution of 1917, Gramsci's Socialism owed much more to his neo-idealist background than it did to any Marxist influence. The article in the January 15, 1916 issue of the *GDP* titled "The Syllabus and Hegel" and signed Alfa Gamma is a good example of the type of socialism Gramsci supported at the time. Analyzing "The Pope and the War," a pamphlet by the journalist and essayist Mario Missiroli,[25] Gramsci expressed praise for the German nation:

> The Germanic nation was born from a religious crisis, the Protestant Reformation, and consolidated and reinforced itself through the slow work of philosophical thought that brought it to the creation of the modern State, in which the Citizen is

also the believer, because philosophical idealism, abolishing any dualism and placing in the individual consciousness the element of knowledge and the creative activity of history, made it independent from any authority, from any syllabus.[26]

On the contrary, the Italian Risorgimento and the French democracy had made the mistake of undertaking a political revolution without first enacting a religious reformation, creating the Catholic syllabus in Rome and the "Masonic syllabus" in Paris. The article went on to praise Hegel, who "has destroyed all possibility of a syllabus, which Rousseau did not do." The last sentence of the article deserves to be cited in full:

> In the struggle between the *Syllabus* and Hegel, it is Hegel who has won, because Hegel represents the life of thought that does not know limits and posits itself as something transient, something capable of being superseded, something always renewing itself just as history does. The *Syllabus* is an obstacle; it is the death of the inner life; it is a cultural problem and not a historical fact.[27]

In his references, and even in the choice of his vocabulary, Gramsci styled himself as the heir of historicist idealism, since he argued for the assimilation of philosophy and history, which were unified in the act of thought, and in this way he adhered to actualism, since he reconciled action and fact by praising the creative function of the self. People would have to wait until the *Prison Notebooks* for Gramsci to express a defined critique of Gentilian actualism. Such an analysis of history was at odds with what he understood as the positivist fatalism of Claudio Treves. We understand that Gramsci, even as he began to think like a Marxist, refused simplified propaganda, as he saw it being administered in public universities or by journalists such as Maria Giudice. This explains his fight to create and promote a cultural association, as the third organ of socialism along with the party and the union, to allow this political doctrine to establish itself by giving each militant a solid vision of the world. It was therefore not surprising that after the failure of the major Turin workers' strikes in August 1917, Gramsci devoted a special issue of the *GDP* (October 20, 1917) to a direct attack on tariff protectionism. This view also explains why, during the secret meeting in Florence on November 18–19, 1917, Gramsci was accused of Bergsonism for the first (and not the last) time, a word his adversaries used to identify the excessiveness of his antipositivist reaction and his resulting anti-Giolittism.[28] The scorn Gramsci displayed for French errors, such as democracy, messianic Jacobinism, Masonic humanitarianism—all trumpeted by Third Republic radicals as abstract ideas of justice, equality, and fraternity—only fueled this critique. Even after he got behind the October Revolution, Gramsci had real difficulty combining Marxism, which he still feared would be reduced to economic determinism, with his view of mankind as the subject of historical creation. All the same, as Leonardo Rapone has quite rightly shown, the October Revolution forced him to think as a Marxist in order to "develop a vision of history in which it would be possible to justify and to rationalize the work of the Russian Revolution within the theoretical perimeter of Marxism."[29] Gramsci would develop a form of Marxism that gave the subject a decisive role, no longer taken individually, but collectively. Gramsci's opening up to Marxist philosophy, and before that, to Leninism, also enlarged his ideological horizon without entailing an abandonment of his idealist background, since he continued to use references that were outside of strictly Marxist terrain, and he still thought, and would always think, that it was fundamental for Socialists to have a solid culture.

Gramsci's first assessment of the Russian Revolution dates from mid- to late April 1917. In an article in the *GDP* on April 29, he attempted to prove that the Russian Revolution was a proletarian revolution that had nothing to do with the revolution in France, as the bourgeois newspapers tried to suggest, since it "has been innocent of Jacobinism . . . a purely bourgeois phenomenon . . . [with] no universal program," furthering "its own, particularist class interests."[30]

The absence of Jacobin contamination within the Russian Revolution indicated that it had not made use of violence, having refused to replace "the dictatorship of one man by the dictatorship of an auda-cious minority."[31] And Gramsci went so far as to offer sweet reveries: "The Russian revolutionaries have not only freed political prisoners, but common criminals as well. When the common criminals in one prison were told they were free, they replied that they felt they did not have the right to accept liberty because they had to expiate their crimes."[32] With this remark that makes us smile, Gramsci advanced the idea that the Russian Revolution was not a simple political fact but, rather, that it had created a new conception of life. We notice, once more, the pervasiveness of actualist vocabulary. By creating a new order and a new ethics, the Russian Revolution achieved the goals of Gramsci's agenda.

But did he know exactly what events were taking place in Russia? As his analysis of the behavior of imprisoned common criminals shows, he had a secondhand and mythical image of this revolution. During the entire first half of 1917, he presented his reports on Russia in major Italian and French dailies that were, let's not forget, sub-ject to censorship because of the war. With the notable exception of the editor of *La Stampa*, Alfredo Frassati (1868–1961), who showed great acuity by affirming in his April 2, 1917 editorial that since the soldiers were tired of fighting, the abdication of the Tsar Nicholas II would set off a revolution that couldn't be stopped, all the bourgeois newspapers praised the February Revolution in 1917. They thought that Russia's liberal and democratic turn would strengthen its en-gagement in the war on the side of the Entente powers. All the same, by stigmatizing Lenin, they committed a grave error, since their criti-cisms of him attracted the sympathy of militant Italian Socialists, for whom "Do it the Russian way" became a 1917 slogan, replacing the one that had been chosen at the start of the war, "Né aderire, né sabotare." Although Lenin became a myth for the Italian workers who wanted an end to the war, he remained almost unknown as a politician and thinker. It was actually very difficult to go to Russia. Oddino Morgari (1865–1944)[33] had tried in vain to reach Moscow in April 1917. Such a situation fostered ambiguity. The Kerensky gov-ernment (July 27–November 8, 1917) had indeed sent three delegates to Italy, the best known of whom were Joseph Goldenberg and Boris Smirnov, two Mensheviks who were opposed to Lenin at the time, while still refusing to see him as the Kaiser's lackey. Their mission was to remind the Allies that the new Russian government intended to advocate for peace, but by fighting beside them in the war. In the interview he gave in Paris to the correspondents of *La Stampa* on July 25, 1917, Goldenberg defended the Constituent Assembly and the idea of fatherland. Despite the statements they gave in Paris and then repeated in London, Smirnov and Goldenberg were nonetheless welcomed in Turin with enthusiastic cries of "Long live Lenin," causing them great embarrassment, since the Kerensky government had banned *Pravda* and the Bolshevik Party, forcing Lenin to go into hiding. The scene repeated itself in Rome, Florence, Bologna, and Milan. What's more, since they spoke in French, Serrati twisted their statements to have an overly pacifist meaning.

For Gramsci, too, Lenin was still only a name. He only started to get to know him better in 1919, by reading the famous interview the Bolshevik leader gave the English journalist and writer Arthur Ransome (1884–1967), printed with the title "Notes of Conversations with Lenin," which was published in translation by *L'Ordine Nuovo* in its September 13 issue, in 1919. Until that year, Gramsci hadn't yet read anything by Lenin—neither the *April Theses* (1917) nor *The State and Revolution* from the same year, nor even *What Is to Be Done* (1902). He also had not followed the developing reports of force in Russia. And so, in an article for the *GDP*, he put Lenin on the same level with Viktor Chernov (1873–1952), a revolutionary Socialist who represented the populist Russian tradition, a minister of agriculture for the Kerensky government before being elected president of the Russian Constituent Assembly that was stillborn in October 1917. In Gramsci's defense, it is true that Chernov's Ligurian exile and his writing about Italian peasants had made him popular in Italy, and that *Avanti!* presented him at the time as the representative of the true revolutionary forces in Russia.

Until 1917, the Bolshevik Revolution didn't change Gramsci's position but rather encouraged him, especially because, for the Socialist journalist, this revolution "consist[ed] more of ideologies than of events," to which he added, implausibly and a bit worrisomely, "(And hence, at bottom, we do not need to know more than we do)."[34]

From July 1917 on, he took a favorable position on the Bolsheviks, whom he referred to by the significant name "Russian Maximalists" like many of his companions in the struggle. In his eyes, these Russian Maximalists were "the continuity of the revolution—they are its rhythm, and hence they are the revolution itself."[35] If "Lenin and his most prominent comrades could be swept away by the onset of the storms they themselves have stirred up, not all their followers would disappear. By now there are too many of them. And the revolutionary fire is spreading, scorching new hearts and minds."[36]

Gramsci hoped that this proposition would become true for Italy as well, since, he said, "What has happened in Russia indicates the route to take. *Avanti!* exalts the revolution, but the revolution is not at all as our leaders imagine it."[37] This statement, which Gramsci had made to Germanetto during their return trip from Florence to Turin, was several days ahead of his article "The Revolution against 'Capital,'" which had a resounding echo within the Socialist world, transforming Gramsci from a little-known and little-recognized journalist into an author whose opinions began to matter on the national level, particularly since it is the first signed article that he published in the national edition of *Avanti!* on December 24, 1917. Though it was heavily censored, it was reprinted in a less redacted form and was signed with his initials, A. G., in the January 5, 1918 edition of the *GDP*.

The central thesis of this article is that the Bolshevik Revolution was made against Marx's *Capital*, which "in Russia . . . was more the book of the bourgeoisie than of the proletariat."[38]

> if the Bolsheviks reject some of the statements in *Capital*, they do not reject its invigorating, imminent thought. These people are not "Marxists," that is all; they have not used the works of the Master to compile a rigid doctrine of dogmatic utterances never to be questioned. They live Marxist thought—that thought which is

eternal, which represents the continuation of German and Italian idealism, and which in the case of Marx was contaminated by positivist and naturalist encrustations.[39]

Therefore,

> Why should they [the Russian people] wait for the history of England to be repeated in Russia, for the bourgeoisie to arise, for the class struggle to begin, so that class consciousness may be formed and the final catastrophe of the capitalist world eventually hit them? The Russian people—or at least a minority of the Russian people—has already passed through these experiences in thought. It has gone beyond them. It will make use of them now to assert itself just as it will make use of Western capitalist experience to bring itself rapidly to the same level of production as the Western world.[40]

This part of Gramsci's article demonstrates his faithful adherence to the Bolshevik Revolution, as living proof of the mistaken interpretation of reformist Socialists for whom History never broke off but rather followed a determined course, perhaps even a fateful one. This revival of the old debate, which began in 1880 between Marx and Vera Zasulich (1849–1919) on the possibility of skipping over certain steps to arrive at communism, was a way for the Sardinian thinker to directly attack the reformist Socialist intellectuals who judged, for their part, that this reasoning was part of his habitual Bergsonism. In this vein, in an article in *Critica Sociale*, Claudio Treves wholeheartedly condemned the statements: "Recently," wrote the reformist leader, "a collaborator of *Avanti!* expounded the doctrine that Lenin's decrees go beyond history, that is, they fly over entire periods in the evolution of property. With these decrees, one jumps right over the industrial bourgeois era, going from patriarchal agrarian economy straight to collectivism."[41] But the position Gramsci advanced was also criticized by intransigent Socialists, and Bordiga was foremost among them, since he could not accept the tone and the idealist arguments of Gramsci's statements, which seemed to him like a vain, dangerous harangue, since it was tantamount to saying the Russian Revolution was "a defeat for the method of historical materialism and, by contrast, a victory for idealist values."[42]

Though the negative comments outweighed the positive, "The Revolution against 'Capital'" marked a turning point in Gramsci's life, since it began to make him known outside of his small circle of Turin regulars. His support of the Leninist revolution also made him into a Bolshevik, even if this transformation didn't yet affect his whole vision of the world, which was still influenced by neo-idealist philosophy. All the same, part of his political position had already changed. By accepting the dissolution of the Constituent Assembly in Russia, elected through universal suffrage, in which, contrary to the meaning of their name, the Bolsheviks were not a majority, he accepted the use of force by a minority in order to impose its dominance. Though the dissolution of the Constituent Assembly did not lead to a positive reassessment of Jacobinism (Gramsci would not recognize the merits of French Jacobinism until 1921, through the influence of historian Albert Mathiez's work), it reinforced his habitual critique of humanist democracy, which was carried out this time in light of the new claim that true sovereignty of the proletariat was not in the Constituent Assembly, "i.e. in a Western-type parliament elected according to the canons of Western democracy. The Russian proletariat has offered us the first model of direct representation of the producers: the Soviets. Now sovereignty has gone back to the Soviets."[43]

At the end of January 1918, Gramsci fixed his attention on the soviets for the first time. Even if he perceived his country as a land of rising social tensions, he didn't think, before 1919, that a revolution was possible on Italian soil. But after the winter of 1917–18, he was convinced that if it did happen, it could take place only by carrying out the soviet idea. In the immediate postwar period, Gramsci's great intellectual and political effort would be toward transmitting the Bolshevik Revolution to Italy as an expression of the soviet state conceived not only as a new economic organization, but also, more

globally, as a new order. He did it by founding, with the other musketeers, a paper with precisely that title: *L'Ordine Nuovo*, whose mission had been a longtime goal for the culturalists, a goal he had tried
and failed to bring into being by creating a cultural organization.
This intellectual and political challenge was accompanied by an increasingly direct and significant engagement in the life of his party—
the PSI, and eventually the PCdI—transforming him in the space
of a few months from a marginal, original Socialist journalist into
a militant Communist and major player in the dramas of his new
party and those of the Third International more broadly.

< 4 >

From the Experience of
L'Ordine Nuovo to His Departure
for Moscow
(1919–1922)

Worker's Democracy

The end of World War I marked a particularly productive period for Gramsci. Though he was no longer part of the new executive committee of the Turin Section of the PSI elected on November 28, 1918, he became, from then on, one of the principal journalists of this political family after being named editor-in-chief of the Turin edition of *Avanti!*, an edition that had previously depended on issues from Milan but became independent after December 5, 1918. He spent most of his time in his new office at the corner of Via dell'Arcivescovado and Via XX Settembre, streets that are close to what is now Via Antonio Gramsci. During the winter of 1918–19, he experienced one of the rare moments when his physical and mental suffering subsided. He joked and laughed, happy to reconnect with his former classmates who had been discharged and to begin new friendships that would become significant in his life—including, first among them, his friendship with Felice Platone (1896–1962), who would become one of the first editors of an anthology of his writing after World War II.

With a print run of fifty thousand copies, the Piedmont edition of *Avanti!*, directed by Ottavio Pastore, was a good forum for Gramsci. The winter of 1918–19 was dominated by the Fifteenth Congress of the PSI and, above all, by the founding of the Third International. The Sardinian thinker understood that he would have to leverage this new political context to create a press organ that closely reflected his political and intellectual ideas and could serve as a compass to orient the minds of militant Socialists who were seized with enthusiasm but also prone to confusion. In fact, though the intransigent maximalists confirmed their hold on the party during the September 1918 congress, they didn't necessarily form a united ideological front, displaying varying sensibilities whose differences would only widen. It was in this atmosphere of both elation and uncertainty that the four musketeers, reunited once again, decided to create a new paper.

Angelo Tasca came up with the six thousand lire that were essential for its launch. Pia Carena took on the administrative work. Everything was in place, on the symbolic date of May 1, 1919, for the release of *L'Ordine Nuovo* (*L'ON*) with the subtitle *Rassegna settimanale di cultura socialista* (weekly review of Socialist culture). The goal was to make this weekly, which comprised eight pages of tightly spaced text, the equivalent of *La Voce*[1] for Italian Socialist workers. In a few months, *L'ON* had four hundred subscribers, the vast majority of whom were Piedmontese, and about ten times as many readers. Piero Gobetti, the young prodigy of liberal journalism who died as a result of injuries inflicted by the Fascist squads, left behind a critical and moving portrait of the founders of *L'ON*, with whom he had collaborated. Though he insisted on the difference between their temperaments—Tasca's sense of propaganda, Terracini's dry intellectualism, Togliatti's knack for strategy, Gramsci's corrosive critical faculties—he also shed light on their common need for action and their commitment, conceived as an apostolate in favor of the revolution. Though the four musketeers were united in their total rejection of reformism, their differences would soon emerge and begin to cause friction between them.

In the first issues, Tasca's ideas dominated. Of the four former "culturists," he was the one with the most political experience who knew best how to speak to the workers' psychology. As someone who had been closely involved in the union battles since the major strikes of 1911–12, he had maintained his "devotion to concrete union organizing,"[2] refusing any kind of extremist demagoguery, for which he endlessly criticized the anarcho-syndicalists. For this reason, he continued to cultivate close ties to Bruno Buozzi, whom he had known since 1911, when Buozzi was elected general secretary of the FIOM. A few months later, Buozzi joined the steering committee of the CGL. Buozzi would continue to occupy these two roles until his 1927 exile to France, where he continued this fight. In his book of first-person accounts, *I primi dieci anni del PCI*, Tasca emphasized the fact that the other collaborators of *L'ON* lacked connections to the Italian trade union movement and its day-to-day existence and battles, citing that deficiency as the principal reason for his 1920 break with his companions in the struggle.

Under the pseudonym of Empedocle,[3] Togliatti, who was in charge of the column *Battaglia delle idee* (Battle of Ideas), endeavored to maintain a dialogue with his former teachers (Croce, Einaudi, Gentile) and with free-market and neo-idealist themes, which had influenced the four musketeers' earliest political positions. Terracini participated much less in the life of the paper and, unlike his three companions, wasn't an editor, prioritizing political action for the PSI on the local and eventually the national level. As for Antonio Gramsci, he threw himself body and soul into this type of journalistic engagement, with its tightly linked political and intellectual challenges.

Though he appreciated that *L'ON* openly supported the Bolshevik Revolution and avoided certain flaws of reformist Socialism, rejecting the coarse anticlericalism that the reformists had often demonstrated, Gramsci criticized the fact that this paper remained, as he saw it, an anthology of texts. He therefore advocated for dedicating this weekly to a central idea that would be anchored in the challenges of the time and would distinguish *L'ON* from the rest of the Socialist press. Keeping this in mind, he decided, with Togliatti and Terracini's help, to organize, in his own words, "an editorial coup d'état"[4] against Tasca by publishing an article called "Workers' Democracy" on June 21, 1919.

Much ink has been spilled about this unsigned article, which was certainly penned by Gramsci, and in which he suggested that the *commissioni interne* (internal commissions, or shop committees) that existed in factories should be thought of and promoted as the seeds of future soviets. Since the article is often praised by his many acolytes in an uncritical way, it is important to put this text back into its precise context. First of all, it is interesting to note that "Angelo Tasca subscribed to the new direction—he did not, incidentally, experience it as a maneuver directed against him at the time—and integrated the new idea into his own conception, approaching it according to his own preoccupations, but those that were linked to this theme."[5] On the other hand, it has been established that this central idea, which was apparently sorely lacking in the first issues of *L'ON*, was formulated for the first time not by Gramsci but very likely by Aron Wizner. Born in 1882, Aron Wizner became a militant at a young age in his hometown of Lodz, where he was one of the leaders of the Social Democratic Party in the Kingdom of Poland and in Lithuania. After experiencing prison, exile, and fighting underground, he spent almost ten years in Italy starting in 1914. Close to the Bolsheviks from 1917 on, he became connected with Gramsci in the same year. He would finish his career as an advisor for Molotov, before becoming a victim of the Moscow Trials in 1937. In his 1920 article "On the *Ordine Nuovo* Program," Gramsci reflected on the genesis of the newspaper's transformation from an anthology of texts into a mouthpiece for the Italian soviet:

> A third person, who had been struck by the following question put to him bluntly by a Polish comrade: "Why hasn't a congress of the internal commissions ever been held in Italy?" answered the same question at our meetings: "Yes, a seed of a workers' government, of a Soviet does exist in Italy, in Turin—it is the internal commission."[6]

It was probably during one of the many impromptu discussions in Gramsci's small office, encumbered with piles of books and proofs of articles to correct, that the metalworker Enea Matta—likely the young comrade troubled by Wizner's question—had first sparked debates about the *commissioni interne* among the proletariat. Even though this idea did not originate with Gramsci (nor did he claim so), he was nonetheless responsible for transforming it into the key concept that had previously been missing from *L'ON*, one that would distinguish the newspaper from the rest of Socialist writing and allow it to respond to the challenges of the time as they played out in Russia.

In the article "Workers' Democracy," he wrote that the *commissioni interne* "must be the organs of proletarian power, replacing the capitalist in all his useful functions of management and administration."[7] The Italian soviet was born, and Gramsci would put all his "apostle's energy"[8] (in Gobetti's words) into its service. Despite his lack of oratorical talent, modest past as a militant, physical weakness, and frequent psychological distress, Antonio fully engaged in political action in 1919. Among his notable acts, which got him jailed for a few hours in July 1919, we can single out his attempt to convince the Sardinian soldiers of the Sassari brigade not to play into a reactionary game by obstructing demonstrations in support of the Socialist republic of Russia and Hungary. But his biggest battle was to transform the *commissioni interne* into instruments of the revolution. To do that, he first had to get to know their reality and understand how they worked. He didn't shy away from endlessly questioning workers at their places of work, at cafés, and on trams. Later on, he came to understand how naïve and sometimes irritating this could be for those who might have preferred to forget about their working conditions on a Sunday!

But what exactly were the *commissioni interne*? Could they embody "the Socialist state in power"? Could they, in Gramsci's words, become "the skeleton of the Socialist state"? Could they represent the authority of the true workers' democracy, alongside the trade unions and the party, which should not, in his mind, stop "its role as the organ of communist education, as the furnace of faith, the depository of doctrine"? Could they transform "internal commissions [that] limit the power of the capitalist in the party . . . [into] organs of proletarian power"? Could they transform "functions of arbitration and discipline . . . [into the] functions of management and administration"[9] that Gramsci called for?

The *commissioni interne* made their first timid official appearance on October 27, 1906, after the FIOM and the leadership of the automobile company Itala signed an agreement to recognize their existence.[10] Contrary to Robert Paris's claim, nuanced though it is, that the *commissioni interne* sometimes appear "as the expression of a spontaneous tendency for direct management,"[11] Paolo Spriano's landmark study shows that they were, first and foremost, arbitration bodies that followed a contractual politics and sought to defend the rights of workers and to promote their interests with respect to salaries, hours, and working conditions. This tendency for class collaboration was reinforced by the creation, in August 1916, of industrial mobilization committees placed directly under the supervision of the minister of war. Actively participating in these committees, the FIOM, which was then led by the reformist triumvirate of Bruno Buozzi, Mario Guarnieri, and Emilio Colombino, defended the idea of a contractual politics, within which the *commissioni interne* were a privileged instrument. This context helped the *commissioni* to gain full recognition, since they had previously been tolerated in theory more than they had been respected in practice. This strategy proved to be effective, since, in February 1919, an agreement was signed under the aegis of Turin's prefect that allowed the *commissioni interne* to be made up of five members elected from a list of candidates. The candidates were chosen from among workers who had been unionized by the FIOM and who had at least one year of experience at the factory. The role of these *commissioni* was to serve in the first instance for examining and trying to resolve disputes between workers and industrialists. In the case of a failed negotiation, the conflict had to be dealt with, in the second instance, by the FIOM and the Management Consortium. This model, which *Avanti!* presented to its readers on February 28, 1919, openly conveyed the FIOM's hold on this body, a hold that would make itself felt ideologically through a preference for reformist actions. In this way, without a rupture in the functioning and strategy of the *commissioni interne*, the series of questions that Gramsci had posed in his article "Workers' Democracy" could be answered only in the negative. In fact, the *commissioni interne* bore a stronger resemblance to arbitration bodies seeking reconciliation than they did to the powerful soviets, which were both instruments of revolution and the first units of a new state. To change this situation (which he knew about even if the tone of his article sought to create enthusiasm), Gramsci helped the other founding members of *L'ON* (with the notable exception of Tasca) to try to reverse this relationship between the unions and the *commissioni interne*, prioritizing demands that the FIOM grant nonunionized workers the right to vote. This step toward actualizing a direct revolutionary democracy for workers found its best expression in Italy through factory councils in Turin, and Gramsci unequivocally became their best theorist and one of their main organizers. But we must remember that, at the time, this initiative was central to a debate in Europe and the United States, and it was among a cluster of experiments that *L'ON* widely publicized in its pages: the Bavarian Soviet Republic, which was destroyed by paramilitary groups in spring 1919; the Hungarian Soviet Republic, which lasted for nearly five months before collapsing after the troops commanded by the French general Henri Berthelot occupied Budapest at the beginning of August 1919; or the experiment of the English shop stewards. Among the theorists who conceived of the factory council as both vector and anticipation of the Socialist republic, it is important to give special mention to Daniel De Leon (1852–1914), one of the founders of the Industrial Workers of the World (IWW), whose work Gramsci encountered at the end of 1918 as he flipped through *The Liberator: The Journal of Revolutionary Progress* created by Max Eastman (1883–1969), a young writer from New York who was a Socialist at the time and who would become friends with Trotsky. This interest in De Leon's thinking would be further supported by the journalist John Reed when he reported that the Bolshevik leader confirmed that De Leon was "the only one who has added anything to Socialist thought since Marx,"[12] inviting Nikolai Bukharin to translate his work into Russian. Aware of the need to adapt the political philosophy of Marx and Engels to the situation created by American industrial development at the end of the nineteenth century, De Leon sought in vain to establish, within the IWW, the idea of a syndicalist organization strong enough to destroy the capitalist state, to put in place a self-governing body of workers who would manage production directly. Two elements of this thinking were surely attractive to Gramsci. The first was his trust in the revolutionary potential of the workers, no longer conceived as citizens and electors, but as producers. The second was De Leon's polemical dimension, which was at the heart of his style and his approach to criticizing union reformism.

Unsurprisingly, the charge against Ordinovist arguments was led by the leaders of the FIOM, led by Bruno Buozzi, whose position was taken up by the leaders of the CGL and the reformist intellectuals of the PSI. Each, in his way, stigmatized the revolutionary-syndicalist character of the theories put forth by *L'ON* and the risk that they would weaken the unions, which had succeeded in holding onto certain essential gains despite the war and the economic crisis of the postwar period, including the maintenance of the *commissioni interne*, which was no small feat. This critique was far from baseless. In fact, anarchists and revolutionary syndicalists shared Gramsci's unequivocal rejection of the political direction of the CGL, which they accused of collaborating with management. Already derided as a Bergsonian[13] by his Socialist comrades for having published "The Revolution against 'Capital,'" Gramsci threw more fuel on the fire by writing a resounding tribute to Georges Sorel, who had written in the oldest liberal newspaper in the whole peninsula, *Il Resto del Carlino* (October 5, 1919) that "the experiment that is currently taking place in the Fiat plants is more important than all the writings published under the auspices of the *Neue Zeit* [Kautsky's journal, representing the best of orthodox theoretical Marxism]."[14] Gramsci confirmed that "Sorel's argument moves in the same direction as Lenin's, which emphasized the importance of councils of shop commissioners. . . . In sum, these arguments are our acknowledgment of the maturity of the Turin proletariat that has been active in this vein."[15] This exaltation of the workers' spontaneity certainly brought the Ordinovists and anarchists closer together. The latter, who had broken with the CGL in 1912 to found the Unione Sindicale Italiana (USI, the Italian Syndicalist Union or Italian Workers' Union), appreciated the tack the Ordinovists had taken, even if the USI continued, by contrast, to deny the necessity of the state.

The Workers' Council, the PSI, and the Third International

Though this experiment with factory councils began and developed in the specific context of the *biennio rosso*—the two "red years" of 1919–20, a period dominated by the revolutionary spirit that was emanating from Russia and moving across all of Europe, and especially across Italy—it is important to keep in mind that the ideas coming from the workers' councils had little impact on the peninsula, even though they were much debated within the Third International. *L'ON* was quick to realize the interest these arguments provoked on an international level, reprinting texts about the councils written by Jules Humbert-Droz in *Le Phare*, Pierre Monatte and Alfred Rosner in *La Vie Ouvrière*, Charles Rappoport in *La Révolution Sociale*, Boris Souvarine in the *Bulletin Communiste*, and giving a lot of publicity to arguments by Grigori Zinoviev (1883–1936) and by Bukharin, who seized on this theme of workers' and peasants' councils. For Gramsci, and for those who shared his conceptions at the time, it was of utmost importance to show that what happened in Turin was fundamentally inspired by the theses advanced by the Third International. So the PSI, which declared its support for the Third International, should have taken this into account. But that wasn't the case.

With two hundred thousand members divided into two thousand sections, the PSI organized its Sixteenth Congress in Bologna in October 1919. Though all its strains decided to follow the Third International, the leadership didn't intend to cut itself off from the powerful CGL, which represented two million members. This strategy, between revolutionary rhetoric and reformist practice, proved to be fruitful, since the PSI became the premier party in Italy. With 1,840,000 votes in the legislative elections of November 1919 and

156 delegates out of the 508 who made up the Chamber of Deputies at the time, the PSI had a hundred thousand more votes than the Partito Popolare Italiano (PPI, Italian People's Party), founded on Catholic teachings, and considered *mutatis mutandis* as the ancestor of Democrazia Cristiana (DC, the Christian Democracy party).

Faced with the risk that electoral success would dampen their Socialist direction, the most revolutionary members within the party called for abstention from the elections, finding that the parliamentary forum overtly favored the reformists. Absent from this debate, which they judged nonessential, Gramsci and the supporters of the workers' council strategy found themselves isolated. It is telling that none of the eleven Socialist delegates from the Turin electoral district took up the ideals of *L'ON*. More generally, the members of *L'ON* searched for their place within the PSI. At the Bologna congress, they fell into step with the party's majority, represented by Serrati, who called for maintaining unity and refused to abstain from elections, as Bordiga argued at the time. Serrati openly defended the revolution that was taking place in Russia, pitting himself against Lazzari's motion uniting the reformists who were careful to protect the role of parliamentary deputies and reject revolutionary rhetoric in all forms. Serrati's wing largely carried the day, with 48,411 votes, compared with 14,800 for Lazzari and only 3,417 for Bordiga, who called for the expulsion of the reformists.

Though he was elected in May 1919 as a member of the executive committee of the Turin Section of the PSI, Gramsci didn't have enough political clout at the national level to foster even a modest discussion of the political experiment under way in Turin. This idea was obviously unilaterally condemned by the reformists: Turati hated the miraculous quality the editors of *L'ON* accorded to the word "soviet." In the pages of *Avanti!* on November 8, 1919, Serrati was no more convinced when he reproached Gramsci for "the aberration of proclaiming the revolutionary capacity of the amorphous masses."[16] But it was especially in the mouthpiece of the CGL, *Battaglie Sindicali*, that Buozzi forcefully criticized the cadre of intellectuals who knew nothing about the life of factories and who, by wanting to give voting rights to nonunion workers—pointedly nicknamed "disorganized" workers[17]—played the role of sorcerers' apprentices, reproducing the fatal mistake of revolutionary syndicalists. The representatives of the most revolutionary minority of the PSI were also against *L'ON*'s arguments. Though his newspaper was called *Il Soviet*, Bordiga, the rising star of revolutionary socialism, emphasized the risk that factory councils would become corporate organisms, which would serve *in fine* only to reinforce the reformist plans of the old Socialists, since he judged that once it had become Communist, the party alone would be the most adequate instrument for delivering workers and peasants from capitalist oppression. Bordiga described the factory council experiment as "the error that the proletariat can emancipate itself by gaining ground in economic relationships at the same time as capitalism holds, with the State, the political power."[18] The only favorable echo came, unsurprisingly, from the revolutionary syndicalists of the Italian Syndicalist Union (USI), whose leader, Armando Borghi (1882–1968), rejoiced, in his paper *Guerra di Classe*, at the birth of a worker's syndicalism that was "true and pure,"[19] far from the compromises of the CGL.

It is important to pay particular attention to Angelo Tasca's reasoned and subtle critique. For Gramsci's friend, "the factory councils were not an end in and of themselves but one way among others to emancipate the proletariat."[20] Unlike the soviets, the *commissoni interne* were not revolutionary except in the circumstances when they transformed into factory councils. It was therefore desirable to reconcile this experience with the policies carried out by the PSI, and, even more, with those of the CGL, which by defending the interests of workers from within the capitalist system, already sought to get the proletariat to "emancipate itself from capitalist slavery."[21] Such a hermeneutic actually came down to placing the gravitational center of the workers' movement within the union, and, in particular, within the FIOM. Tasca openly supported this interpretation by publishing an article called "Cercando la verità" [Seeking the Truth] in the October 4, 1919 issue of *L'ON*. October 4, 1919 therefore marks a better date for the political rupture between the two men than the

June 21, 1919 publication date of "Workers' Democracy." This rupture would grow during the summer of 1920, when Tasca once again put forth his views with vigor and practicality on the occasion of the Congress of the Chambers of Labor. The pages of *L'ON* would become a space for this ideological and strategic confrontation. It was during this time period (summer 1920) that Gramsci justified, after the fact, the reasons for his "editorial coup d'état," by attacking Tasca directly:

> What was the *idea* of *L'Ordine Nuovo* in its first numbers? There was no central *idea*, no inner organization of the literary material published. What did Comrade Tasca mean by "culture"— what did he mean in concrete, not abstract terms? This is what Comrade Tasca meant by culture: he meant "recollection" and not "thought"—and recollection of the discarded, useless junk of working-class thought. He meant letting the Italian working class know, "recalling" for the benefit of the worthy Italian working class—which is so retarded, so rough and uncultured—that Louis Blanc had some thoughts on how work should be organized and that these ideas were tried out in actual experiments.... What was *L'Ordine Nuovo* in its first numbers? It was an anthology, nothing but an anthology. It was a review like any other that could have come out in Naples, Caltanisetta, or Brindisi, a journal of abstract culture, abstract information, with a strong leaning towards horror stories and well-meaning woodcuts. This is what *L'Ordine Nuovo* was in its first numbers: a mess, the product of a mediocre intellectualism, which sought on all fours an ideal place to land and march on to action.[22]

The virulence of this position conveyed Gramsci's isolation. Without managing, at the national level, to establish his arguments in favor of transforming the *commissioni interne* into factory councils, he chose to devote most of his energy to defending this strategy locally, all the while demonstrating that the Third International encouraged him to take this route. For the entire second half of 1919 and until the spring of the following year, he didn't write about national political questions or about the PSI, but rather about the question of workers' councils. This double strategy—of betting on both the international and the local—initially paid off. In fact, the factory councils had real success with Turin's workers, who saw them as a more effective organization than the old *commissioni interne* as well as a way of enacting the revolution they had voted for. Starting in September 1919, the first factory council was established within the Fiat Brevetti business, quickly followed by an identical initiative on the part of the Fiat Centro workers. Two months later, more than thirty thousand metalworkers belonging to thirty-two industrial businesses had elected their councils, the representatives of which met on October 6, 1919, at the Casa del Popolo in Turin. At the beginning of December 1919, the movement had reached one hundred and twenty thousand workers. The Industrial League was forced to react. *L'ON*, for its part, could not avoid the question of how the workers' councils would relate to the PSI and CGL. One of the first responses was a *Manifesto* written by Togliatti, calling for a national congress of all the councils at the end of March 1920. On March 20, 1920, Olivetti, Agnelli, and De Benedetti, who was the president of the Industrial League, went on the offensive by announcing to the prefect of Turin that they intended to close their factories under the pretext that there couldn't be two powers coexisting in their businesses. Eight days after this ultimatum from the Italian bosses, the showdown began.

The accumulated tensions between the former *commissioni interne* (which had become workers' councils) and the Industrial League exploded on March 28, 1920, with the so-called strike of the clock hands (*sciopero delle lancette*). After the dismissal of three of their comrades who were *commissioni interne* members, the workers decided to stop the hands of the clock in their factory, protesting against the push to reestablish the so-called *ora legale* (daylight savings time) that had been used during the war. Metalworking and automotive industrialists reacted swiftly, and a lockout was put in place. The confrontation between management and the Piedmontese workers would last for a month. This tension reached its peak with the decision to begin a general strike on April 13, 1920, after the Industrial League offered to end the lockout in exchange for reducing the power of the *commissioni interne*. Though the movement wasn't limited to the Turin metalworkers and reached many agricultural workers in the Piedmont,[23] the general strike was a failure. Almost all of the workers engaged in the movement were from the Piedmont, and displays of solidarity on the national level were all too rare: dockworkers in Livorno and Genoa, Ansaldo factory workers, and railway workers from Florence were the only ones who responded to the call.

Despite Gramsci and Togliatti's presence on the executive committee of the Turin Section of the PSI, the party proved to be quite reluctant to support the general strike. During its national council from April 18 to 22, 1920, which was initially supposed to take place in Turin but actually happened in Milan, the leadership of the PSI judged that an immediate revolution was unrealistic in Italy as long as Turin was besieged by soldiers and the management bankrolled hitmen to combat the workers—an unprecedented measure in postwar Italy prefiguring the "preventative counterrevolution" carried out by the Fascist squads.[24]

After ten days of strikes, they signed a compromise that had been drawn up by the prefect of Turin. Though this text neither put an end to the *commissioni interne* nor disputed the electoral process of choosing representatives, it was henceforth clear that the internal government of factories was determined by the sole jurisdiction of the management. The last memo from the strike committee clearly recognized, in the face of the Turin movement's failure to spread throughout Italy, that "the captains of industry, supported by the armed force of the bourgeoisie, have once again imposed their will. . . . This battle is lost, the war goes on."[25]

Gramsci came to the same conclusion, but he understood how to extract lessons from this episode at a deeper level. In the pages of *L'ON* on May 8, 1920, he published "Towards a Renewal of the Socialist Party," an article with an agenda in its title. For the first time, he clearly laid out the alternative that was facing Italy: either the working class took power or the bourgeoisie clamped down with violence.

Toward a Renewal of the Socialist Party

After "Active and Operative Neutrality," "The Revolution against 'Capital,'" and "Workers' Democracy," "Toward a Renewal of the Socialist Party" was the fourth of Gramsci's articles to gain a wide reception for his ideas. The article initially derived from a report the Turin Socialist representatives planned to present at the national PSI Council in April 1920. This is why it was written in nine points, which were in some ways Gramsci's April Theses, or what he would later call, in a letter to Alfonso Leonetti on January 28, 1924, his "Theses of the April Scission," anticipating by a few months the break that would take place in Livorno and lead to the creation of the PCdI.

The principal arguments in this article were: that the situation in Italy was revolutionary; that the bourgeoisie was organized "to smash once and for all the working class's organ of political struggle (the Socialist party) and to incorporate its organs of economic resistance (the trade unions and cooperatives) into the machinery of the bourgeois state"; that the workers and peasant forces had not attained that degree of discipline "because the leading organisms of the Socialist party have shown themselves to be incapable of understanding the stage of development of national and international history . . . [or of showing] its own autonomous stance as a party typical of the revolutionary proletariat." As a consequence, he wrote, "non-Communist revolutionaries must be eliminated from the party, and its leadership, freed from the preoccupation of preserving unity and balance between various tendencies and leaders, must devote all its efforts to putting workers' forces on a war footing."[26]

This text, published unsigned in *L'ON* on May 8, 1920, was hailed by Lenin himself in paragraph 17 of his pamphlet *Theses on Fundamental Tasks of the Second Congress of the Communist International* (July 1920):

Concerning the Socialist Party of Italy, the Second Congress of the Third International considers that the criticism of that party and the practical proposals submitted to the National Council of the Socialist Party of Italy in the name of the party's Turin Section, as set forth in *L'Ordine Nuovo* of May 8, 1920, are in the main correct and are fully in keeping with the fundamental principles of the Third International.

Accordingly, the Second Congress of the Third International requests the Socialist Party of Italy to convene a special congress to discuss these proposals and also all the decisions of the two Congresses of the Communist International for the purpose of rectifying the party's line and of purging it, particularly its parliamentary group, of non-Communist elements.[27]

But once again, though the ideas Gramsci put forward were welcomed in a significant way at the international level, they were almost completely overlooked on the national stage, to the point that, during the national conference in Milan in April 1920, Tasca and Terracini both stopped supporting the Gramscian hermeneutic. The Sardinian thinker was therefore forced to ally himself with Bordiga, for two main reasons. The first, positive reason was that *L'ON*, like *Il Soviet*, was pushing for the emergence of a Communist Party following the logic of the Third International; the second, negative reason was related to Gramsci's political isolation. After his polemic with Tasca, his friendships with Togliatti and Terracini also suffered. The reasons for this rupture, which was only temporary with Togliatti and Terracini but much deeper in Tasca's case, were essentially ideological, as Gramsci later explained in a January 5, 1924 letter to Mauro Scoccimarro:[28] "At that time [summer 1920] it was I who wanted to maintain relations with the left [hence his choice to ally himself with Bordiga's abstentionist tactics] rather than the right, while Palmi and Umberto had joined up with Tasca, who had broken away from us as early as January."[29] In fact, when the executive committee of the Turin Socialist Section turned over on July 24, 1924, Tasca, Togliatti, and Terracini aligned themselves with the position Serrati had taken at the national level, in favor of the PSI's revolutionary faction participating in elections. Though Gramsci thought the debate between abstentionists and those who wanted to participate in elections was fundamentally unimportant, he aligned himself with the first camp, represented in Turin by Giovanni Boero and Giovanni Parodi, two of Bordiga's faithful, for he judged the Neapolitan's position to be more revolutionary than Serrati's. This divergence, which could be explained as simple political tactics, nonetheless revealed an underlying divide: Togliatti and Terracini intended to act on the short-term, concrete situation with the support of the Turin Socialist Section (with Togliatti becoming its leader in August 1920), while Gramsci, faithful to his first battles, conceived of political combat over the long term (as he had with the Cultural Association during World War I). In fact, it was during this time that he created a Group for Communist Education that would prepare its members culturally and ideologically for the revolution. But it attracted only seventeen workers, none of whom carried particular political or union clout, and Gramsci's strategy was a failure that continued to aggravate his political isolation. Of the seven hundred militants who participated in the election to turn over the Turin Section of the PSI on August 16, 1920, only thirty-one followed Gramsci's advice to keep their ballots blank. The abstentionists got only 186 votes; the rest of the votes were carried by those who supported the elections: Togliatti was elected with the most votes at 466, Terracini with fewer was second. Gramsci wasn't elected. And he didn't wish to be.

Gramsci's isolation during that summer of 1920 was shared by *L'ON*, which stopped its publication for a time to allow its backers to directly support the workers' movement to occupy the factories.

The Occupation of the Factories

Unlike the "strike of the clock hands," which had broken out spontaneously, the occupation of the factories from August to September 1920 was the result of two months of fruitless discussion about met-

alworkers' salaries. After the Industrial League had unilaterally broken off negotiations on August 13, 1920, the leaders of Alfa Romeo
establishments in Milan chose a lockout. This decision set off the
powder keg. The workers countered by occupying their factories. The
movement spread from Milan, extending to Genoa and especially to
Turin after the FIOM got involved in this action, which it judged
to be less dangerous than a general strike and more effective at provoking government intervention to obtain a compromise solution.
While the factories were surrounded by the police and the army, who
were not intervening, the workers organized to restart production.
Considering the context, this continuation of production was a real
success, particularly in Turin. Paolo Spriano, the author of a pioneering, classic study on this occupation, estimates that the Fiat Centro
factory, the jewel of the Agnelli business, produced the equivalent
of 55 percent of normal production—or thirty-seven cars a day as
opposed to sixty-eight as usual—while the workers dealt with the almost complete lack of clerical staff and technicians and compensated
especially for the lack of raw material deliveries.

This experience was exhilarating for the four musketeers. Tasca,
secretary of the Turin Labor Council, unreservedly hailed this occupation movement. In the pages of *Avanti!* (since *L'ON* had been temporarily put on hold, the PSI newspaper published Gramsci's writing),
Gramsci urgently analyzed this episode, from which he drew three
fundamental lessons. First, he argued, the theses on the *commissioni
interne* "are not simple ideological abstractions, but the precise impression of actual reality." Second, the occupation of the factories prefig-
ured "the imminent transformation of social and historical values . . .
[because] it indicates the extent of the proletariat's power." But—and
this is the third lesson—"The occupation of the factories in and of
itself—without the proletariat possessing its own armed force, having
the means to ration basic necessities according to its own class interests,
or having the means to physically punish sabotage by specialists and
bureaucrats—cannot be seen as an experience of communist society."[30]

While the failure of the April 1920 strike was still on everyone's
minds, the workers had a compelling need for support from the PSI,

which could erase the memory of the excuses and criticisms during spring 1920. But this support didn't materialize, and it was old Giolitti, elected prime minister for a last time between June 15, 1920, and July 4, 1921, who maneuvered to find a way out of the crisis, armed with his political experience and his sense of strategy. He succeeded without a drop of blood being spilled, demonstrating for posterity that he was one of the greatest liberal Italian statemen of the twentieth century. Aware that the proletariat could not hang onto its producers' role for long, since it would soon lack all raw materials, and aware, too, that the FIOM had supported a movement that had escaped its control and that it was waiting for the slightest indication of the right moment to put an end to it, Giolitti initially played for time. He let the FIOM act, which gave the workers occupying the factories a choice: put an end to the movement or unleash an insurrection. A false choice. How could the workers have taken on the task of unleashing a revolution? Especially while the CGL Congress, which was held in Milan from September 9 to 12, resulted in a clear victory for the reformist plan, advanced by its leader D'Aragona, over the notion of revolution, which Togliatti and Tasca had supported with their votes. As for the PSI, both the reformists and the supporters of the majority, regrouped behind Serrati, declined to devise the transformation of this agitation into a revolution. In this context, Giolitti's decree offering to maintain workers' control of the factory (which amounted to empty rhetoric), in exchange for Socialists' agreeing to stick to economic and social demands, appeared to be the only solution, especially since the old political leader overcame any resistance from the Industrial League rather easily. All the same, this plan greatly embittered the hundred and fifty thousand workers who had, for almost a month, kept their factories running by themselves. On September 28, the occupation ended. On October 4, work resumed. Gramsci shared the sadness of the workers, "men of flesh and blood,"[31] forced to open the door of their business with their heads down, and he lamented that his call to create workers' militias had not been heard.

With the birth of the PCdI in January 1921, the *L'ON* experiment that began with the article "Workers' Democracy" came to a

conclusion that was both anticipated and foregone. It was anticipated because the supporters of the workers' councils knew from
then on that they had to liberate themselves once and for all from the
contradictions and inclinations of the PSI. And it was foregone because, in the final months of 1920, these supporters were not central
to the dynamics that led to the Communist scission at the Livorno
conference. In a pattern that would·be confirmed in the following
months, the debate in September among the Turin Socialist Section
already turned on the necessity of a new party. Gramsci and Togliatti
openly called for creating a Communist Party in Italy, as an answer
to the dictates of the Twenty-One Conditions passed by the Second
Congress of the Third International (July 1920)[32] and also as a way of
avoiding a reprisal of "the reformist sabotage of the revolution."[33] A
decisive clarification was taking place. While the reformists gathered
their strength during the conference they organized at Reggio Emilia
on October 10–11, 1920, the Communist fraction was officially created and gathered its supporters at Imola on November 28–29 of the
same year.

Though Gramsci had the honor of seeing his theses in favor of
the workers' councils upheld by Lenin, and though the experiment
L'ON supported was the most significant the Italian proletariat had
known during the *biennio rosso*, his ideas occupied very little space
at the Imola conference compared with those of Bordiga, who, more
than ever, proved to be an unparalleled organizer in the fight against
reformist Socialists and Serrati's centrist followers.[34] Therefore, the
last issues in this first run of L'ON reflected Bordiga's logic for breaking away, founded on the creation of a PCdI as the vanguard of the
proletariat. After the leadership of the PSI had decided to suspend
the Piedmont editions of *Avanti!* as a retaliation against the insubor-
dination of the Turin Section, L'ON came back to life as a daily starting on January 1, 1921. Gramsci was the director and Togliatti was the
editor-in-chief. As the newspaper of the Communist fraction, which
had come into existence in Imola, L'ON logically became one of the
press organs of the PCdI after the Livorno conference. But in becoming one of the Communist dailies, L'ON lost two characteristics:

its openness to international problems and its sensitivity to cultural issues.

Did the experiment with the councils disappear from Gramsci's politics once he became a Communist? Certainly not. Without subscribing to the argument put forth by certain critics of Gramsci who take this as his most fertile theoretico-political contribution, it is clear that an Ordinovist thread runs through Gramsci's thought. After the *biennio rosso*, in a totally different context, when he had become general secretary of the PCdI and was attending its congress in exile in Lyons in January 1926, Gramsci continued to draw from this experience. In the thirtieth thesis of the motion he put forward during that conference (see chapter 6), he wrote: "The practice of the factory movement (1919–20) has shown that only an organization adapted to the place and system of production makes it possible to establish a contact between the upper and lower strata of the working masses."[35] Though this experience isn't central to the *Prison Notebooks*, it nonetheless nourished Gramsci's reflections on three points: the spontaneity of the masses and the need to educate them, the idea of a "democracy of the producers" as an alternative to bourgeois democracy, and last, the need to create a new type of intellectual whose culture would be founded on industrial work.[36] But above all, we should keep in mind that although there wasn't a smooth transition between Gramsci the journalist for *L'ON* and Gramsci the militant Communist, the experience of transforming the *commissioni interne* into soviets nonetheless marks a decisive break in his political thought.

The Livorno Conference

During the *biennio rosso*, Gramsci abandoned his reading of history in which liberalism and the free market had a positive role, insofar as they allowed Italy to become a true capitalist nation. Though Gramsci had once admired Einaudi, he came to denounce him as "one of the writers who built the most sandcastles in the air. Serious as a child absorbed in his game, he wove an endless shroud like Penelope, which was dismantled daily by cruel reality."[37] In an article with the revealing title "Einaudi, or the Liberal Utopia," we read that "Marxist theories are actualized with rigor, while Einaudi's discipline falls to pieces and while the liberal world falls apart."[38] By working to transform the *commissioni interne* into soviets, Gramsci meant quite concretely to translate the Bolshevik Revolution into Italian. His difficulty in imagining the full potential of bourgeois democracy, already reduced in his first writings to a stale humanitarianism, found its logical conclusion in his interest in the producer, whom he considers the only truly concrete individual, while the citizen remains an abstract being. While he had long been attentive to civil society and would become so once again, the shift of his attention toward the producer goes along with his statements that favor the state, bringing him much closer to Bordiga than an entire critical tradition would care to admit. In truth, the Socialist state he wished for had to be substituted for the bourgeois democratic and parliamentary state, not only so that a republic of soviets could be put in place, but also so that it could be confirmed as a power capable of bringing about the dictatorship of the proletariat through its authority. In short, to realize this Communist revolution, the Communist Party had to be strong enough to blow up the old PSI.

It is outside the scope of this project to describe the stages of evolution within the Third International and the PSI that led to the schism in Livorno, but we do want to shed light on a few episodes that are particularly significant in understanding the evolution of Gramsci's political and intellectual trajectory during the postwar period. While the experiment of the workers' councils was ending, the PSI began to seem like a colossus with feet of clay. Despite its electoral successes, five major weaknesses undermined the party internally. It suffered from a lack of policy adapted for the peasantry, who represented most of the workers in Italy. The call to socialize the land seduced only a fringe group of fieldhands (*braccianti*) but could not quench the thirst for land that the great majority of peasants felt. The PSI's divorce from the petty bourgeoisie had equally unfortunate consequences, as this group quickly become the sociological incubator for the National Fascist Party (Partito Nazionale Fascista, PNF), with bourgeois sons who had been petty officers and subalterns during World War I rejecting the defeatism of the PSI that they judged "Caporettist," a neologism formed from the major defeat at Caporetto (see the previous chapter). The third weakness came from the lack of a party militia. The organizing of the Red Guards in Turin in 1919 was an isolated experience, and one that the PSI didn't encourage. Before this lack was dramatically revealed through the rise of Fascist squads, it was one of the elements that explained the rapid failure of the factory occupations in September 1920. Along with these three weaknesses, there was the distance between maximalist and internationalist discourse, on the one hand, and, on the other, the lack of any concrete revolutionary action. The moment the party leadership, with 65 percent of the votes, decided to join the Third International in March 1919, they should also have broken effectively with the political culture of the PSI elaborated when it was founded in 1892. Filippo Turati, a historic figure in Italian socialism and the head of the reformists, saw things clearly when he emphasized the divergence between the PSI's original aim of leading bourgeois democracy in a Socialist direction and the wish to establish a dictatorship of the proletariat. It is further proof of a rare lucidity that he criticized his companions for mythologizing the Bolshevik Revolution and conceiving of it as a social palingenesis. It is therefore not surprising—and this was the PSI's fifth great weakness—that the party's leadership was steering blindly, yet with a main focus that was strong enough to slow down the crash: maintaining the unity of the party at all costs, and Serrati was the man who embodied this "unitary passion"[39] (Gramsci).

Though the minority led by Bordiga and by his two lieutenants, Alfonso Leonetti (1895–1984) and Ruggero Grieco (1893–1955), could take credit for being the first to endorse the necessity of creating a PCdI, these three militants' dedication and great organizational capacity should not make us forget the important gaps in their strategy. Though the fights between internal factions of the PSI are inescapable to any reader of *Il Soviet*, there are, on the other hand, very few analyses of an original economic or political nature. Despite its name, Bordiga's newspaper wasn't much interested in the newness created by Leninism, which it considered to be mainly the pursuit of Marxism. In gathering all their energies to create a vanguard of the party, the Bordigists ultimately forgot to defend the twelve million Italian workers (four million small farmers, four million *braccianti*, and four million workers), while the experiment led by *L'ON* at least had the merit of trying to organize the urban proletariat.

In the pages of *L'ON*, Gramsci endeavored, for his part, to understand the innovations Leninism created. In this way, the theoretical horizon of this review was directly linked to the Third International. This was surely the reason why the latter took an early interest in Gramsci. It has been claimed that not only Aron Wizner but also another member of the Comintern, Cain Haller (alias Chiarini),[40] had sought to get in touch with Gramsci starting in October 1919. At the same time, Bordiga's efforts toward the Third International were unsuccessful. Though the Neapolitan leader's letters were likely intercepted by the Italian censors, in spring 1920, Moscow considered his wish for a clean, definitive break with the PSI to be premature, while Lenin stated loudly and clearly that the theses put forward by Gramsci in "Toward a Renewal of the Socialist Party" were in perfect agreement with the Comintern's plans.[41] Everything seemed to be going well for Gramsci. While Lenin indirectly condemned Bordiga, publishing his famous pamphlet *"Left-Wing" Communism: An Infantile Disorder*, the principal speeches given at the Second World Congress of the Communist International, like Zinoviev's on the system of Soviets or Karl Radek's (1885–1939) on workers' control, were in line with the theses Gramsci advanced. But that didn't apply to the reactions of the Italian Socialist delegates present in Moscow. Serrati and Antonio Graziadei (1872–1953) warned the congress against overrepresenting the undisciplined minority of the Turin Socialist Section. For his part, the maximalist leader Nicola Bombacci (1879–1945) criticized the syndicalist tendency of *L'ON*'s theses. Bordiga—who had only a mandate to deliberate—also defied Gramsci, since he thought Gramsci was trying to defend the unity of the PSI through his tactical subtleties. At the time, Bordiga was undoubtedly correct. In fact, Lenin's worry was that Serrati, the popular leader of the PSI who had just been elected a member of the Comintern executive committee, would take over the Second-and-a-Half International. He therefore had to consolidate the Communist fraction while creating a place for the centrist current of the PSI. At the Imola meeting, Chiarini, who was likely acting on Lenin's orders, incited Gramsci to get closer to Bordiga and try to moderate the latter's desire to secede. Serrati's reaction was swift, since he suppressed the Turin edition of *Avanti!*

The last act played out at the Goldoni theater, where the Seventeenth Congress of the PSI was held between January 15 and 21, 1921. Each camp was represented. Serrati's centrists wanted to reconcile both belonging to the Third International and maintaining the unity of the PSI. Turati's reformists and the Communists—Bordiga, Terracini, Togliatti, and Gramsci—played to their own agendas. Since Zinoviev and Bukharin were not able to make it to Livorno, the Comintern was represented by the Bulgarian Khristo Kabakchiev and by Mátyás Rákosi, who was not yet known as "Stalin's best Hungarian student." With 98,000 votes, Serrati's camp defeated Bordiga's 59,000 votes, while the reformist camp had only 15,000.

The atmosphere was electric, and the tone was one of invective rather than discussion. Despite attempts by the German Communist Paul Levi, assisted by Graziadei, to avoid the fragmentation of the Socialist Party, the Comintern wanted the rupture, and the Bulgarian Kabakchiev led the charge against the maximalists and their followers, drawing applause from the Communists while the majority of the congress ironically cried, "Long live the Pope! Long live *papachiev*! We are not slaves and we don't want the papal legate."[42] According to Zinoviev's report to the Third Congress of the Comintern in June 1921, in this circus-like atmosphere, Turati's speech directly reaffirming his political platform was one of the rare moments in which dignity and seriousness triumphed over disorganized passion, to the point that the speech was applauded even by the maximalists.

In this supercharged atmosphere, Gramsci kept silent. With the exception of Alfonso Leonetti's account, which explains this silence by the fact that his voice did not carry (since microphones did not yet exist at the time), it is quite likely that Gramsci avoided expressing his views because he was aware of his poor abilities as an orator, and because his name continued to be associated with interventionism.

On January 21, the Communist minority left the Goldoni theater to go to the San Marco theater while the delegates who had remained at the Goldoni voted unanimously in favor of belonging to the Third International. Turati would have liked to speak out against it, but his old companion Modigliani whispered in his ear: "Let it go! In six months, no one will be talking about the Third International."[43] The break between the maximalists and reformists was merely postponed: it would happen in October 1922.

During the afternoon of January 21, the PCdI came together. Bordiga's stamp was everywhere: the party seat was in Milan, his faithful dominated the Central Committee. Gramsci was the only prominent person elected who wasn't a Bordiga acolyte. In fact, Terracini, the other representative of *L'ON*, had already become closer to the Neapolitan leader. Under these conditions, it was obvious that Gramsci played a secondary role in the first months of the PCdI. The whole message and philosophy of *L'ON* (from its days as a weekly) did not find a foothold in this organization, which became as ultracentralized and disciplined as an army, with its soldiers obeying the decisions of the Central Committee. As a known militant, receiving the still discreet but quite real attention of the Comintern, Gramsci nonetheless participated in the first successful and unsuccessful battles of this organization, and from then on, he would pledge and sacrifice his life to it.

From Livorno to Moscow (January 1921–May 1922)

Before he left for Moscow, Gramsci continued his journalistic work as he had been doing all along. As the director of *L'ON*, he was earning 1,200 lire per month,[44] and his life revolved around his work.

Around two or three in the afternoon, every day, he left the little room he still rented on the Piazza Carlina. Accompanied by Giacomo Bernolfo (a tall, well-muscled comrade and former artillery sergeant who proclaimed himself Gramsci's bodyguard once the Fascist militias cracked down), he would go to a *trattoria* on the Via Po or the Piazza Solferino to eat his main meal of the day. He would then go up Via dell'Arcivescovado to the building that housed many PCdI groups, a true stronghold for this party. The PCdI had the building guarded by workers and went so far as to fortify it to prevent a squadrist takeover. With its run of 45,000 copies, *L'ON* was the principal Communist daily, ahead of *Il Lavoratore* directed by Ottavio Pastore in Trieste, which had a run of only 16,000 copies, and *Il Comunista*, which became a daily only in October 1921, when Togliatti became the editor-in-chief.

Gramsci directed a small team of two editors, a lead editor, three freelancers, a stenographer, a typist, three errand runners, and five secretarial employees. Extremely hard on himself, Gramsci was also demanding with his subordinates. His rages were Homeric. Alfonso Leonetti, a young editor under his leadership, relayed some of the comments he shouted furiously after reading the proofs of an article: "This isn't a newspaper, it's a sack of potatoes! Agnelli can call all his workers together tomorrow and say: 'Look, you see! This lot can't even put a newspaper together, yet they want to run the State!'"[45] He didn't leave his little office until dawn, when the grates of the first cafés were rising on Via Po and Via Roma. He worked for almost fourteen hours straight, pausing only to swallow a frugal dinner.

When we examine his duties, Gramsci seems like an important person. Wasn't he a member of the executive committee of the PCdI and the director of its main daily? Without denying that he had become important in the eyes of his comrades, especially after the experiment with the workers' councils, he still remained a secondary figure in the workers' movement. As we have seen, the PCdI was firmly controlled by Bordiga on both organizational and ideological levels: the principal theoretical magazine of the new party, the *Rassegna Communista*, was directed by Giovanni Sanna, a fervent supporter of the Neapolitan leader. Another sign of Gramsci's persistent marginality was his failure in the legislative elections of May 1921. Though he gathered 30,000 votes, several ballots were thrown out since his name, still unfamiliar to the voters, had once again been misspelled as Granoschi and Gramischi. The Communist voters in Turin preferred the old militant workers Francesco Misiano and Petro Rabezzana, two former *rigidi* who had become Bordiga supporters. This failure can also be explained by his lack of charisma and oratorical talent. Last, he still couldn't manage to rid himself of the accusation that he had been an interventionist. This original sin in the eyes of his comrades had already prevented him from being a candidate in the municipal elections of autumn 1920.

After the enthusiasm of the *biennio rosso*, the year 1921 was disastrous for Gramsci. He was once again felled by a physical and mental collapse that was aggravated by setbacks with his family. In December 1920, he lost his sweet sister Emma and could not make it to Ghilarza in time for the funeral. His brother Gennaro refused, for his part, to marry the mother of his daughter, while Mario became the federal secretary of the Fascist group in Varese after serving as a secretary for the PNF in Ghilarza. This "blackshirt Gramsci" did not help his brother, the "red Gramsci," become any more popular with militants who were quick to remind him of his first article, "Active and Operative Neutrality."

But for this mind entirely devoted to engagement, the main source of trouble had to be political. It can be summed up in one sentence: he was ill at ease in the new PCdI, but he either didn't want to formulate his unease or couldn't openly do so. Several accounts report that Gramsci criticized several decisions by the PCdI, but that he always did so in private conversations. We must not see this as cowardliness on his part, but more as concern for preserving the unity of his party, which was still young and quite fragile. Indeed, the majority of workers in Livorno remained in the old party, as had an even greater majority of renowned intellectuals. The historian and philosopher Zino Zini (1868–1937) was one of the few who joined the ranks of the PCdI (and he had been a student of Arturo Graf before becoming Antonio Gramsci's professor). According to Paolo Spriano's calculations, intellectuals made up less than 1 percent of the PCdI at the start. Gramsci also suffered from the dismantling of his former culturist group. Though the four musketeers were all members of the PCdI, some of them no longer lived in Turin, and they were thinking along different ideological lines. With the philosopher and deputy Antonio Graziadei, Tasca established himself as the right-wing figurehead of the party; Togliatti and Terracini were faithful to Bordiga at the time; Gramsci was too, but in his own way, with more nuance and critique.

This ultracentralized party, whose structure was molded on an underground organization, controlled only a few chambers of labor and municipalities. How could it expand when it had only sixteen deputies and fewer than forty thousand militants divided into cells that were not implanted within workplaces like the *commissioni interne*? Faced with this situation, Gramsci made his personal opinions heard on only two points: his openness to Catholics, on the one hand, and, on the other, his aborted attempt to parlay with D'Annunzio, who was then in conflict with Mussolini (the meeting was planned at Gardone in Lombardy). This choice to get closer to the *comandante*, a title the poet received from his legionnaires when they were occupying Fiume under his orders, demonstrates Gramsci's desire to organize a vast front against rising Fascism. He thought his own party's analysis of Fascism was full of gaps. All the same, he refused to rule out the interpretation of the Italian Communist leadership, who saw the blackshirts as simply the "White Guard" of the bourgeoisie, guessing that violence by the *squadristi* was intended only to establish a counterrevolutionary coalition founded on the alliance between the Giolittian bourgeoisie and the social democracy represented by the PSI. And Gramsci criticized his former comrades from the PSI along with Giolitti, the pioneering character whose policies he had never understood. His argument was particularly vehement against the militant Socialists when he denounced, in a full article, actions taken by the CGL and the PSI to institute a peace treaty with the Fascists, a pact that was effectively signed on

August 3, 1921. Another sign of his fealty to the Bordigist line was his abandoning of support for the Arditi del Popolo movement after the PCdI leadership threatened to expel any members of the party who were affiliated with it. Though Gramsci was one of the first intellectuals to have an intuition of the petit bourgeois sociological character of Fascism, including its desire to get closer to D'Annunzio and his legionnaires, and though he was perfectly aware that the lack of workers' militias was one of the determining factors in the failure of the factory occupations in September 1920, he was forced to bend to Bordigism. Though he refused to admit that the Arditi del Popolo movement was contrary to a Communist movement,[46] he was nonetheless forced to agree that it needed to be strictly defined by the PCdI,[47] which ultimately wound up condemning it.

Why did Gramsci sweep his own ideas under the rug this way, forcing himself to keep quiet, or at least erase his differences with the leadership of his party? He would have to wait until 1923–24, and a completely different context, for a break with Bordiga. He would do it by giving free rein to his own conceptions, but in the capacity of a Bolshevik agent, careful to follow the ideological line of the Comintern. Before his departure for Moscow in the spring of 1922, his concern was to avoid stunting the young organization he had joined, a concern that outweighed his loyalty to the Comintern. Until the Second Congress, which was held in July 1920, the Comintern supported *nolens volens* Bordiga's effort for ideological purity, clearing the old accusations of intolerance and antiparliamentarianism that had dogged him. But the military setbacks of Soviet Russia and the choice of the New Economic Policy would lead the Comintern to elaborate the united front doctrine designed to put an end to sectarianism among the European Communist parties. The Italian situation was of particular interest to the 605 delegates who gathered in Moscow in June 1921 for the Third Congress of the Comintern. Radek's report laid out the challenge clearly: Communist parties couldn't just organize the vanguard anymore—they had to conquer the masses. This plan meant that the PCdI had to reconcile with the PSI, especially since the Comintern's efforts to create a current within the PSI that was favorable to the PCdI's efforts had not met with the success they had expected. At the Eighteenth Congress of the PSI, which took place in Milan in October 1921, the motions by the *terzinternazionalisti*, who were still called *terzini*, garnered only 3,765 votes, as opposed to 47,628 for Serrati's supporters, and 19,916 for the reformists.

Terracini, one of the four representatives of the PCdI at the Third Congress of the Comintern, placed himself at the head of a revolt supported by a number of German, Austrian, Bulgarian, and Polish delegates who were hostile to the new direction that was being promoted and heralded by Radek, and attracted the ironic criticism of Lenin: "plus de souplesse, camarade Terracini, plus de souplesse"[48] (more flexibility, comrade Terracini, more flexibility). This phrase is all the more meaningful alongside Lenin's comment to Serrati on the eve of the Livorno congress: "Separate yourself from Turati, then make an alliance with him."[49]

Before the Comintern had formalized its new tactic of a united front by publishing a manifesto of directives in twenty-four points on December 18, 1921, it tried, once again, through the intermediary Chiarini, to convince Gramsci to take leadership of the PCdI at the beginning of October. The Comintern hoped this might be a way to solidify the support of a man who had the ideological approach that corresponded with their strategy. Gramsci refused. He gave several reasons for this refusal. It was likely that he didn't feel he had the stature to assume such a role. Moreover, in the stances he took for *L'ON*, he didn't have any major divisions with Bordiga, whom he appreciated for doing more than any of his other comrades to open the way for the creation of the PCdI. Last, he was especially preoccupied with the unity of his party, which seemed especially threatened by its right-wing minority, led by Tasca and Graziadei, who, for their part, unhesitatingly followed the Comintern's strategy of a united front. And so, at the Second Congress of the PCdI which was held in Rome in March 1922, the Comintern supported these two intellectuals, but their motions received only 4,151 votes, eight times fewer than Bordiga's. Gramsci backed the Neapolitan leader once again, not only opposing this attempted takeover from the right of the party, but also intending to demonstrate his admiration for Bordiga as a person. In a letter to Togliatti on July 14, 1923, Mario Montagnana—a worker who had been very close to Gramsci since 1914 and who had become a representative of the PCdI for the Comintern—understood this state of mind, in which political clarity ceded to the need for loyalty:

> I still remember that, at the Rome Congress [second PCdI congress, March 1922], Antonio had the aim of making known his divergences from the action of the executive committee. He abstained from doing so only to avoid playing the game of Bombacci, Sanna, Tasca, Graziadei, etc.... We felt and still feel so united to Amadeo [Bordiga's] group and we felt so distanced from the minoritarians not because our ideas were the same as those of Amadeo but because, in Amadeo and Ruggero [Grieco], we found marvelous companions in terms of faith, disinterestedness, and spirit of sacrifice, and in the others we found instead ... the opposite.[50]

After being instated at the Rome congress, the executive committee of the PCdI submitted only formally to the Comintern, while refusing the united front in actuality. Gramsci subtly subscribed to the same line as Bordiga, while advancing the argument that the strategy of a united front supposed, in an agricultural country like Italy, that this front would be extended to the PPI (a mass organization of Catholics)—an expansion that would run the risk of depriving the working class of its guiding role. With this argument, he conciliated both Bordiga and the Comintern. But he had to observe that, while the PCdI was preoccupied with finding a way to coexist with the Comintern, the party paid little attention to the Italian question—it underestimated the Fascist danger, failed to take the peasant world into account, and proved its sectarianism by refusing all initiatives that didn't give the party full and total control (in 1920, it was the Arditi del Popolo movement; in 1922, it was the Labor

Alliance trying to unite all the unions against Fascism). In the second instance, Tasca, who agreed perfectly with its arguments, became the director of the Turin Section of the Labor Alliance. As for Gramsci, he once again returned to the themes of *L'ON* to condemn this creation as a bureaucratic operation focused only on unionized workers, neglecting the worker as a producer.

Among these lackluster outcomes of the Second Congress of the PCdI, wasn't the most important result the nomination of Gramsci as a representative of this party within the Comintern? This choice owes as much to the wishes of the Comintern, which had already approached Gramsci several times and knew that it could count on him, as it does to the PCdI's Bordigist leadership and its wish to see a subtle, crafty militant distance himself from its sectarian ideology. Whatever the cause, this step would radically change Gramsci's life.

On May 26, 1922, after living in Turin for eleven years, Gramsci left the Piedmont capital for Moscow. He would not return to Italy until two years later—in love, a father, and a committed Bolshevik.

PART III

The Bolshevik

(1922–1926)

< 5 >

In the Service of the Comintern

(May 1922–May 1924)

"There Is No Happy Love"

Gramsci left Italy on May 26, 1922. That same day, Lenin suffered his first brain hemorrhage two months after a surgeon had removed a bullet that was lodged deep in his shoulder, refusing to run the risk of taking out the one that was lodged in his neck. The Bolshevik leader recovered, and though he was weakened by the ordeal, he remained the uncontested master of the Soviet Union, a country that was still extremely poor, yet nonetheless beginning to overcome the dramatic effects of war communism thanks to the early successes of the New Economic Policy.

Invited via a radio-telephone message by Zinoviev himself, Gramsci, Bordiga, and Graziadei attended the meeting of the executive committee of the Comintern (ECCI) that took place in Moscow from June 9 to 11, 1922, to prepare for the Fourth International. This Italian delegation arrived in the Soviet Union by passing through the Latvian border. The Livorno deputy, Ersilio Ambrogi (1883–1964), was added to this group, though he was already present in Moscow in his capacity as first representative of the PCdI within the Comintern (before Gramsci occupied that role). Bordiga, Gramsci, and Ambrogi shared the same ideological line, the minority opinion within their party at the time, while Graziadei represented the right-wing majority, guided by Angelo Tasca. Though part of this session was devoted to the Italian question, Gramsci did not speak up as they worked, but his public and private writings show that under Bordiga's influence, he was not convinced by Zinoviev and Radek's arguments for an alliance with the PSI and thought the idea of a united front was poorly adapted to the Italian context. Upon his return to Italy, Bordiga explained to his comrades that this maxim had been accepted out of sheer discipline, but that under no circumstances should it change the PCdI's strategy as it had been developed at the Rome congress in March 1922. Gramsci and Ambrogi, who had remained in Moscow, also didn't intend to succumb to pressure from Radek, and they continued to support the Bordigist line. In particular, they used this policy to discredit Serrati,[1] the leader of the maximalist current of Socialism, by demonstrating that his influence over the Italian masses boiled down to very little. In this way, Tasca was right to emphasize that the Comintern was forced "to work in Italy under conditions of illegality regarding its Section"[2] by trying, over the heads of the PCdI leaders, to establish a direct contact with the fraction of the PSI that was furthest to the left.

Split between several trajectories, the PSI was especially torn between two fundamental attitudes: one reformist, the other revolutionary. Always in conflict, these two "souls" of Italian socialism (as Spriano put it) increasingly had trouble coexisting, and the break between them, which had up until then been avoided,[3] finally took place at the Nineteenth Congress, which was held in Rome at the beginning of October 1922. This split resulted in the departure of Turati and Treves, the most prestigious leaders of reformist Socialism, who would create the Partito Socialista Unitario (Unitary Socialist Party, or PSU), naming Giacomo Matteotti as their secretary, and taking the great majority of deputies and most of the unions and cooperatives with them. Though this process of clarification was going the Comintern's way (the PSU adhered to the Second-and-a-Half International or Vienna International that rejoined the Second International after 1923, while the PSI maintained its membership in the Third International),

Bordiga and the majority of Italian Communists saw this episode just as more proof of maximalism's failure.

Despite the reticence of the Central Committee (CC) of the PCdI, the Comintern didn't give up its strategy, and on October 12 it sent a delegation to Italy led by Rákosi to prepare the fusion of the PCdI and the PSI. Once again, the Communist leaders went through the motions of following the Comintern's request for them to serve on a committee to prepare for this fusion, but they actually did nothing to allow this initiative to become realized (neither, incidentally, did the maximalist Socialists). The Italian question, which was far from settled, had to be discussed at the Fourth Congress of the Comintern, which opened in Moscow on November 5, 1922. While the Italian delegates began their long journey to Berlin to reach the Soviet capital, Mussolini's march on Rome (October 28, 1922) brought Fascism to power.

Gramsci followed these events only from a distance, since, immediately after attending the ECCI meeting in June 1922, his health deteriorated rapidly, requiring him to be urgently hospitalized. As was often the case during his life, he was both physically and psychologically exhausted. Bordiga and Zinoviev were so worried about him that they advised him to go to the Serebryany Bor (silver forest) sanitarium in Ivanovo. The sweats that soaked his forehead, the tics, the convulsive trembling, and his involuntary grimaces provoked fear among the other patients, especially after they learned that he was Sardinian, and therefore, in their imaginations, naturally savage and disposed to violence. As for the doctors, they feared that these physical symptoms were a prelude to paralysis of the lower limbs. Though the five months he spent at the Serebryany Bor clinic didn't cure his perpetually sickly state—he continued to suffer from insomnia and experienced several instances of memory loss—his hospitalization spared him the paralysis of the legs that his psychiatrists had feared.

At the Serebryany Bor sanitarium, Eugenia Schucht[4] had been hospitalized since 1919 for paralysis that was likely neuropsychiatric in origin. A friendship formed between Gramsci and the young woman, who was two years his senior, and it turned into an idyllic romance. Eugenia was the third daughter of Apollon Schucht and Julija Girschfeld, who had six children,[5] three of whom would play a decisive role in Gramsci's life: Eugenia, Julia, the great love of his life, and Tatiana, who would be his main supporter and confidant during his imprisonment from 1926 to 1937.

Born into a Saxon family that was ennobled during the Russo-Turkish war of 1877–78, Apollon married Julija, a pretty young woman from the Ukrainian Jewish bourgeoisie. Contrary to the story that has often been told to make Schucht and Girschfeld into pioneering Bolsheviks, Tatiana, Eugenia, and Julia's parents were ideologically close to the populist movement Land and Liberty (Zemlya i Volya), which led to the emergence of the terrorist organization People's Will (Narodnaya Volya) in 1879. This organization believed in a gradual movement toward socialism after Russian society became democratic and liberated itself, though violence, from the tsarist regime. In 1917, the populists separated into two factions, one supporting Kerensky's provisional government, while the other, taking the name of the Socialist Revolutionary Party, passed into history as SR, which formed an alliance with the Bolsheviks, even though very few of them took the step of joining the ranks of the Russian Communist Party (Bolsheviks) (RCP(b)). The tie this family claimed to Lenin and to his wife Nadezhda Krupskaya was therefore primarily an affectionate one. Lenin had made several private visits to the Schuchts. Apollon's political choices forced him to leave Russia with his loved ones, going first to Switzerland, then to Montpellier, and ending up in Rome after 1908. In 1913, the Schucht family returned to Russia in a scattered way, with the exception of Tatiana, who remained in Italy. In 1917, all the Schuchts joined the RCP(b), with Apollon first and Eugenia dead last, since they had to wait until February 1919 and the intervention of Krupskaya, whom Eugenia had worked with at the Ministry of Education, to finally obtain the precious party card. It bears noting that after spending four and a half years at the sanitarium, and despite her many requests, Eugenia would never be fully reintegrated into the RCP(b). By the time Gramsci entered into contact with this family, the father, Apollon, no longer held important duties within the new Soviet state. While in 1918 he had been director of the treasury, responsible for the sector of current accounts for the Soviet bank on its way to nationalization, before being charged with the smooth functioning of the internment of White Russian prisoners of war, he left Moscow at the end of 1919 to work in an obscure library in a little town in the Ivanovo district. Though he was very fortunate not to be considered an enemy of the people, Apollon's aristocratic origins and his past involvement prevented him from being part of the Soviet *nomenklatura*.

In this multilingual, cultivated family where aptitudes for sciences vied with the arts, particularly music, they all spoke Italian very well. Gramsci could communicate with Eugenia easily, though he didn't speak Russian (thanks to his phrasebook, he could say that much, at least). In the language of Dante, the two thirty-somethings shared their enthusiasm for the new regime being built in Russia, and they likely evoked sweet Italy, a source of nostalgia for all the Schucht sisters. Analyzing one of Antonio's letters to Eugenia dated February 13, 1923—one that critics have long thought was meant for Julia—allows us to understand that the friendship kindled between these two patients had become a romantic interest. But this interest would soon change once Gramsci met Julia.

Antonio and Julia met for the first time at the end of summer 1922, when Julia was visiting her sister in the hospital. The love story between the Italian and the Russian that developed over the next few months was hard on Eugenia, who was hurt to no longer be the center of the Sardinian revolutionary's attentions. As a result, the relationship between Antonio and Eugenia would always be difficult, and it even took a pathological turn after the birth of Delio, the first of Antonio and Julia's two boys, whom Eugenia was so passionately attached to that she considered herself his second mother, relegating Gramsci to the rank of uncle. After Gramsci's imprisonment, Eugenia did nothing to encourage the epistolary relationship between Antonio and her sister. She seemed to want to cut ties with the Italian revolutionary and rarely mentioned him to his son, forbidding Delio to speak Italian. After Gramsci's death, her position softened, but the positive portrait she sketched of the Italian revo-lutionary was mainly intended to make him a Communist hero in accordance with the ideological schemas that were prevalent in the Soviet Union, which she fervently supported for the rest of her life, for better or worse. However, it would be unfair to make Eugenia into the black sheep of the Schucht family. She was, above all, an energetic woman, capable of making good decisions. In this role, her influence was beneficial, for Apollon and his loved ones had a rather bohemian attitude, without much initiative. She was fiercely attached to her sister Julia, whom she jealously protected. Aware of the straitjacket of Fascism descending on Italy, she was the one who convinced Julia, who was pregnant with Giuliano, Antonio's second son, to leave Italy on August 7, 1926, while there was still time.

If relations between Antonio and Eugenia were complicated, they were far from simple with Julia. Before we examine them, it makes sense to review a few historiographic controversies. Though we cannot formally rule out the idea that Julia informed the State Political Directorate (GPU)[6] about Gramsci's activities, no proof exists that she was charged with this sinister task. In a letter from March 5, 1924, Gramsci evokes the possibility that Julia could be "a Cheka agent sent to sound out how corruptible I am . . . ," but in the same letter, he lets slip that this (mainly ironic) supposition was intended only to provoke Julia to explain the temporary difficulties in their relationship. Julia did actually work for the GPU starting in 1924, but only as a translator of French and Italian documents. Though she kept this low-ranking job with the political police until 1930, her two children and the weakness of her physical and psycho-logical constitution (she fell ill in 1927 and even more gravely so in 1929) don't add up to an image of her as a Mata Hari in a red hat, charged with seducing and surveilling one of the rising stars of the PCdI, though the Comintern did place great hope in Gramsci for several years. Only the archives of the KGB, if any exist on this point, could "definitively" answer this question.

Another, more anecdotal controversy is the question whether Julia and Antonio were ever married. It is very likely that they were not. How else to explain that Julia never mentioned this marriage, not even in the biographical profile of Gramsci that she furnished to the executive section of the Comintern in 1938? And what to make of the marriage certificate that actually does exist, dated September 1923? It was likely a fake created by the Soviet authorities to make Tatiana's role as a sister-in-law official for the Italian government, so that she could be authorized to help Antonio Gramsci in prison.

Beyond the questions of spying and marriage, and even beyond the disruptive role Eugenia played, the difficulties in Julia and Antonio's relationship can primarily be explained by the piecemeal quality of their union. These two didn't see each other except between the end of summer 1922 and November 1923 in Moscow, between February and the end of April 1925, and finally between October 1925 and August 1926 in Rome. In this way, during the four years after they met and before Gramsci was arrested, the two lovers were only together for two years and three months, without ever living together. Until the end of October 1922, Gramsci remained at the Serebryany Bor sanitarium; then he stayed at the Lux Hotel, which served as a general headquarters for the members of the Comintern, in a small room on the third floor that he often had to share with a comrade. In Moscow, Julia's work for the GPU constituted the only source of income for her entire family for a time, and her parents and her sister Eugenia stayed with her. When she finally joined Antonio in Rome, he preferred to rent her a little apartment, which she continued to share with her sister and her father, while Gramsci lived with a family of pensioners on Via Morgagni.

This separated life was not a choice—it was dictated by necessity. Gramsci didn't want to compromise the Schuchts in the eyes of the Fascist authorities, who kept them under tight surveillance. The love between Antonio and Julia was therefore clandestine, but rather than making their relationship more exciting, this situation was a source of sadness and misunderstanding. The letters he wrote in Vienna, where he was living from December 1923 to May 1924 on the orders of the Comintern, are particularly heartbreaking. In the six missives that survive from Gramsci's first separation from Julia, he complains repeatedly of his solitude: "I'm very isolated where I live ... I miss you and feel a great void all around me."[7] You miss a single person and the world empties of people! Vienna seemed terribly sad to him with its snowy streets that reminded him of the desolated landscapes of the Cagliari salt mines. His life was "sad and monotonous," brightened only by the dream that Julia would join him so he could "embrace and caress [her] at length."[8] But this dream would never materialize. "My imagination is dried up and dead. I can think only of you and the probabilities of your coming. It's an idea that is an obsession with me, always dominating my mind, and leading me to build one castle in the air after another."[9]

Stuck in a body that had been deformed by Pott's disease, Gramsci had been living only for and by his wits, in service of political engagement. Of course, his political fight continued, as he himself recognized elsewhere—"my life is one long wait for you interrupted by practical activities that absorb me"[10]—but this engagement no longer occupied the exclusive place in his life it once held. Until he met Julia, Gramsci didn't believe himself capable of loving, not to mention being loved. He was therefore forced to find a new balance in his life. This search was painful. In fact, if the Italian revolutionary saw his life expand through the private roles of lover and father, the long periods of separation, the violent political climate in Italy, the nervous illness of his wife, and the urgent and significant character of his political combat made it almost impossible for him to combine private life with public action. At best, these two spheres of his life might find a way to coexist. Along these lines, when Julia and their son joined him in Rome in the autumn of 1925, Gramsci visited the apartment he rented for them as often as possible so he could play with his son while Delio's mother worked at the Soviet embassy in Rome. But during the dinners they ate together, he carefully avoided discussing politics. There was surely a great deal of prudence behind this decision, but this disjunction between the familial sphere and his public engagement also shows the impossibility of reconciling *chorosaja, slavnaja, lubjmaia, rodnaja* Julia—beautiful, good, beloved, dear Julia—with *tovarich* (comrade) Julia. Political analysis wasn't absent from their letters, but it was always a secondary theme. Antonio and Julia shared the same Communist ideal, but they didn't pour much passion into this theme, and it would ebb over time. When they went out together in Moscow at the start of their relationship, they visited factories and attended political meetings and cultural ceremonies, Julia translating the speeches for Antonio. But they were too busy living in two different sociological realities that were both oppressive to be able to speak freely. In this way, Julia had to prove her Soviet purity by sharply refusing the small pecuniary assistance to help with Delio's education that Antonio tried to give her through an intermediary (his friend Vincenzo Bianco, then a political émigré in Moscow). Besides, it is significant that Gramsci devoted few articles to the education of Soviet society and that they almost all deal, unsurprisingly, with the defense and illustration of decisions made by the Central Committee of the RCP(b).

The incompleteness of his relationship with Julia was replicated in his relationship with his older son Delio, whom his parents had thought of calling Ninel—an anagram of Lenin—then Lev, as an homage to Trotsky. By all accounts, Gramsci loved his son with all his heart, seeing him for the first time eight months after his birth. A poor but pampered child, Gramsci had always been attentive to young people. When he was in Ghilarza for the last time in his life, at the end of October 1924, he took advantage of one of his rare moments of free time to play with Edmea, the daughter of his brother Gennaro, who was then four years old and much amused by the toys her uncle made for her and by the extraordinary stories he told. In the little living room of the apartment on Via Trapani in Rome, Gramsci experienced some of the happiest hours of his life with his son. Like all fathers, he was blinded by love for dear Delio, seeing him as a budding musical prodigy when he was able to match music notes to animals by the sounds they produced. In 1926, in the mountains near Bolzano under the blue, late August skies, Gramsci experienced his last moments of paternal happiness with his son, who looked so much like him. In the first days of September 1926, he kissed Delio for the last time. He would never see him again. Gramsci would never meet Delio's brother, Giuliano, who was born on August 31, 1926.

Imprisoned on November 8, 1926, he received regular news of his two boys, writing them little animal-themed fables inspired by his childhood.[11] The Schucht family led them to believe their father was absent because he was working abroad. The two boys didn't learn the truth until their father died. Delio and Giuliano's childhoods were sad, taking place under circumstances that were "unhealthy . . . mainly surrounded by women, among them their gravely ill mother; educated by a touchy, authoritarian aunt [Eugenia], by elderly grandparents, and 'distanced' from a foreign, unknown father."[12]

In autumn 1929, a long silence began between the two former Serebryany Bor lovers. Suffering from amnesia and sometimes aphasia, to the point of being hospitalized in a psychiatric institute in 1930, surrounded by her parents and by her sister Eugenia, Julia no longer wrote to Antonio, who resigned himself to a sad accounting: only one letter between July 1929 and July 1930. How to explain these long silences? For political reasons, certainly, Gramsci was no longer in good standing within the Comintern after his letters from October 1926 (see chapter 6), and more generally because of the oppressive political climate of the USSR (the politics leading up to the Great Purge made Soviets who had relationships with foreigners particularly suspect). But it was also for personal reasons. The Schucht family tried to hide the severity of Julia's illness from Antonio. At this point, Gramsci was so discouraged that he planned to stop writing to her. Luckily, Tatiana managed to convince him otherwise. In 1931, the correspondence between Julia and Antonio resumed at more regular intervals, but from then on, it was Tatiana who would play a decisive role in the life of Antonio the prisoner (see chapter 8).

At Bordiga's Side (November 1922–June 1923)

Gramsci left the Serebryany Bor sanitarium to go to the Fourth Congress of the Comintern that opened on November 5, 1922. The Fascists' seizure of power created much conversation fodder for those who attended the congress. Without immediately ruling out the interpretation that this phenomenon was a specific outgrowth of the local Italian situation, the vast majority of Comintern and RCP(b) leaders (Trotsky first among them) saw this situation as the sign of an international reaction that conveyed the difficulty of achieving revolution in the West and, consequently, the failed strategies of Western Europe's Communist parties. More than ever, those parties therefore had a duty to defend the last bastion of the revolution, namely, the Soviet Union, which was starting to emerge from its diplomatic isolation and to progress economically thanks to the New Economic Policy. This situation resulted in an intensification of the Bolshevik hegemony within the Comintern, whose organization was henceforth modeled on that of the RCP(b). In this way, meetings of the Enlarged ECCI had to be held twice a year from then on, while the different Communist parties were asked to gather after these meetings, to align their political strategy with the one chosen by the decision-making body of the Comintern.

With the exception of Radek, the orators who succeeded each other at the dais of the Winter Palace called for creating a vast front against the reactionary forces that were sweeping Europe from France to Hungary, by way of Germany and Italy. At the time, this strategy of a united front was conceived as a "ground-up" alliance of all the leftist militants, but also as a fusion "from above" of the different parties that made up the Third International. Faithful to the dynamics that had been at play since the Livorno congress, and that were confirmed by the one in Rome in March 1922, Bordiga refused the strategy of a united front, which could only deliver, in his eyes, a transitional government that subscribed, by its very nature, to the logic of bourgeois society and, for this reason, betrayed the interests of the working class. For the first time, a member of the CC of the PCdI openly opposed Bordiga on the Comintern stage. It was Antonio Graziadei, a figure from the right of the PCdI who was close to Tasca, but who would keep his distance from him after this, finding that he questioned Marxist economic doctrine too much.[13] All the same, Graziadei was not strong enough to undermine the majority united behind Bordiga. It was also true that Graziadei's argument against what he saw as the leftist extremism of his party's majority coincided with the views of the Comintern at the time. In the eyes of everyone, this skirmish showed that a right-wing minority[14] existed within the PCdI that was in favor of a reconciliation with the PSI.

What was Gramsci's position? Suffering from insomnia and memory loss, he attended the congress, but he barely spoke. Rákosi asked him once again to take the reins of the party against Bordiga. As he would later explain in a letter on March 1, 1924, addressed to both Togliatti and Mauro Scoccimarro (1895–1972), who had joined the Central Committee of the party in 1923 and quickly became a distinguished member, he refused the offer. At the time, he thought it was totally inappropriate, not hesitating to call Rákosi a "nitwit, without the tiniest measure of political intelligence."[15] Certainly, moving in the direction the leaders of the Comintern wanted would have betrayed Bordiga, for whom Gramsci felt sincere friendship (which was reciprocated) and whom he saw as an extremely capable and devoted leader. Still more seriously, agreeing to Rákosi's demand would have meant entrusting the PCdI to men who planned to liquidate it: we have already analyzed Gramsci's strong inclinations against Tasca, and his judgments of Graziadei were even sharper and would take their definitive form in his *Prison Notebooks* (particularly in the seventh). And so, when the Comintern devoted two days to the Italian question (November 13–15, 1922), Gramsci clearly placed himself on Bordiga's side against Tasca and against the Comintern, refusing any fusion between the PCdI and the PSI. He didn't shy away from a direct polemic with Zinoviev, using irony as a weapon: "Joining together the two parties is like wanting to marry Gianduja[16] with the daughter of the king of Peru, which has no king and thus no king's daughter. When the Commission will ask the Maximalists what forces they currently have in Italy, the latter will not be able to give any explanation."[17] In response to this volley from Gramsci—a militant whom the Comintern had been courting for several years— the latter brought out the heavy artillery, publishing a letter from the

RCP(b) signed by Lenin, Trotsky, Bukharin, Zinoviev, and Radek in favor of the fusion of the two parties. That left the members of the Comintern with no choice but to unanimously approve this fusion. The Italian delegates from the PCdI (those from the right-wing minority obviously had no problem with this political demand) refused to run the risk of a divorce from the RCP(b) but, as he explained in his letter of November 24, 1922, Bordiga didn't intend to go back on his analysis: "After your invitation, your brotherly advice, we declare to you that the representatives of the majority of the PCdI will be quiet. It will not support the opinions you are familiar with and of which it remains convinced."[18] This reasoning did not reassure all the members of the CC of the PCdI. Scoccimarro, first, then Gramsci, considered that their political platform was facing a problem they could not avoid, namely, carrying out the fusion between the PSI and the PCdI that the Comintern wanted while making sure that this operation didn't allow the revolutionary ideal to be engulfed by the maximalists. The maximalist alliance with the right-wing majority of the Communists would lead to the liquidation of the PCdI, which had been created in Livorno precisely to avoid a repetition of the tragic error of the *biennio rosso* (1919–20), in which the revolutionary drive had been a victim of the maximalists' hesitations, crushed on the rocks of reformism. Not wanting to abandon the fate of their party to the right-wing minority, Scoccimarro and Gramsci accepted (unlike Bordiga, who refused to cede to Zinoviev's pressure) the invitation to become members of the interparty commission to prepare the fusion of the PCdI and the PSI to create a new Partito Comunista Unificato d'Italia (Unified Communist Party of Italy). This new organization, which was baptized in 1923, never saw the light of day, since both the PCdI and the PSI were hostile to it. Also, the PSI was more and more ideologically dominated by the Socialist National Defense Committee led by Arturo Vella and Pietro Nenni, who were resolutely opposed to any reconciliation with the Communists. For its part, Fascism feared a united front of the two parties: Bordiga was arrested at the beginning of February 1923, followed by Serrati on March 1.

Among the victims of this wave of Fascist repression (not the first and certainly not the last), was the unfortunate Gennaro Gramsci, Antonio's older brother, who was violently struck and stabbed with a bayonet. He lost a finger during this attack. Pia Carena organized his exile to France. Could he have been mistaken for his brother Antonio? Whatever the case, the PCdI was a target for the Fascist authorities, who succeeded in arresting almost all the members of its CC and no less than three-quarters of its federation secretaries. Forced into hiding, the PCdI had to adopt a sectarian attitude that made any fusion with the PSI impossible, so much so that this party decided at its twentieth congress (Milan, April 1923) to vote against fusion by a clear majority.[19] Faced with increasing Fascist repression and the failure of any reconciliation between the political families of Socialism and Communism, Tasca, who had worked hard at Togliatti's side to reorganize the party after the wave of arrests in winter 1923, asked the Comintern to put him in charge of the party so that he could approach the next meeting of the Enlarged ECCI (planned for June 1923) with a clear strategy. In May or June of 1923, confronted with this hasty course of events, Bordiga wrote a *Manifesto for the Comrades of the PCdI* to defend his position from his prison cell. With a tone of finality, he critiqued the strategy of the Comintern, which was in the process of liquidating the PCdI, though its platform had been created in Livorno precisely to break with the maximalists. At the time, Gramsci's own analysis was similar, and it was very poorly received in Moscow. The Comintern rejected Bordiga's *Manifesto* by taking up Tasca's arguments accusing the PCdI of having chosen the wrong enemy, preferring to concentrate its attacks against Serrati, the leader of the *terzini*, rather than against Mussolini. Zinoviev's diatribe against the Italian Section of the Comintern didn't spare Gramsci: "Gramsci had promised to write letters in favor of fusion, he wrote letters that were against it."[20] Upon closer inspection, this accusation of playing a double game makes us think that unlike Bordiga, the Sardinian revolutionary intended to spare the Comintern. This prudence regarding the institution of which he was a representative was not the sign of a servile attitude but conveyed a difference in temperament and political acumen between Gramsci and the Neapolitan revolutionary. This difference did not escape his contemporaries, and it is apparent in Ruggero Grieco's portrait of these two PCdI figures:

> It is interesting to compare the two most characteristic mentalities of our movement: Gramsci and Bordiga. The first has a philosophical temperament, the temperament of one who studies incessantly, of someone "hungry for doctrine" with a tendency toward analysis, the patient gatherer of elements around a question or situation. The other, Bordiga, is a synthesizer, distrustful of books, wishing to fight over any and all terrain; enamored of battle, extremely jovial and extremely strong. In the former, judgment develops more slowly because it needs to find all its elements. In the latter, judgment is speedier thanks to the speed with which it selects useful and necessary elements from useless and superfluous ones. Gramsci tends toward divulgation, schooling, teaching; Bordiga would rather command armed battalions.[21]

Despite Gramsci's propensity to display more flexibility, and perhaps more intellectual agility, than Bordiga, the Comintern didn't seem to want to give him the reins of the party anymore, logically preferring to hand them to Angelo Tasca. All the same, after the meeting of the Enlarged ECCI in June 1923, Zinoviev would not go so far as to entrust the destiny of the party to the established leader of its right-wing minority, for both the Comintern and the RCP(b) thought that this would show too much authoritarianism and that the message would not sit well with the leaders of other sections of the Comintern (i.e., other Communist parties). This involvement in steering the party was still too much for Bordiga, who objected to the Comintern's naming members of the CC of the PCdI, creating a careful blend of majority and minority leaders, and even inviting him to be part of the Presidium of the Comintern.

Though he hoped to return to Italy with Julia, Gramsci had to stay in the Soviet Union because a warrant for his arrest had been issued by the Fascist authorities. From his arrival in Moscow in May 1922 until his departure for Vienna in December 1923, he was able to follow the life of his party thanks to epistolary exchanges with his comrades who remained in the country, and because he had conversations with all those[22] who came to Moscow. Nonetheless, the geographical distance from Italy allowed him a certain perspective and offered him leisure to reason more serenely than if he had been on Italian soil, under attack from the persecutions of Fascist militias. Before he reached Vienna, where he was tasked with creating an information bureau for the Comintern (another one already existed in Berlin) to maintain the link between the PCdI and the other Communist parties, he lucidly analyzed the challenges of the moment. These could be summed up by the attempt to avoid a break between his party and the Comintern without entrusting the destiny of the PCdI to Tasca's minority group. Such a position would require him to demonstrate a great deal of diplomacy, going so far as to "undulate like an eel,"[23] as he described the tactic, which would get him a reputation for being "a devilishly cunning fox."[24] From the middle of 1923, on a theoretical level, he began to put in place a strategy to reluctantly argue against Bordiga and the majority of the PCdI and without enthusiasm against Tasca and the right-wing minority.

The Difficult Break with Bordiga (June 1923–May 1924)

At this turning point within the PCdI, Gramsci's first step toward becoming its main architect was the brief he presented to the meeting of the Enlarged ECCI. In it, he denounced the very principle of minorities existing within a party, since the latter always served to gather the opposition:

> political adversaries polarize themselves toward the minority, widening and generalizing its position, they conspiratorially publish manifestos, programs, etc. signed by the opposition or by a group of their friends, and enact a form of agitation that can become extremely dangerous in a specific moment.[25]

This text, which confirmed how much Gramsci had cut his ties with any form of democratic culture, was also dictated by his analysis of Fascism, which he saw as "decomposing."[26] The PCdI could not allow itself to approach a decisive battle while it was undermined by internal tensions.

The second step was the letter he addressed to the EC of his party, on September 12, 1923. The context of this missive was the expulsion of the *terzini* faction from the PSI[27] in August 1923 and the Comintern's wish to publish a newspaper that would be strong enough to compete with *Avanti!* and could accept both Communists and former *terzini*. This paper was a way of compensating, through a small fusion, for the consummate failure of the larger one between the PSI and the PCdI. Gramsci was not content simply to agree with the Comintern's wish and started to actually design this new political project for his party. The first powerful idea he put forward was to assure the PCdI "a legal tribune that will allow it continuously and systematically to reach the widest section of the masses."[28] If this newspaper was to be for all those on the left (the reasoning behind calling it *L'Unità*), keeping "faith with the program and tactics of the class struggle," then they had to be careful not to give too much space to Serrati, the former director of *Avanti!*. The second part of Gramsci's letter is more interesting, defending the idea that *L'Unità* should be the newspaper of workers and peasants, as the Comintern wanted. For the first time since he had become a Communist, Gramsci offered his take on the southern question, which he defined as the "question in which the problem of the relations between workers and peasants is posed not only as a problem of class relations, but also and especially as a territorial problem, that is to say, as one of the aspects of the national question."[29] This framework perfectly followed the logic that was being promoted in Moscow at the time, with the March 1923 creation of the Krestintern, the international peasant council, still currently called the Red Peasant International. This council's brief existence[30] should not make us forget its importance, since it was led by Bukharin, the main theorist of the alliance between the proletariat and the peasantry. The near simultaneity of

Gramsci's letter and the creation of the Red Peasant International demonstrates how much Gramsci and the Comintern shared a similar political approach to the problems of the time. Therefore, it is clear that from this moment on, Gramsci would have to distance himself from Bordiga's sectarian approach that flatly refused the goals of the united front. The Sardinian thinker's political savvy would truly reach its full potential in his effort to convince the militant Italian Communists that the Comintern's choices were correct, a step that corresponded with his charisma as an educator, as Grieco had clearly seen.

All that remained was to complete the break with Bordiga, a friend whom Gramsci respected. It took place in Vienna, where he arrived in the first days of December 1923, staying until May 1924. Was he acting of his own accord or on the orders of the Comintern? It's a difficult question to answer. He was working toward the political strategy the Comintern wanted, but the latter still would not risk a frontal attack against Bordiga, whom they planned to co-opt into their executive leadership (the Presidium) to better control him while giving him a position that would correspond with his historic role. Gramsci's offensive against Bordiga can also be explained by the publication of the Neapolitan leader's open letter, written from prison in spring 1923, in which he informed the leaders of the PCdI of his fundamental disagreements with the Comintern and demanded that they sign it, so it would become a sort of anti-Comintern manifesto. This document shook the consciences of many leaders, beginning with Togliatti, Terracini, and Scoccimarro, who were on the point of signing, since they saw the letter as a continuation of the coherent ideology and strategy they had followed since the Livorno congress. On the other hand, Gramsci immediately expressed his firm refusal to sign. He organized a counterattack by calling on militants to form a center within the party between Bordiga's left and Tasca's right. At first, Terracini, Scoccimarro, and Togliatti were against this initiative by Gramsci, considering it divisive. It certainly was divisive, but for the first time, and in the open, Gramsci was totally aligned with the Comintern, whose directives he had once followed out of sheer discipline and with private reservations. Now he championed the conception of the PCdI as a section that was completely faithful to the Comintern. Gramsci didn't intend to "undulate like an eel" anymore, but positioned himself in unreserved opposition to Bordiga's attitude, which he found to be sectarian and dissident—sectarian because it was cut off from the masses, and dissident since it was permanently at odds with the Comintern. Helped by Bordiga's stubbornness, since he refused any form of compromise with the Comintern, he succeeded in convincing Terracini, Togliatti, and Scoccimarro that this was the right step. His own intellectual ascendancy was certainly the deciding factor in this rallying process, but we must also consider the ties of brotherhood that had been established around L'ON.[31]

From October 1923 on, after the Rome trial had absolved all the accused Communists who were quickly liberated,[32] a period began in which the Fascist pressure lightened a bit, allowing the PCdI to rebuild its strength. This new situation facilitated the ideological reorientation that Gramsci began to orchestrate. One of the signs of his party's health was the circulation of its newspapers. L'Unità, directed by Ottavio Pastore, whose first issue came out on February 12, 1924, had a run of forty thousand copies. This daily became the advocate for the platform upheld by Communist and *terzini* candidates who were running on the Proletarian Unity (Unità Proletaria) list in the 1924 legislative elections. More modest, with four to six thousand copies, was the circulation of the third run of L'ON,[33] which had become biweekly, and whose first issue Gramsci edited almost entirely by himself, in his room in Vienna. The idea to (re)publish L'ON was one editorial project among many that germinated in Gramsci's mind during his time in Moscow and in the Austrian capital. For a while, he had imagined publishing a theoretical journal, which he wanted to call *Critica Proletaria*, as well as a newspaper devoted to the peasant question, *Il Seme*. Though these two initiatives didn't materialize, it's interesting to notice that they were aligned with the political strategy the Comintern desired. It was the same for the relaunching of L'ON, which enjoyed quite a large amount of autonomy from the PCdI, and which would therefore become one of the privileged vectors for Gramsci's defense of the anti-Bordigist strategy. "The Comintern Section for Agitation and Propaganda made no mistake about it, signaling in 1925 that the *Ordine Nuovo*'s role was to lead 'the fight against a drift to the extreme left.'"[34]

From then on, the PCdI was the principal force on the left. With twelve thousand members, ten times more than the CGL whose membership had foundered, the PCdI's outlook was healthy, given the circumstances. Sociologically, it corresponded to the makeup of its class, since its militants were practically all workers and peasants. The vast majority of the Communist candidates were also workers and *braccianti*. The situation was more nuanced when it came to the elected officials, many of whom were journalists. Thanks to its network of 815 underground sections, the Proletarian Unity lists successfully reached thirteen of the fifteen electoral districts that made up the country in the legislative elections of April 6, 1924. One hundred and eight Communist candidates and forty-eight *terzini* would therefore campaign alone, without ever forming an alliance with the PSI or the PSU, which both categorically rejected the idea of fusing their lists. Still hostile toward playing the parliamentary game, Bordiga refused to be a candidate. This was a harsh blow to his party, for he still had great influence among the militants. On the other hand, Gramsci agreed to be a candidate in Veneto and not in Sardinia, which, along with the Abruzzo, was the other of the two districts in which the Communists and the *terzini* hadn't been able to present a list. Despite many irregularities tarnishing the vote, and the unleashing of violence by the *squadristi* (Fascist squads) during the electoral campaign, the lists opposing the *Listone*[35] succeeded in collecting a third of the votes. With slightly more than 268,000 votes and nineteen elected (thirteen Communists and six *terzini*), the young PCdI, which had existed for only three years, pulled off a great success beyond what even the most optimistic had hoped.[36]

Gramsci was among the Communist deputies. From then on, he was, at least in theory, a beneficiary of parliamentary immunity, and he would be able to return to Italy. What was his position, then, on

Fascism and the fight his party was leading against this regime? In Austria, Gramsci lived alone in an outlying area of Vienna, in a little room that was poorly heated and poorly furnished, with a bed made up in the German style, meaning it had an eiderdown that slipped, causing him to wake up each night with his feet uncovered and frozen. The wife of his host, Joseph Frey, an old Communist militant, had no appreciation for this lodger, unshaven, uncombed, and poorly dressed, who risked getting him into trouble with the police. This "sad and monotonous" life far from Julia wasn't even brightened by (always banal) conversations with his secretary, Mario Codevilla. Though the secretary was a devoted Communist, he lacked intellectual scope, and he was increasingly weakened by tuberculosis. In this little room, which he left only to go to dinner or to attend a few political meetings, Gramsci gave in to pessimism on a personal level, but never on a political one.

Against Pessimism

Gramsci had by this time lived outside of Italy during the first eighteen months of Fascism, from the March on Rome to the legislative elections of April 1924. Though he was relatively well informed about the persecutions the Communists had endured (he still didn't seem to know about the one his brother had suffered), he could not, given the state of things, take part in the daily fight his comrades waged. They undertook a task that rivaled Penelope's, reconstructing the legal and clandestine structures of their organization after they were regularly dismantled by the Italian police and by the Fascist militias. This distance likely provides one explanation for why he was less susceptible to the pessimism that was overtaking a number of his companions in the fight, along with the fact that he'd witnessed the consolidation of the revolution in Russia. But as he explained in a letter to his old professor Zino Zini, he knew how to resist the "contamination of pessimism," for he guessed that "Fascism really has created a new permanently revolutionary situation, just as tsarism did in Russia . . . this is the source of my optimism, which I would like to communicate to all the friends and comrades with whom I am coming back into contact, and who have, it seems to me, been oppressed by the spiritual pressure of Fascism."[37] This was the whole point of his article "Against Pessimism" that was published in *L'ON* on March 15, 1924.

"Against Pessimism" opened by recalling Gramsci's early and consistent critique of fatalism that prevents any form of action. He saw its confirmation in the real situation of the PSI, which the PCdI had to distinguish itself from more than ever (the article was written in the middle of the campaign period, when the PSI and the PSU had refused any alliance with the Communists). The article continued by recommending that militant Communists remain hopeful about their undertakings, for their party had succeeded in bringing together "a phalanx of steel, too small, certainly, to enter into a struggle against the enemy forces, but large enough to become the framework for a broader formation."[38] Gramsci invited his comrades to forge this great army capable of commanding a decisive victory against Fascism. It was therefore a question of applying the decisions of the Third and Fourth Congresses of the Comintern, whose theses he considered fully workable for Italy. In this effort to create a great party of the masses, "The activity of the International was for a time the only activity that allowed our Party to have an effective contact with the broad masses and that kept up a ferment of debate and the first stirrings of movement in significant strata of the working class—something it was impossible for us to achieve in any other way in the circumstances."[39] This success was so important because it constituted "the only physical and ideological defeat of Fascism and reaction"[40] since 1922. After this appeal to educate a party of the masses as the best instrument for combating and defeating Fascism, Gramsci laid out three principal steps that would allow such a party to materialize.

He first of all proposed to concentrate the party's action in the factories, since it was through action at the level of the workplace that they could "create a clandestine, centralized trade union organization that would work toward creating a new situation in the working class."[41] By clearly formulating this proposal, he was both following the tradition of *L'ON* and responding to a reform the Comintern wanted. In a February 1924 document from its presidium to all the national sections, the Comintern made it known that the base organizational unit of the different Communist parties should no longer be territorial but rather founded on cells within the factories. The reform was validated a few months later at the Fifth Congress of the Comintern (June 1924), which has passed into history as the congress that bolshevized the Communist parties, something that was considered essential for expressing the class character and the revolutionary dimension of Communist political organizations. Unsurprisingly, Bordiga was hostile to this decision, while Gramsci gave it his full support.

The second method put forward by the Sardinian thinker was the attempt to collaborate with intellectuals who were not card-carrying members of the PCdI, but who felt close to it. On this point, it is interesting to note the link he fostered with Piero Sraffa (1898–1983), especially because this Ricardian specialist would later play a decisive role in allowing Gramsci to write his *Prison Notebooks*. From a rich Jewish family based in Pisa and Livorno, Piero Sraffa was the son of Angelo Sraffa, a prominent lawyer, who was an expert in Italian commercial law and the first to hold a professorship in this field at Bocconi University, a brand new but already renowned private institution. Rector of this university, then president of the faculty of law at the State University of Milan, Angelo Sraffa was a dedicated anti-Fascist but, like his friend Luigi Einaudi, not a militant. Like many people of his generation, his son Piero was first influenced by the neo-idealist philosophy of Croce and Gentile, before becoming influenced by socialism. After having begun his studies in economics under the wing of Luigi Einaudi and Pasquale Jannaccone—one of the main figures in Italy's marginalist school—Piero was mobilized as an officer. After the war, he pursued his university studies in Turin, where Umberto Cosmo put him in touch with Gramsci, most likely in 1919. After an initial period in England, where he met John Maynard Keynes, who took Sraffa's highly critical take on the Banca

Commerciale Italiana and published it in the *Manchester Guardian Commercial* and in the prestigious *Economic Journal*, Sraffa enjoyed a real intellectual renown when he was very young, a renown that would earn him a professorship in economics at the University of Cagliari in 1926, when he was only twenty-eight. But he chose to live in England from September 1927 on, knowing he was under surveillance from the regime, which did not appreciate his ties to anti-Fascist circles and his critique of the Italian banking system. He became a lecturer in economics at King's College.

In contact with the leadership of *L'ON* from 1919 on, he published three articles in 1921 that criticized workers' unions in England and in the United States. Between June 1922 and January 1924, Piero Sraffa no longer kept in touch with Gramsci or with the other members of *L'ON*. He distanced himself from Communism, as much out of concern for building his university career—which seemed compromised for a time after Mussolini personally expressed his ire against the publication of his articles on the banking system—as for ideological reasons, since he became closer to the reformist Socialists during that time. He fostered a particularly close relationship with Carlo Rosselli (1899–1937), who became a major anti-Fascist figure and who was close to the PSU at the time. Starting in January 1924, Gramsci sought to renew his ties to Sraffa, whom he saw as one of the intellectuals who could reinforce the PCdI's foundations in its fight against Fascism. In a letter of February or March 1924, the young economist thought that, in the first place, there would be no anti-Fascist revolution so long as the workers were thinking of saving their jobs and their salaries to feed their families. In the context of shrinking political and unionist freedoms, "the union and the [Communist] party cannot be of any help, on the contrary . . ."[42] Therefore,

> the urgent problem, arising before any other, is that of "liberty" and "order": the others will come up later, but they cannot for the moment interest the workers. I do not believe that the Communist Party can today lessen Fascist pressure: it is the time

for democratic opposition movements and I feel we should let them act and even help them along. Before anything else, we need a "bourgeois revolution," and only then will labour politics be able to develop.[43]

The consequence of this reasoning was that the PCdI was making a grave mistake when it gave the impression of sabotaging an alliance of the opposition, since "today's problem is urgent . . . it seems to me to be, more than a problem of class, a problem of police."[44] For Sraffa, it was therefore necessary for a bourgeois revolution to precede a Communist revolution. Ultimately, he advocated for a two-part strategy, reasoning that a direct transition from Fascism to a dictatorship of the proletariat was impossible. As Paolo Spriano rightly points out, this ideological line, hostile to the "splendid isolation"[45] of the PCdI, was shared by Tasca, who held the same political position as Sraffa, sensitive to the importance of trade unionism's role, even if the young economist was rather severe on the leaders of trade unions.

Part of this letter was published in *L'ON*'s issue for the first two weeks of April in 1924. It was accompanied by a response from Gramsci titled "Problems of Today and of Tomorrow." Gramsci reproached his young friend for not yet being fully Marxist, since he had not "been able to rid himself of all the ideological residues of his democratic-liberal intellectual background."[46] His second critique was weightier and more significant:

> S. believes that the future belongs to our party. But how can it continue to exist, how can the Communist Party continue to develop, how can it hope to be in a position, after the fall of Fascism, to dominate and guide events, if it destroys itself in an absolute passivity such as that suggested by this same S.[47]

Last, Gramsci subtly denounced the weakness of the constitutional opposition:

The truth is that the constitutional opposition will never realize its programme, which is a pure instrument of anti-fascist agitation. It will not realize it, because to do so would mean that so great a "catastrophe" would occur so soon; and because the entire development of the situation in Italy is controlled by the armed force of the national militia. Nevertheless, the development of the opposition and the features which it assumes are extremely important phenomena. They are the proof of fascism's powerlessness to resolve the vital problems of the nation. They are a daily reminder of the objective reality which no volley of insults can annihilate. For us, they represent the environment in which we must move and work, if we wish to remain in contact with historical reality, and not become a meditational sect; the environment in which we must seek the concreteness of our slogans and our immediate programmes for action and agitation.[48]

Between 1924 and 1926, there is no trace of further exchanges between Sraffa and Gramsci, but it is likely that after the murder of Matteotti and the failure of the Aventine Secession (see chapter 6), Sraffa drew closer to the Communists once again, or at least turned away from the Socialists, condemning their political helplessness. For his part, Gramsci used articles by the young, brilliant economist to feed his reflections on the state of Italian finance and banking.

Continuing to support the Comintern's drive to build a party of the masses, the third and final means Gramsci advanced was to call on his comrades to pay particular attention to the Mezzogiorno, which seemed to him to be the ideal terrain for a strategic alliance between the workers and the peasants. He explains this idea in an article, "The Mezzogiorno and Fascism," published on March 15, 1924 in *L'ON*.

He began with the claim that Fascism was not taking root in the peninsular, insular southern half of Italy (except for part of Sicily), while it was implanted successfully, and through violence, in the north and center of the country. The attachment to the monarchy, the clout of elites and clientelist networks, not to mention the anti-unitary feeling among a large part of the population, made it "an enclave for the constitutional opposition,"[49] heralded mainly by Giovanni Amendola (1882–1926), a figure within liberalism who was just as hostile to revolutionary ideas as he was to *squadrismo*. As Salerno's deputy since 1919, Amendola established himself as the leader of the bourgeois and monarchical opposition to Fascism after the speech he gave against the Acerbo Law in the Chamber of Deputies on July 12, 1923, a speech that was the first to label Fascism as a totalitarian movement. This brave position made him a target for Fascist harassment, harassment that rapidly escalated to violence after his newspaper, *Il Mondo*, founded in 1922, became the principal mouthpiece of the Aventine Secession. It is interesting to note that there were rumors Amendola would be kidnapped and killed, and not Matteotti. After a first attack in December 1923, and then two others in April and July 1925, he was forced to take refuge in France, where he died of his wounds at a clinic in Cannes on April 7, 1926. In a related way, Gramsci hypothesized that, unlike *La Stampa* (close to Giolitti and in favor of a hegemonic northern government, if not a strictly Piedmontese one), the *Corriere della Sera* (a newspaper for the conservative Italian bourgeoisie) wanted "an 'Amendola' government—that is, it wants the petite bourgeoisie of the South and not the cream of the Northern factory workers to be incorporated officially into the real power system."[50] Faced with this coherent agenda, the Fascist bosses were dismayed, so much so that in destroying all the workers' organizations (cooperatives, labor leagues, unions), "Fascism has deprived the 'democrats' of their strongest weapon in the fight to turn the hatred of the peasant masses against the industrial forces."[51] Henceforth, though Fascism had not created the southern question, it exacerbated it without meaning to by showing that "In the present situation, with the depression we are seeing at the moment in the proletarian forces, the southern peasant masses have assumed an enormous importance in the revolutionary arena." Gramsci could therefore conclude by advancing the following alternative:

> Either the proletariat, through its political party, will succeed in creating a network of allies in the *Mezzogiorno*, or else the peasant masses will look for political leaders in their own region—in

other words, they will put themselves entirely in the hands of the Amendolian petite bourgeoisie and become a storehouse of counter-revolutions, prepared to resort to separatism and appeals to foreign armies in the case of a purely industrial revolution in the North. The guiding idea of the workers' and peasants' government must then take special account of the *Mezzogiorno*. The problem of the Southern peasants must not be confused with the more general question of the relations between the cities and the rural areas within an economic whole which is organically subjected to the capitalist regime. The Southern question is also a territorial question and it is from this perspective that it must be considered if a program of worker and peasant government is to be established that will win large-scale support from the masses.[52]

When he was getting ready to return to Italy after a two-year absence (he had left his homeland on May 26, 1922, and would return on May 12, 1924), Gramsci had a clear plan that willingly leaned on the Comintern to renew the PCdI by giving it a new political and ideological direction. That direction was opposed to Bordiga, from whom Gramsci had gradually begun to keep his distance, without openly breaking with him. All that remained for Gramsci was to convince the majority of cadres and party leaders of his theses. No sooner had his feet touched Italian soil than he began tackling this new task.

< **6** >

At the Head of the
New Communist Party of Italy
(May 1924–November 8, 1926)

The Fifth Congress of the Communist International

A little over a month before Gramsci reached Italy, the CC of the PCdI met without the Bordigists. Tasca led the charge against Togliatti, Scoccimarro, Terracini, and Gramsci, accusing the new center of being a faction that had converted to the Comintern with the sole purpose of driving out the right-wing minority that was, for its part, always faithful to the international organization. Tasca then decided to resign from the Central Committee of the PCdI. Above all, this decision was due to political reasons: he didn't want to work with his centrist comrades, much less share with them the political responsibility for divorcing from the Comintern. Nonetheless, he agreed to present a programmatic platform at the meeting in mid-May, which would gather the members of the CC and all the federation secretaries so they could consult about their feelings toward the Comintern.

With the greatest secrecy (the police caught wind of the meeting but didn't know the location until after it had taken place), sixty-seven cadres of the party (eleven members of the CC, forty-six federation secretaries, a representative of the Socialist Youth Federation, a representative from the propaganda sector, five leaders of interregional committees, and three bureaucrats) met in the Como region during the second half of May. Staying in a chalet, they passed themselves off as company employees taking advantage of the joys of a mountain excursion. At lunch and dinner, they joked and sang Fascist songs, but in the afternoons, they discussed political strategy far from prying eyes in "beautiful valleys, white-carpeted with daffodils."[1] The meetings were organized around the discussion of three motions. Bordiga's directly opposed the Comintern's policy of a united front, asserting the heritage of the Rome Theses in their entirety. Tasca's proposition advanced the classic arguments of the right-wing minority, opposing Bordiga's point by point. On the one hand, he took up the accusations the Comintern had leveled against the PCdI during the meeting of the Enlarged ECCI in June 1923, and on the other, he proposed a strategy of vast alliance between the anti-Fascist forces, which was not unlike the one put forward by Sraffa in his March 1924 letter (see chapter 5). The third motion carried Togliatti's signature, but it was the result of a joint project in which Gramsci had played a significant role. As a faithful agent of the Comintern, whose latest orders from Zinoviev himself were transmitted via Terracini in a letter of April 25, 1924, Togliatti attempted to spare Bordiga in hopes that he would rejoin the new majority that was being built. Unlike Togliatti and Scoccimarro, who still believed it was possible to convince Bordiga, Gramsci knew that it was time to clarify the situation once and for all, especially since the Neapolitan had pushed away the olive branch they had offered him. The vast majority of comrades seemed to support this refusal, since they remained unmoved by Gramsci's argument that Bordiga's strategy was a failure because it had not been able to convince the majority of the proletariat, drawing this spirited sectarian response from the Neapolitan leader: "we would have it if we hadn't changed our tactic toward the Socialist Party! After all, we are not in a rush." Gramsci lamented this final sally, affirming, "We *are* in a rush! There are situations in which not being in a rush leads to defeat."[2] This exchange shouldn't mislead us. The debates in the "beautiful valleys, white-carpeted with daffodils" had almost no bearing on the concrete situation of the country and the ways to fight Fascism, remaining confined to questions of internal strategy.

Unsurprisingly, a crushing majority voted in favor of Bordiga's ideological line, which received the support of thirty-five federations, four of the five interregional secretaries, the representative of the Socialist Youth Federation, and one member of the CC. The right did better than the new center, with the support of five federation secretaries, one interregional secretary, and three members of the CC. The new center received only eight votes: from four federation secretaries and four members of the CC (the center held a majority only within that body). So while the Fifth Congress of the Comintern was on the point of opening, the PCdI traversed a new crisis. Not only had the majority of cadres renewed their trust in Bordiga, who had resigned from the CC, but the representatives of the right-wing minority had also decided to leave the CC. As for the centrist group, it was still very much in the minority. Even though the Como meeting had only an advisory role, it was already clear that the fate of the PCdI was once again in the hands of the Comintern.

On June 17, 1924, 406 delegates representing 41 nations and 51 Communist parties met at the Bolshoi. The Italian delegation was made up of eighteen members, including the notable figures Bordiga, Grieco, Leonetti, Tasca, and Togliatti, who was visiting the Soviet Union for the first time, in addition to Serrati and Maffi, who represented the *terzini*. This delegation was joined by Terracini, who was already in Moscow as a PCdI representative within the Comintern. Gramsci, who was also supposed to leave for Moscow, was held back in Rome, during the dramatic hours after Matteotti's murder. Through the decisive action of Zinoviev, who was still the strongman of the triumvirate at the head of the RCP(b) at the time (Stalin and Kamenev were the other two), the Fifth Congress of the Comintern's plan was the bolshevization of the Communist parties so they would henceforth be organized on the basis of workplace cells, as we described in the previous chapter. As a result, the Comintern had to become a true global party, centralized and disciplined. Compared with the Fourth Congress, the speeches by sixty-two orators were characterized by a very evident leftist turn, expressed as a frank hostility toward social democracy, represented as the left wing of the bourgeoisie, while Fascism was represented as the right wing. Karl Radek paid the price for this swerve to the left, since he was criticized for having underestimated the danger represented by social democratic forces. All the same, the united front was still the major theme, and from then on, it was conceived of as a unity that could be realized from below, at the level of the workers, and not from above, at the level of partisan organizations. Zinoviev tasked himself with maintaining a good relationship between the Comintern and the PCdI by refusing to favor this or that current. For its part, the Italian delegation declared itself officially and unanimously in agreement with the conclusions of his report. Bordiga, for one, proved himself capable of diplomacy, but the guarded tone of his speech didn't prevent him from letting his profound disagreements with the Comintern and with the RCP(b) show. In this way, though he accepted, like it or not, certain aspects of bolshevization (like that of greater centralization), he believed that the decision-making power should pass from the Comintern to the Communist parties of Western Europe, which had an industrial proletariat that was historically more advanced. They also had a more developed Marxist experience, from which the Bolsheviks themselves had learned many lessons. This analysis, running counter to Comintern decisions, was fiercely denounced by Bukharin. He was a proponent of the theory that consolidating Socialism within the Soviet Union was more important than extending the revolution outward; he feared that an alliance between Bordiga and Trotsky would shift the epicenter of the revolution from Moscow to Western Europe.

As the debates of the Fifth Congress of the Comintern wrapped up on July 8, 1924, Bordiga was "both conquered and victorious. Conquered because his intransigence isolated him in a way that would soon become definitive. Victorious because the left turn that the Congress took was in line with his ideas and his positions."[3] The Comintern's agreement with the Neapolitan revolutionary's analysis of anti-Fascism was particularly distressing. Even though Matteotti had just been murdered, Bordiga continued to think that non-Communist anti-Fascism was just as dangerous as Fascism, as he had during the Fourth Congress of the Comintern, which had taken place just after the March on Rome. By trusting Bordiga with the speech on Fascism during the plenary session on July 2, 1924, the Comintern deprived itself of a serious analysis of this movement, mainly displaying their ambivalence when it came to Italian Communism. This ambivalence was also part of the decision by Comintern leaders to display a turn to the left, all the while eliminating Bordiga's group from the leadership of the PCdI. The Communist International decided to put an end to the opposition from Bordiga that really hadn't flagged since 1921, ratifying the resignations of all the Bordigists from the CC and allowing the *terzini* to join instead. From then on, the new CC had seventeen members: nine for the center, four for the right, and four *terzini*. The EC of five members was formed by Togliatti, Scoccimarro, and Gramsci (who was included for the first time) in the center, Gustavo Mersù on the right, and Fabrizio Maffi for the *terzini*. This new leadership faced colossal tasks. They still had to win over the local leaders and the militants of the PCdI, of whom a majority were will attached to Bordigism, all the while confronting the new situation that had been created in Italy as a result of Matteotti's murder.

Gramsci and the Conquest of the PCdI

On June 10, 1924, Matteotti's kidnapping (his corpse would not be found until August 16) unleashed the most serious crisis that Fascism faced outside of World War II. Matteotti, the deputy from Rovigo, incarnation of the soul of reformist socialism and general secretary of the PSU, accused the Fascists of fraud during the April 1924 elections. From the podium of the Chamber, in the midst of cries of hate, he demanded the dissolution of the newly elected Chamber of Representatives. Though the immediate political reaction to Matteotti's speech aimed at preventing Mussolini from implicating several figures within his government who were important to the CGL,[4] the deputy's critiques of Fascism were leveled in the name of law and justice that transcended the political divisions of the anti-Fascists. And so Matteotti became "a mythical figure" while his murder would stain the Fascist regime forever, becoming their "original crime."[5]

While their comrades were participating in the Fifth Congress of the Comintern, Gramsci and Scoccimarro had assumed the de facto leadership of the PCdI in Italy. They thought they had been presented with a splendid opportunity to bring the tactic of the united front into being as a bottom-up alliance of all workers, since there was, objectively, a historic chance to strike a decisive blow against the Fascist regime. But while the Communists called for a general strike, the CGL leadership was opposed to that measure, which they thought was as ineffective as it was dangerous. For their part, the deputies of the PSU and the PSI joined with their colleagues who had been elected on the PPI lists and on those of different liberal movements. These deputies decided, on June 21, to no longer participate in the operations of the Chamber of Deputies until a new government could be established, one that would reaffirm constitutional legality. This began what its contemporaries called the Aventine Secession, a reference to the first secession by the Roman plebeians in 494 BC when the Roman people, after revolting, withdrew en masse to the Aventine hill. This spectacular event would quickly devolve into an impasse, culminating in a bitter failure. In fact, the Liberal, Socialist, and People's deputies—the latter acting without the support of the Holy See—had only their hostility to Fascism in common, and this eclectic coalition very quickly found itself confined to a legalist position that prevented it from calling on public opinion, or forming a parallel chamber. As for the hand they extended to Victor Emmanuel III, it was met with royal silence by the king, who continued to trust Mussolini. Along with the support of the monarch, the head of the government continued to hold several trump cards: a solid majority in the Senate chamber, the unwavering support of the PNF and the Milice, not to mention access to the good old squadrist recipes of bludgeonings and castor oil, a terrible combination that caused numerous deaths within the opposition ranks, including those of Piero Gobetti and Giovanni Amendola. After six months of indecision,

Mussolini's famous speech on January 3, 1925, in which he assumed all political responsibility for the events, allowed him to take the upper hand openly. From "dictatorship that was legal," Fascism moved on to "legalization of the dictatorship" (Pierre Milza). This transformation was carried out on three levels: the PNF went back to work with the firm support of the state, they pursued and destroyed any form of opposition, and last, they created a whole legislative arsenal that was traditionally called the Leggi Fascistissime (Fascist laws).[6]

In the acute phase of the Matteotti crisis, the PCdI intended to lead a frontal attack against Fascism in the press and on political and union grounds. Though its call for a general strike on June 23, 1924, was not answered by the CGL or relayed by the Socialists, it could be considered a success, since there were as many strikers that day as there were Communist voters on April 6, 1924. This proved the stability of the party's numbers though it had been hard hit by repression, since, at the time, one in every two political prisoners was a Communist and several militants were forced into exile. In terms of tactics, the leadership of the PCdI succeeded in distinguishing themselves radically from the forces of the Aventine Secession. During a speech before the CC of the party in August 1924, Gramsci described the opponents of the Aventine Secession as "semi-Fascism that wants to reform the Fascist dictatorship by softening it."[7]

The Communist forces and those behind the Aventine Secession actually shared the same false interpretation of the situation. Though Amendola, a major figure in the Aventine Secession, thought that the king would depose Mussolini and restore constitutional legality, Togliatti and Gramsci believed that the fall of Fascism (which they thought was imminent) would be settled by putting a conservative government in place, probably dominated by Salandra, with the support of the king's court and the military caste. Though the Aventine Secessionists' diagnosis of the situation was as mistaken as that of the Communists, we must acknowledge that the latter had a discourse and a practice that were less contradictory and more dynamic. While the Aventine coalition, undermined by internal fault lines, seemed incapable of developing a clear and effective strategy for building another chamber parallel to the existing one, the Communists called for battle on all fronts. They were undoubtedly encouraged in this aggressive strategy by the growth in their party's numbers, which doubled during the second half of 1924, as well as by the fact that the *terzini* also joined their line after their own fell apart. Among the two thousand new militants who abandoned the PSI to join the PCdI, a few, like the doctor Fabrizio Maffi or the journalist Giacinto Menotti Serrati, had had a glorious past, while others, like Girolamo Li Causi (1896–1977), had a promising future.[8]

Despite these encouraging signs, Gramsci knew that when it came to convincing the leaders and local militants of the ideas the new PCdI leadership put forward, the argument was far from won. And so he redoubled his efforts. For the whole autumn of 1924, he traversed the peninsula from north to south, increasing, with the utmost secrecy, his contacts with community activists in backyards or in huts in the middle of fields to escape the surveillance from the Fascist authorities. This propaganda work gave him the opportunity to go to Sardinia at the end of October 1924. He decided to visit his loved ones, who were still living in Ghilarza at the time. He was greatly moved to be with his parents once again. This was the last time he would see them. With his stained jacket, his worn and dirty shirt, hatless, his beard poorly groomed, his hair combed every which way (this account is from Nino Bruno, the young Sardinian Communist metalworker who accompanied him during his trip to his native island), Gramsci was the antithesis of what a conventional deputy was supposed to look like. Most deputies wore carefully maintained clothing, and when they did display extravagances of dress, they were perfectly controlled. Gramsci remained, above all, a militant devoted to his engagement, refusing any compromise with bourgeois values. Even if he hadn't experienced prison, it is unlikely that he would have become an apparatchik profiting from privileges. Besides, one of the reasons for his success in convincing his comrades was that he seemed like one of them. In Sardinia, the peasants and notables (*prinzipales*), including Fascists, came to greet him, the latter to take pride in the fact that a child of their land now sat in Montecitorio, the former to express their incredulity: "But why leave Sardinia, which is so poor, then join up with another lot of poor folk over there?"[9] But only the militant Communists whom he met with near Cagliari in a field between the salt mines felt complete trust in one of their own. Leaning against a tree, he spoke calmly. He had always preferred little circles to large assemblies. He spoke to them in Sardinian dialect, joking and sharing a bit of cheese with them. In his capacity to connect naturally with people, Gramsci resembled Garibaldi, and it's not surprising that they both figure in the Italian pantheon.[10]

Along with this psychological element, Gramsci was helped in his task of conquering the PCdI by objective factors. While the FIOM and the FEDETERRA (a contraction of the name National Federation of Workers of the Land) were lamenting a considerable fall in their numbers, the union organizations that were organically linked to the PCdI experienced promising beginnings. The same was true for the Association for the Defense of Southern Peasantry, which had regrouped seventy-five thousand members as soon as it was created in November 1924, half the number of unionized people who remained faithful to FEDETERRA. The other signs of the party's health were the class demographics of the PCdI, since of the twenty-five thousand members, 75 percent were workers and 20 percent were peasants. The party had also been implemented across the whole territory, even if the north had the lion's share of supporters, with the Genoa-Milan-Turin industrial triangle and its fifteen thousand supporters, as opposed to five thousand from central Italy and five thousand from the continental and insular Mezzogiorno. Though this positive overview should not mask the weak points of the PCdI, particularly its dire lack of weapons, Gramsci could reasonably convince his comrades that the creation of workers' and peasants' committees was the best way to enact the united front the Comintern wanted. Taking up the Ordinovist questions of the immediate postwar period, he once again considered these committees to be the soviets of a new Socialist state that was waiting to be built.

The PCdI's choice to be present at the opening of the new parliamentary session was another way of breaking with the passivity of the Aventine Secession. Not without difficulty, the governing bodies of the Comintern agreed that a single deputy would speak on behalf of the party on the day the Chamber reopened, which was planned for November 12, 1924. The PCdI pulled off a small tactical masterpiece. In fact, while the return of all the deputies would have meant giving importance to the bourgeois parliament, sending no deputies would have been tantamount to depriving themselves of a platform from which they could make their criticisms heard. Moreover, the three hundred deputies elected from the *Listone* could not unite against the lone Luigi Repossi (1882–1957), who was close to Bordiga and very popular with the Milanese workers. Though the deputies of the Aventine Secession cried that it was a scandal, thinking the Communists were playing Mussolini's game, the Communists kept on fighting tirelessly for the PCdI while the press and the organizations gathered around them, recognizing the PCdI as the principal opponent to the Fascists. After the speech on January 3, 1925, which marked, as we've seen, a decisive step in Italy's transition to Fascism, the persecution of the PCdI intensified. In this context, the party had to expand its clandestine network, but it also had to play the card held by its deputies, who took advantage of the fact that parliamentary immunity still existed, an immunity that was entirely relative, since the Communist speakers always got their share of insults, often getting spit on or even hit.

In his introductory speech before the CC which gathered on February 6, 1925, Gramsci nonetheless had to acknowledge the poor results of attempting to update the workers' and peasants' councils, but he remained loyal to this strategy, criticizing Tasca and Maffi for wanting to relaunch a political initiative toward the PSI leaders, to whom the Comintern remained opposed, preferring to adhere to the idea of a united front from below. Beyond his prophesying on Aventine anti-Fascism and on the approaching end of Fascism, the Sardinian thinker began to form a more interesting theory about the role of the intermediate layers in every partisan organization, and particularly those that saw themselves as democratic, layers that formed the link "between the higher executive group and the masses of the party and the population influenced by the party, [specifying] that a notable portion of the medium strata of the various popular parties is subject to the influence of the movement for a unified front."[11] So in his eyes, more than ever, it was imperative to continue demonstrating political openness toward both the intellectuals (Gobetti, for example) and the parties (such as Lussu's Sardinian Action Party) that were ready to join the united front.

Such a strategy meant an honest, clean break with the Bordigists' sectarian mindset. This work was even more urgent because the Comintern demanded it, and Gramsci faithfully followed their decisions. The Fifth Congress of the Enlarged ECCI,[12] which was held in Moscow from March 21 to April 5, 1925, clearly raised the question of Bordiga, after the latter had decided to take Trotsky's side in a February 1925 article sent to *L'Unità*, but whose publication the EC of the PCdI decided to block.[13] For the first time, on February 6, 1925, the CC of the PCdI had evoked the question of Trotsky, taking stock of where Lenin's *enfants terribles* diverged, with Trotsky on one side, and Zinoviev, Kamenev, Stalin, and Bukharin on the other, differences that could not be swept under the rug or softened, not after the international press had given so much publicity to Trotsky's *Lessons of October* (published in October 1924), in which the latter attacked Zinoviev and Kamenev, reminding people of their Menshevik (and therefore anti-Leninist) behavior in 1917. This awareness of the conflicts within the RCP accentuated the divorce between the new leadership of the PCdI and Bordiga. All the same, more than the debate between the strategy of Socialist consolidation in the Soviet Union and the Trotskyist theme of permanent revolution, the Italian Communists proved to be especially sensitive to the risk of division their party ran if an alliance formed between Trotsky and Bordiga. Being faithful to the decisions voted in at the Fifth Congress of the Comintern meant recognizing the necessity of bolshevizing the PCdI and accepting that it was subordinated to the RCP in both word and deed. Also, during the meeting of the Fifth Enlarged ECCI, which unfolded during the context of an ebb in the revolution after Hindenburg's victory in Germany and the consolidation of Fascist power in Italy, Scoccimarro openly, and for the first time, established the parallel between Bordigism and Trotskyism. Though Scoccimarro didn't take up Zinoviev's outrageous terms and accuse Bordiga of being such an opportunist that he had switched from the far left of his party to the right, Scoccimarro shared this analysis, since he emphasized the formalist character of Trotskyist and Bordigist thinking, where they should have instead been taking the concrete situation into account.

Gramsci, who had attended the meeting of the Fifth Congress of the Enlarged ECCI without speaking at it, came back to the Bordiga question during meetings with the CC of the PCdI on May 11 and 12, 1925. In his opening remarks, he wholeheartedly reiterated the necessity to bolshevize the Communist parties of Western Europe so they could work in the same ideological direction going forward. After this preamble, he confronted the Bordiga question directly, taking care to distinguish it from the one surrounding Trotsky, since he presented Bordiga's position as a provincialist reaction that conveyed the PCdI's refusal to "form part of a global organization."[14] According to this reasoning, Bordiga reproduced the same error that had been Serrati's five years earlier, when "out of patriotism for the party,"[15] he had acted to exclude the maximalists from the Comintern. For fear of being contaminated by social democracy, the PCdI (as it had been created in Livorno and structured by the Rome Theses under Bordiga's wing) had turned in on itself, developing a set of sectarian behaviors that amounted to closing itself off, meaning it paid attention only to national experiences. Rather than subscribing to a polemical alignment between Trotsky and Bordiga, who were both stigmatized for being right-wing opportunists, Gramsci proposed a historical reading of Bordigism as part of the Italian tradition of Socialism that had always been inclined toward a fractionist mindset.

On May 16, 1925, five days after presenting this take, which received the support of all the CC members, Gramsci showed the full measure of his talent by giving his first and last speech at the Chamber of Deputies.

He left us this account, from a letter to his companion Julia, dated May 1925:

> The fascists reserved special treatment for me and, from the revolutionary viewpoint, I therefore got off to an unsuccessful start. Because my voice does not carry, they gathered around me in order to hear me, and they let me say what I wanted, interrupting me only in order to drive me off the point, but with no attempt at sabotage.[16]

This description is corroborated by several accounts and immortalized by a photograph of Mussolini concentrating, his hand cupped behind his ear so he could better hear this speech by a man he described in 1921 as a "Sardinian hunchback, professor of economics and philosophy, with an unquestionably powerful brain."[17] The two adversaries met at the café in Montecitorio, but Gramsci refused to shake the Fascist leader's hand when he congratulated him on his speech. He drank his coffee and left the Chamber of Deputies, having made a permanent impression.

Gramsci's only speech as a deputy took place within the framework of a discussion about the planned law against secret societies, presented by Mussolini and Alfredo Rocco, his minister of justice. This text was officially directed against Freemasonry, an organization that Mussolini had always wanted to destroy.[18] This plan marked an important moment in Fascism's takeover of power. Gramsci wasn't fooled, for he saw in it "a form of systematic persecution which precedes and will justify the application of the new law" to disperse opposing parties.[19] In his speech, he first demonstrated that if Fascism took on Freemasonry, it would be because "given the initial weakness of the Italian capitalist bourgeoisie, Freemasonry was the only real and effective party which the bourgeois class had for a long time." He went on to argue that attacking Freemasonry came down to being "against the political tradition of the Italian bourgeoisie." In wanting to realize "the spiritual unity of the Italian nation" at the expense of Freemasonry, as confirmed by the deputy Gilberto Martire, a populist elected on the *Listone*, Fascism was only reproducing the strategy that the Vatican and the Jesuits had used in the first decades of the new Italian state. This process of submission was one in which "the most backward classes of the population bring under their control the class which has been progressive in the development of civilization." This movement of "historical regression" was happening not only in Italy, but also in Germany, with the election of Hindenburg, and with the conservative victory in England's legislative elections of 1924. Continuing his arguments on the failure of both bourgeois solutions for accomplishing national unity (the Giolittian theory of an alliance between the bourgeoisie and the northern industrial aristocracy and Salandra's wish for an agreement between northern industrials and agrarians of the Mezzogiorno, see above), Gramsci confirmed that "In reality Fascism struggles against the only effectively organized force which the bourgeoisie had in Italy, to supplant it in the posts which the state gives its civil servants. The Fascist 'revolution' is only the replacement of one administrative personnel by another."

After this skillful analysis, in the second half of his speech Gramsci criticized the systematic attacks the regime had carried out against the PCdI, provoking in return ironic remarks from Mussolini and from other Fascist deputies recalling the violence committed by Communists in Russia to establish their revolution, getting them this awesome—an adjective intended in its etymological sense— reply from the Communist leader:

> We are sure of representing the majority of the population, of representing the most essential interests of the majority of the Italian people; proletarian violence is thus progressive and cannot be systematic. Your violence is systematic and systematically arbitrary because you represent a minority destined to disappear. We must say to the working population what your government is, how your government conducts itself, to organize against you, to make it ready to defeat you. It is most probable that we too

will find ourselves forced to use the same systems as you, but as a transition, occasionally. Certainly: use the same systems as you, with the difference that you represent the minority of the population, while we represent the majority.

This speech concluded by affirming the coming victory of an alliance between the masses of workers and peasants. Gramsci's presentation showed both the nuance of his analysis of Fascism, which he repositioned within Italian and European history, and the limits, emphasized by Sraffa, of a hermeneutic that places the fight against Fascism within the narrow perspective of class struggle between the bourgeoisie and the proletariat. A corollary was his idea of an objective alliance between Mussolini and Amendola, the principal figure of the Aventine Secession, who was labeled a "semi-Fascist" in the pages of *L'Unità*. All the leaders of the PCdI, including Gramsci, denied the democratic dimension of anti-Fascist political culture, for the simple reason that they were incapable of feeling it. This was surely a moral failing but also a political mistake, especially when the main crisis of Fascism had begun with the murder of Matteotti, who represented law and liberty in the face of unpredictability and violence.

The Lyons Theses

From autumn 1925 on, the Fascists no longer pulled their punches, understanding that the most acute phase of the crisis threatening their regime had passed. In November 1925, Roberto Farinacci, head of the squadrists, quickly chased the Communist deputies out of Montecitorio, though they were still theoretically protected by their immunity, and he encouraged the militias to physically and verbally harass them. Once again finding themselves the target of persecutions (which had tapered off at the height of the Matteotti crisis, though they had never truly stopped), the PCdI sank into hiding, especially after the wave of arrests in October and November 1925, which forced the CC to push back the date of the congress that had initially been planned for autumn 1925. Gramsci continued to expand his travel. He was fully aware that, unlike the advisory meeting in Como in May 1924, the next congress would not only have a deliberative vote but also reflect both the positions of the leaders and those of all the militants. His propaganda work was surely paying off, since more than 90 percent of the votes at the Lyons congress (the third congress of the PCdI, which took place from January 20 to 26, 1926) were for the centrist motion, whose principal theses he had co-written with Togliatti (see below).

Gramsci's action to make sure he had control of the party meant a direct confrontation with Bordiga, which became impossible to defer once the Neapolitan had offered his official support to the leftist Entente Committee, created in 1925 as a way of regrouping his main supporters. This committee published three documents in May and June 1925: the first protested against the accusations the Comintern had leveled at Bordiga; the second put in place some coordination between leftist militants; and the third called for a democratic discussion during the next party congress. In the pages of *L'Unità*, Gramsci reacted forcefully against "the seeds of fractional contamination" that pushed the comrades of the Entente Committee to "position themselves outside of the party and the Communist International," meaning they would assuredly "reinforce the counterrevolutionary elements."[20]

To prepare for the Third Congress of the PCdI, the centrists created five documents: the first on the international situation, the second on the national and colonial situation, the third on the agrarian question, the fourth on the Italian situation and bolshevization, and the fifth on the unions. The main document, which passed into history as the *Lyons Theses*, is the fourth, not only because it summarizes the principal themes developed in the four others, but also because it can be considered an expression "of the politico-theoretical elaboration of the Gramscian direction, in the same way the Rome Theses were for the Bordigist direction."[21]

Written by Gramsci and Togliatti, the *Lyons Theses* included eighteen paragraphs articulated around three big ideas, which took positions against the strategy of the past, and especially against Bordiga's strategy of the moment. Right away, unlike the Neapolitan revolutionary who saw the template for the PCdI in the extreme maximalist left of the PSI, Gramsci saw the founding act in the October Revolutions and, on the doctrinal level, Leninism's contribution to Marxism. It would be a mistake to interpret Gramsci's reading as just that of a faithful servant of the Comintern and the RCP—it was also the reworking of ideas he had already developed during the *biennio rosso* in the pages of *L'ON*, arguments that were already in opposition to the positions Bordiga put forward in his review *Il Soviet* (see chapter 4). The theses went on to say, and this is the second key idea, that the bolshevization of the PCdI was a necessity that should not be compromised. Unlike Bordiga, who thought it was better to keep the party organized around territorial sections, they argued that the basic organism of the PCdI should henceforth become the cells embedded in each workplace. On this exact point, Gramsci followed the directives from the Fifth Congress of the Comintern to the letter, which delighted him in that they directly echoed the thematic of the *commissioni interne*. For Gramsci, the bolshevization of the PCdI meant once again rejecting any form of faction within the party, which had to react with iron discipline, conceived as one section of a vast body, the Comintern, in which the RCP had a dominant leadership function. Last, where the Bordigists saw Fascism as the homogeneous expression of the dominant class, the Sardinian thinker, in line with his writings that had been published in *L'ON* and in *L'Unità*, and without forgetting his parliamentary speech, detected an alliance between the urban petite bourgeoisie and the reaction of the agrarians, an alliance that made Fascism not a revolution, as its supporters proclaimed, but the replacement of one leadership elite in power with another. This analysis showed, in his eyes, the tight ties that existed between Russia and Italy. On a social level, Italy, like Russia, was characterized by the presence of a labor class that was still the minority in an agricultural society. It followed that Italy had a revolutionary potential that was more significant than the one that existed in countries where the capitalist system and industry were more developed. The united front strategy was therefore, more than ever, an indisputable reality.

The other documents on the international, agrarian, and union situation corroborated "this effort to translate the Soviet experience"[22] for Italy that would be endorsed at the Third Congress of the PCdI.

The organization of this congress was proof of the PCdI's capacity to act in a way that would elude the surveillance of Mussolini's political police who were well aware of this meeting but who, once again, didn't know where it was held until after it had taken place. The PCdI leadership had first imagined that its Third Congress would unfold in the Austrian capital, but they gave up that idea owing to the worsening tuberculosis of Mario Codevilla, their representative in Vienna, who was no longer strong enough to prepare the logistics. Lyons seemed like a better choice. In fact, the militant Communists could count on the dedication and efficiency of their many compatriots who had emigrated and who were able to deal, as best they could, with the material aspects of the congress, especially the lodging of seventy delegates elected by the different sections of the PCdI to represent them in Lyons. Though they could count on relative benevolence from the French authorities—the Cartel of the Left, already in crisis, was still in power—the delegates, who had crossed the Franco-Italian border using no less than eleven different routes, some without passports, others with false papers, and even some among them entering with real passports, were all aware it was a hidden congress that would take place in different locations. From January 20 to January 26, the only applause at the congress was fueled by Gramsci's speech. He chided the left of the party for doubting the legitimacy of the chosen delegates, since the secretary general had the easy job of reminding people of the courage of the militants who planned the event and those who were taking part, despite the risks they ran.

This applause was a good omen for Gramsci. The congress was dominated by his confrontation with Bordiga, a confrontation where the internal battles of the RCP didn't seem to have much of a role.

Incidentally, Jules Humbert-Droz (1891–1971), representing the Comintern in Lyons, minimized the internal conflicts running through the RCP while also clearly letting Bordiga know that he would have to work with the Comintern or be expelled if he continued to criticize their positions. This congress was also characterized by a retreat in the right-wing minority's positions. Tasca remained faithful to his views, but his attachment to old structures of workers' syndicalism wasn't as convincing as it once had been once the latter were whittled down to nothing. The same was true of his refusal to consider social democracy as the left wing of Fascism and his call for a united front between the leadership, conceived as an agreement between his party and the PSI. These positions could no longer hold the same relevance they'd held even eighteen months earlier in Como in May 1924. Therefore, Tasca no longer seemed to be the protagonist of an alternative politics and played only a secondary role in the confrontation between Bordiga and Gramsci, who attempted a four-hour presentation in response to the three-hour one from the Neapolitan leader. (These two speeches combined approached General Fidel Castro's record-length political speech in 1998.)

Without a transcript of Gramsci's and Bordiga's speeches, it's not possible to determine the precise themes they broached, but in reading Togliatti's summary of the meeting, it becomes clear that each of the two revolutionaries staked out his positions and repeated the arguments we have already examined. Gramsci's victory is conclusive, since the *Lyons Theses*, his motion co-written with Togliatti, received 90.8 percent of the votes compared with 9.2 percent for the motion from the Bordigist left. Tasca rallied to Gramsci's motion. The latter's victory was even more brilliant in that the right (Tasca) and the left (Bordiga and Carlo Venegoni) accepted Gramsci's proposal to include their representatives in the CC next to supporters of the center, who were largely in the majority.[23] As secretary general of the CC, Gramsci was also part of the EC, which was designated as a political bureau (henceforth PB), along with Scoccimarro, Togliatti, Terracini, Camilla Ravera, Paolo Ravazzoli, and Ruggero Grieco, who all agreed with the Gramscian line. It was decided that Togliatti would be sent to Moscow in March as a representative of the PCdI within the Comintern.

From then on, Gramsci was the uncontested leader of the party, but his reign began at a time when, more than ever, the hand of Fascism was bearing down on the Communists. Out of the sixty-six delegates present at Lyons, sixty were arrested in the following months. As for the members of the PB, only Grieco, Togliatti, and Ravazzoli escaped prison (Camilla Ravera would not be imprisoned until 1930).

Some Aspects of the Southern Question

The year 1926 was a black year for Italian communism, since it was the year Stalin's dictatorship began and the PCdI went underground. At the Fourteenth Congress of the RCP (December 18–31, 1925), Stalin emerged as the great victor. As a man of the unified party, defender of the alliance between the proletariat and the peasantry, and promoter of the consolidation of socialism's roots in the Soviet Union, Stalin held all the cards to marginalize Trotsky, whose theories had won Zinoviev's and Kamenev's support. Going directly from Lyons to Moscow, where the sixth meeting of the Enlarged ECCI opened on February 17, 1926, Bordiga[24] met Trotsky on February 21. The two men talked until dawn, yet a real alliance did not form between them, since Bordiga defended his traditional arguments (Leninism was not a developmental part of Marxism's original creation, Russia was economically backward and therefore less primed for a Marxist revolution than the industrialized West) more than he subscribed to Trotskyite analyses. He also refused the bolshevization of the united front. Nonetheless, the two men agreed on two fundamental points: on the one hand, they refused to give the peasantry too large a role, and on the other hand, they wished to orient the foreign policy of the RCP toward extending the revolution rather than turning inward toward the Soviet Union.

By expounding his ideas in a long, four-hour speech, Bordiga presented himself as the main opponent to Stalin and Bukharin, who took it upon themselves to answer him personally. Bukharin went so far as to devote three-quarters of his own speech to refuting Bordiga, criticizing him for thinking in an abstract way without considering the balance of power that demanded stabilizing the USSR to give a counterweight to the stabilization of capitalism.

Bordiga didn't succeed in influencing the balance of power between the Comintern and the RCP by arguing that the decisions of the latter, as the vanguard of the proletariat, influenced the politics of the former. Bukharin's nomination as head of the Comintern during the Seventh Congress of its Enlarged Executive Committee in November 1926 put an end to then-imprisoned Bordiga's efforts to reverse policy and ensure that the sixth full congress of the Comintern would take place quickly. In fact, it did not take place until 1928, when Stalin's power was already consolidated. After losing ground against Gramsci on the national front, Bordiga was therefore also vanquished at the international level, since he had "spiritually placed himself outside of the Comintern" and his "position was forever compromised,"[25] according to these harsh words from Grieco, his former lieutenant, who had rallied to Gramsci and the politics of bolshevization.

While Stalin began a decisive political battle against his opponents in Moscow, a prelude to their physical elimination a few years later, Mussolini intensified his actions against all anti-Fascists, and especially against Communists. During what he called his "Napoleonic" year (1926), when the ultra-Fascist laws became official, Mussolini prevented the PCdI from having any public presence. While it was not explicitly forbidden, the Communist press, and particularly L'Unità, could only reprint official notices. Under tight surveillance, the Communist deputies had to content themselves with a few protests on principle against Fascist policy. The life of the PCdI became almost illegal, since no public action by the party was permitted. A sharp decrease in its numbers followed, and the party probably lost more than 10,000 members in 1926. All the same, with around 15,000 supporters, the PCdI remained the principal force of opposition. By contrast, the very powerful FIOM, whose numbers had once reached up to a million members, had only three hundred! However, from then on, the balance of power was entirely on the side of the Fascists. The two hundred committees of workers and peasants that the party had assigned the immense tasks of working in favor of the united front, of fighting against the monopoly of the Fascist union, and of defending the material interests of the proletariat—what could they do? What could the activist committees for the unity of the proletariat accomplish when almost all Communist workers were automatically fired? How could the strategy of a united front be realized when tensions between Socialist militants and Communist militants were increasing?

During the dark year of 1926, the only bright spots (whose shine would last a long time) were two texts by Gramsci: his unfinished essay on the southern question and the two letters he wrote to Palmiro Togliatti on the operations of the RCP and the Comintern.

With the title "Some Aspects of the Southern Question" (Alcuni temi sulla questione meridionale), Gramsci wrote a pamphlet that he could neither finish nor revise because he was imprisoned. Published for the first time in January 1930 in the exiled PCdI magazine *Stato Operaio*, this essay has since been published in many editions. For many decades, it has been considered a classic in the discourse surrounding the southern question. Originally titled "Notes on the Southern Problem and on Communist, Socialist, and Democratic Attitudes toward It," it was very likely written in October 1926, in response to the publication of an article by the writer and journalist Tommaso Fiore (who was close to Gobetti) in the Socialist magazine *Il Quarto Stato* on September 18, 1926, with a preface by Carlo Rosselli (1899–1937) and Pietro Nenni (1891–1980). More than the content of Fiore's article, Gramsci hated the introduction by Rosselli and Nenni, which denounced what they saw as the erroneous politics of Turin Communists who called for dividing up the large, private agricultural estates (latifundia). "This formula is at the antipodes from any sound, realistic vision of the Southern problem."[26] In responding to this accusation, Gramsci first intended to demonstrate, in a slightly forced way, that Communist policies in favor of the southern agricultural proletariat had existed since 1921.

Though Gramsci, Leonetti, and Giovanni Sanna had been aware of the southern question from the time of the Livorno congress, neither Bordiga nor Graziadei mentioned it, though Graziadei had been in charge of writing the theses on the agrarian question for the Rome congress of March 1922. Gramsci, above all, is therefore responsible for the PCdI's attention to the southern question, though he was seconded in this task by Leonetti and especially by Grieco, who, in August 1924, was named head of the agrarian section of the PCdI attached to the Krestintern. After establishing the southern question on a theoretical level, Gramsci made it into a centerpiece of the new PCdI strategy, along with his *Lyons Theses*.

In "Some Aspects of the Southern Question," he takes up and develops many of the arguments we have already considered, nonetheless specifying and adding several fundamental ideas. The southern question was no longer in its "indistinct, intellectualistic"[27] phase, when it was raised by several great thinkers like Giustino Fortunato or Gaetano Salvemini[28] who could be sensitive to the divide between the north and the south of the peninsula. Thanks to the Turin Communists, it had since become the business of the northern proletariat whose hegemony could not be realized without an alliance with the southern peasants. After dispensing with the ideology that the "the Southerners are biologically inferior beings, semi-barbarians or total barbarians,"[29] the proletariat had understood that its duty was to work toward resolving the peasant question. In Italy this meant the question of the Mezzogiorno, in which the poor peasants were ideologically subjected to the agrarian bloc founded on the agreement between the industrialists and the big landowners.[30] The mortar of this agrarian bloc was made up of the group of individuals, the priests first among them, who depended economically on the latifundia:

> Southern society is a great agrarian bloc, made up of three social layers: the great amorphous, disintegrated mass of the peasantry; the intellectuals of the petty and medium rural bourgeoisie; and the big landowners and great intellectuals. The Southern peasants

are in perpetual ferment, but as a mass they are incapable of giving a centralized expression to their aspirations and needs. The middle layer of intellectuals receives the impulses for its political and ideological activity from the peasant base. The big landowners in the political field and the great intellectuals in the ideological field centralize and dominate, in the last analysis, this whole complex of phenomena. Naturally, it is in the ideological sphere that the centralization is most effective and precise.[31]

The PCdI's goal was to break this double bloc by proposing not only to give land to the peasants but also to organize them in an autonomous way, seeking "to break up the intellectual bloc that is the flexible, but extremely resistant, armor of the agrarian bloc."[32]

Communist analyses on the difficulties of the Italian economy grafted themselves onto this clear plan, analyses which placed the emphasis on overproduction (Scoccimarro), on the risk of a headlong rush toward adventurous imperialism (Tasca), or on the monetary crisis Gramsci had himself examined, no doubt leaning on information provided by Piero Sraffa. Despite the pertinence of their diagnosis, the Communist leaders continued to believe that a revolution was in the relatively near future. In this way, hailing the general strike by English workers in solidarity with the miners in autumn 1926, Gramsci had the PB of the PCdI vote on a resolution confirming:

> The period of the temporary stabilization of capitalism has not ended; we are not at the beginning of a new revolutionary period. Nonetheless we can today affirm that the negative elements of stabilization tend to take over, that capitalism's forces of dissolution tend to act with renewed vigor; stabilization has thus entered into a period of decline.[33]

This relative optimism, which seems absolutely unfounded to us after the fact, was fueled by the weakness of Gramsci's analysis of Fascism. Sensitive to the opposition within the PNF between the legalistic and the revolutionary tendencies,[34] Gramsci's interpretation turned out to be subtler than Bordiga's, since the latter saw Fascism only as a form of reaction by the bourgeoisie. All the same, the Sardinian thinker underestimated the importance of the ultra-Fascist laws, which displayed Fascism's formidable capacity to regulate society[35] by systematically eliminating its opponents but also by overturning the old frameworks of bourgeois power. He ultimately didn't see the totalitarian tendency that was already at work within this movement. This myopic view of Fascism explains why the new secretary general of the PCdI compared Mussolini's Italy in autumn 1926 with Kerensky's Russia in autumn 1917, and therefore refused the plan, proposed by what remained of the Aventine forces, to focus the anti-Fascists around the idea of a republic. In 1930, in his *Prison Notebooks*, Gramsci would come back to his theses of 1924–26 in a critical way, proposing to reactivate the old Mazzinian maxim of a constituent assembly. But in 1926, he judged, "Only one republican concentration has a 'permanent' and historically stable perspective of success in Italy today: that which has the proletariat as its fundamental axis."[36] The underestimation of Fascism and the overestimation of the Communists' revolutionary capacity would have the dramatic effect of diminishing the sense of danger among the leaders of the PCdI, almost all of whom would be arrested. They would also prove to be incapable of organizing the exile of their general secretary.

But before we move on to the conditions of Gramsci's arrest in the next chapter, it makes sense to detail the last, spectacular act of his life as a militant Communist who was still a free man.

The Testament of a Free Bolshevik

To understand the weight of Gramsci's last act before he was arrested, we must return to Moscow to grasp the context. Three months after the Fourteenth Congress of the RCP ended, Kamenev, Zinoviev, and Trotsky decided to unite forces and go on the offensive. But it was already much too late. The three men could count on only a tiny fraction of the RCP's militants, the vast majority of whom had by then already been won over to the line represented by Stalin and Bukharin. With the loss of the Leningrad Section, which had until then been a bastion for Zinoviev, and which Kirov, Stalin's young protégé, was "taking in hand," the three revolutionaries no longer had any reserves of power left. Also, none of the critiques formulated for the first time by Trotsky to the CC of the RCP on July 1926 against the New Economic Policy (NEP) and the politics of consolidating socialism exclusively within the Soviet Union found any echo within the RCP. The CC of the party not only rejected all of the Troika's proposals but also decided, unanimously, to remove Zinoviev from the Politburo.

The vicissitudes of Soviet politics were widely commented on by the Italian press. *La Stampa* placed the emphasis on the rivalry between Lenin's heirs, emphasizing "Stalin's common sense."[37] This Turin newspaper, which was close to Fascism at the time, guessed that under the aegis of Stalin and Bukharin, the RCP intended first of all to undertake agrarian reforms that would put an end to the feudalism of the Russian economy and society. This argument, by which the Bolshevik Revolution would ultimately be reduced to a bourgeois revolution to allow for the development of capitalism, was taken up by *La Voce Repubblicana* and by *Il Mondo*, the newspaper of G. Amendola, which published an article devoted to the USSR on September 9, 1926, with the unambiguous title "Communism without Communism."

Initially, the PCdI's strategy (one that Togliatti particularly wanted) was to avoid discussing the problems with Russian policies with other parties. All the same, Gramsci felt obligated to refute the theses upheld by the anti-Fascist press, which was not yet totally muzzled. In the pages of *L'Unità*, he unambiguously supported the majority line that was confirmed by the Fourteenth Congress of the RCP, but he didn't intend to dwell on the debate between the Russian Bolsheviks. Instead, he argued that the Russian Communists were the only ones to have given land to peasant cooperatives. Making Stalin and Bukharin's reasoning his own, he emphasized that the peasants creating primitive capital served to feed the production apparatus that was in the hands of the proletariat. If this mechanism of growth led to the birth of a rich peasantry, the latter not only would reinvest part of its riches in industry but would also form only a minority both in the present and in the future. There was therefore no reason to fear that "their political influence will therefore become dangerous, since the alliance between the poor peasants and the workers will be reinforced by these very developments."[38]

The polemic could have stopped there, especially as Trotsky appeared more than ever as a prophet unarmed (to use the title of the second volume of the first big biography written about him by Isaac Deutscher) after he proposed a truce at the PB of the RCP, which published the contents in the October 16, 1926 edition of *Pravda*. In this document, which felt like a reissue, Trotsky, Kamenev, Zinoviev, and a few of their supporters set out to distinguish themselves from the dissidents of other Communist parties, particularly Karl Korsch in Germany, Boris Souvarine in France, and Amadeo Bordiga in Italy. But two years later, the publication of Lenin's *Testament* in the *New York Times* by Max Eastman, Trotsky's American friend, revived the tensions. Lenin's clearly expressed reservations about Stalin's brutal character led the latter to convene the CC of the RCP, who unanimously approved Trotsky's expulsion from the PB. They also removed Zinoviev from the presidency of the ECCI.

At first, *L'Unità* contented itself with publishing the communiqué that had appeared in *Pravda*, accompanied by the official commentary of the PB of the RCP. But the leaders of the PCdI had to react to the latest Soviet events, which challenged their militants and sympathizers. Unlike the ex-Spartacists—who were kicked out of the Kommunistische Partei Deutschlands (KPD)—Bordiga, who was directly implicated in the declaration signed by Trotsky and his comrades, did not regret that the left of the RCP had disowned him, since he saw it as only a tactic to more effectively combat the ideological orientation of the Comintern from within.

Probably at the request of the PCdI leadership, Gramsci wrote a letter to the CC of the RCP. Though it was not dated, the most likely hypothesis is that it was written on October 14, 1926, in any event before the October 16, 1926 article from *Pravda* came out and before Lenin's *Testament* was published in the *New York Times*. Togliatti received the letter on October 16, 1926. Two days later, Togliatti (the new representative of the PCdI within the Comintern) replied to Gramsci, provoking a new missive from him dated October 26, 1926.

The first of this set of three documents (Gramsci's letter from October 14, 1926) was not published for the first time until April 1938 by Angelo Tasca in *Problemi della Rivoluzione Italiana*, a magazine run by anti-Fascist Socialist émigrés and published in Nancy. Tasca had already supplied fragments of it in the article he wrote after Gramsci's death for *Il Nuovo Avanti* on May 8, 1937. Reproduced once again by Tasca in *I primi dieci anni del PCI* (1953), the letter was deliberately not circulated among Communist militants, and most of them were unaware of its existence. It was only in 1953 that Togliatti halfheartedly admitted that it existed, before authenticating it in 1964 and making his response public. We had to wait another six years for Gramsci's second reply—his letter of October 26 that Togliatti thought was lost—to be published in the Communist magazine *Rinascità* in April 1970. Togliatti's great difficulty in recognizing the existence of these three documents and his discomfort with publishing them raise the question of a deep ideological divide between the two Communist leaders, who would no longer have any direct contact after this epistolary exchange. Indeed, Gramsci never sought to personally reconnect with Togliatti from prison. Regarding the complex role that Togliatti played in the circulation of Gramsci's writings, a role that was both decisive and problematic, this episode should not be downplayed but rather merits a detailed study, even though much critical literature has been written about it. Does it signify a passing split or a deep divide in how they understood Communism?

What did Gramsci's first letter contain that he wanted Togliatti to communicate to the CC of the RCP? First of all, the letter was signed by the PB of the PCdI. Though this doesn't call into question the fact that it was written by Gramsci, who was then the secretary general of the party, this collective signature involves the governing bodies of all the PCdI.

The first argument developed by the Sardinian thinker was that if the unity of the RCP was indispensable, it must be forged by "having achieved a greater ideological and organizational homogeneity through such discussions."[39] By beginning his argument this way, Gramsci certainly would have had his own strategy in mind for convincing militants to distance themselves from Bordigism. He continued by writing that "the present attitude of the opposition bloc and the sharpness of the polemics within the Communist Party of the USSR necessitate intervention by the fraternal parties."[40] Was this not placing the Comintern before the RCP? And hammering in the nail by reminding them that the risk of a schism within the RCP was a windfall for both the bourgeois and social democratic parties and a drama for the Communist parties for whom "the Republic of the Soviets and the CPSU[41] [are] today a formidable element of revolutionary organization and propulsion"?[42] Gramsci particularly emphasized that the Fascist newspapers were full of articles that were

> technically well constructed for propaganda purposes, with a minimum of demagogy or insulting comment, in which an attempt is made to demonstrate with a manifest effort to achieve objectivity that now, as is proved by the best-known leaders of the Joint Opposition in the CPSU themselves, the State of the Soviets is inexorably becoming a purely capitalist State.[43]

Gramsci continued his analysis by praising bolshevization

> under the guidance of the CPSU as a united ensemble and of all the great leaders of the CPSU.... You are degrading, and run the risk of annihilating, the leading function which the CPSU won through Lenin's contribution. It seems to us that the violent passion of Russian affairs is causing you to lose sight of the international aspects of Russian affairs themselves; is causing you to forget that your duties as Russian militants can and must be carried out only within the framework of the interests of the international proletariat.[44]

In the second part of his letter, whose beginning is clearly marked by the way he skips a line, the leader of the PCdI openly guessed that of the underlying problems (NEP, importance paid to the peasantry, priority of stabilizing socialism in the USSR), the majority of the CC of the RCP was right and that the opposition bloc was wrong, for it had proved incapable of thinking in Leninist terms about the contradictions at work in the Soviet story, namely, that a dominant class, the proletariat in the USSR, had been, "in its entirety, experiencing conditions of living inferior to those of certain elements and strata of the dominated and subjected class."[45] In his letter, Gramsci logically defended theses that were identical to the ones he was in the process of laying out in his essay on the southern question. The document concluded by a call for unity and discipline which "in this case cannot be mechanical and enforced [but] must be loyal and due to conviction."[46] This critique of their approach reached its height at the end of the letter, which is worth citing in full:

> This, dearest comrades, is what we wished to say to you, brothers and friends, even if we are your younger brothers. Comrades Zinoviev, Trotsky, Kamenev have contributed powerfully to educating us for the revolution; they have at times corrected us with great force and severity; they have been among our masters. To them especially we address ourselves, as those principally responsible for the present situation, because we like to feel certain that the majority of the Central Committee of the USSR does not intend to win a crushing victory in the struggle, and is disposed to avoid excessive measures. The unity of our brother party in Russia is necessary for the development and triumph of the world revolutionary forces. To this necessity, every communist and internationalist must be prepared to make the greatest sacrifices. The damage caused by the error of a united party is easily mended; that caused by a split, or a prolonged condition of latent split, may easily be irreparable and fatal.[47]

Not finding it advisable to bring Gramsci's letter to the CC of the RCP, Togliatti had Bukharin read it, who then transmitted it to the PB of the RCP, which was careful not to pass it on to the CC. This missive provoked a small earthquake and started to create suspicion on the part of Stalin and his accomplices toward the PCdI, suspicions that would be directly revealed several times up until the 1940s. While the fight against the Trotskyist opposition entered a decisive phase, this distrust of Gramsci briefly reflected even on Togliatti, who was forced to react if he wanted to keep the trust of the Comintern and therefore that of the RCP. And so he began his response to Gramsci with this very clear sentence: "I do not agree with this letter . . ."[48] In the eyes of the PCdI representative within the Comintern, Gramsci had laid out the problem poorly. The most important fact was not, as he believed, the risk of division within the leading group of the RCP, but to confirm the rightness of the line followed by the majority of the CC of the party. Since Lenin's death, "the Leninist old guard" had lived on and people could not speak "indiscriminately of all the Russian comrade leaders [without establishing] any distinction between the comrades who are at the head of the CC and the leaders of the opposition,"[49] and call the first to order like the second. The CC of the RCP was not at fault at all, since all the errors were on the part of the opposition. By the same token, the majority of the CC of the PCdI could not be held responsible whatsoever "for Bordiga's fractionist activity."[50] Gramsci's letter was therefore "an error" which gave the upper hand to the opposition, which "would make use of the slightest waverings"[51] it could detect in European Communist parties. Last, to this arsenal of critiques, Togliatti added two others: Gramsci's letter was too optimistic about the degree of bolshevization attained by Communist parties, but it was too pessimistic about the capacity of European Communists to understand and therefore to adhere to the ideological line of the RCP.

Unable to leave these attacks without a response, Gramsci wrote a new letter, this time signed with his name only. Though he recognized that the RCP was "the most powerful mass organizer that has ever appeared in history," it did not automatically follow that it had attained "a stable and decisive form."[52] And for the great masses, and even for the Communist militants who were in the vanguard, gifted with the most developed awareness of history, "The question of unity, not only of the Russian Party but of the Leninist core is . . . the most important question in this historical period."[53] Even if this unity couldn't match the unity of Lenin's era, it was their "absolute duty to recall to the political consciousness of the Russian comrades, and recall to them forcefully, the dangers and weaknesses that their approaches are about to bring into being." Though such a duty would also serve the opposition, this flaw was not a serious one, since "it is our aim to contribute to maintaining and creating a unitary plan in which the different tendencies and different personalities may once again come closer together and even fuse together ideologically."[54] Gramsci continued his argument by refuting the double accusation of being too alarmist about the consequences of a schism within the RCP and too optimistic about bolshevization, before concluding by denouncing the character of Togliatti's reasoning as "tainted by 'bureaucratism.'"[55] This epistolary exchange and this last accusation clearly carry considerable historic weight, going so far as to outline two conceptions of communism, one that would be that of Soviet orthodoxy, the other, a freer one, which would find its full measure in the *Prison Notebooks*.

At the time, Gramsci's letter of October 26 was not transmitted to the PB of the RCP but provoked a secret meeting of the CC of the PCdI which was held at Valpolcevera, near Genoa, on November 1–3, 1926, so that Jules Humbert-Droz, the Comintern representative for the Latin countries, who was then fully aligned with Stalin's majority, could explain the RCP situation to his Italian comrades. On October 31, at the Milan train station on the way to this meeting, Gramsci was firmly told by a police commissioner to go back to Rome. Not wanting to compromise his comrades, he decided to take the first train leaving for the capital. Though no account of this meeting remains, it emerged that Gramsci's critiques of the methods used by Stalin's majority to combat the Trotskyist opposition had been swept under the rug, and only the Bordigist Carlo Venegoni raised them. The meeting in Valpolcevera concluded with the obedient alignment of the members of the PCdI's PB and CC with the RCP. Mauro Canali therefore had reason to write that Valpolcevera, a week before his arrest, was the beginning of "Gramsci's political and personal solitude."[56]

After he was arrested on October 8, 1926, Gramsci would begin the last stage of his life. From then on, this child of Sardinia who became a poor student in Turin, this militant Socialist who became the secretary general of the PCdI and the architect of its bolshevization, was a prisoner and a philosopher whose analyses and concepts would affect political thought well beyond the Communist political family. Experiencing the darkness of his cell while Mussolini oppressed his country and while Stalin distorted, in the deepest sense, the ideals of his life, Gramsci produced free thought. His personal drama was a boon for his posterity. All the same, this polemic with Togliatti, which was his last public act, allows us to imagine that even if this ordeal of prison had not cut him off from active militant life, Gramsci would probably not have foundered into Stalinism as so many of his companions did.

PART IV

The Prisoner

(November 8, 1926–April 27, 1937)

< 7 >

For Twenty Years, We Must Stop This Brain from Functioning
(November 8, 1926–July 19, 1928)

The Arrest (November 8, 1926)

At 10:30 p.m., on the night of November 8, 1926, two policemen came to arrest Antonio Gramsci at his home at 25 Via Morgagni in Rome. Since 1924, Antonio had been lodging with the Passarge family from Germany, who had come to live in Italy and who he wrongly believed were ignorant of all his activities, at least until the police searched his room on October 24, 1925.[1] Even though he probably wasn't informed that Mario Passarge, the son of the couple, was a friend and protégé of Carmine Senise (1883–1958), who held the post of vice-director of the Italian police,[2] it is undeniably shocking that Gramsci hadn't tried to move and that the party, which he had led since the Lyons congress, had not decided to find him a more secure place to live. All the same, rather than reasoning as if everything were suspect, it seems to us that the Communist leader's naïveté can be explained by his lack of experience with living in secrecy, and by his continued difficulty with perceiving the true illiberal nature of Fascism, a regime that considered parliamentary immunity no more than a fiction from a world governed by principles that had already been irrevocably condemned.

That same night, thirteen other Communist deputies and many national and federal cadres from that political family were also taken, in manacles, to Regina Coeli, the largest prison in Rome, where the Fascists habitually detained their political prisoners.

A close reading of the chronology of events shows that this arrest was completely illegal. In his report, Arturo Bocchini (1880–1940), the brand new chief of the Central Police (Pubblica Sicurezza) named by Mussolini after the attack by Anteo Zamboni (see below), lets slip that the removal of parliamentary immunity from the Communist deputies was decided in accord with the law for the protection of the state (*Provvedimenti per la difesa dello Stato*). The one little problem is that this law was not passed until November 25, 1926, fifteen days after Gramsci's arrest! This chronological gap explains why the Sardinian was not officially registered at the Regina Coeli prison. Though the decision flouted the letter of the law, also disrespecting its substance, it clearly revealed a political logic.

As we have seen, once it overcame the Matteotti crisis, the Fascist regime legalized its dictatorship and began to give it a totalitarian bent.[3] The November 25, 1926 law for the defense of the state reinstated the death penalty (which did not exist in the penal code passed in 1890 by the Minister of Justice Giuseppe Zanardelli) and established a Special Tribunal for the Defense of the State charged with prosecuting offenses and crimes committed against state security and also against the Fascist regime. This law was passed three weeks after a revolver shot was fired at Mussolini while he was inaugurating the Bologna stadium to celebrate the fourth anniversary of his nomination as prime minister. Much has been written about this October 31, 1926 act, carried out by a very young Anteo Zamboni (he was born on April 11, 1911). Though the theory of an isolated act, which the authorities, on Mussolini's orders, kept as the official version, is not completely improbable since the young Anteo had been fed a diet of political culture that was both Anarchist and anti-Fascist, it is undoubtedly more relevant to remember that such an attack would have been very difficult to realize without the complicity of certain hardline Fascists who were disappointed in Mussolini. Either way, this assassination attempt helped to sanction a strategy of fear, beginning with the lynching of the young shooter, as a way of preventing his act from being fully brought to light. This new step in Fascism's evolution resulted in the passage of a series of measures to curtail freedom, which were approved by the Chamber of Deputies during its November 9, 1926 session. To prevent the debate about the laws concerning defense of the state from turning into an oratorical joust that would have given the anti-Fascists a platform, Roberto Farinacci, the representative of the most intransigent, revolutionary wing of Fascism, and one of the earliest *squadristi*, led the charge against the Aventine deputies. In several newspapers, including the Roman Fascist daily *Il Tevere*, he demanded votes for a motion depriving the deputies who had taken part in the Aventine Secession of political rights, which would be the de facto end of their parliamentary immunity. Based on legal arguments that were unsubstantiated but politically obvious, the motion was put forward by Augusto Turati, the general secretary of the PNF (not to be confused with Filippo Turati, leader of the moderate Socialists who was then in exile in Paris) at the opening of the November 9, 1926 session.

Therefore, the deputies were arrested during the night of November 8–9 by virtue of a motion that would be voted on the next day and not yet passed into law until two weeks later. But this judicial aberration was mirrored by a political oddity. In fact, though the Communist deputies had participated for a time in the Aventine Secession, they had later rejoined the ranks in Montecitorio, judging it more politically fruitful to use the parliamentary podium against Fascism—including Gramsci's first and only speech, which had made a strong impression. So why add the names of Communists to the list of Aventine deputies? With the air of a scorned virgin, even Farinacci seemed to refuse, before falling back into line, and leaving his rival, Augusto Turati, with the responsibility of presenting the motion. During the afternoon of November 8, 1926, Bocchini received an order to arrest the Communist deputies from the minister of the interior, who was none other than Mussolini. Rumor has it that the king, Victor Emmanuel III, had imposed that condition for approving the Fascist regime's final blow to the last vestiges of the liberal system.[4] Such a decision must have pleased Il Duce, since it permitted him to put an end to any form of opposition, particularly that of the Communist deputies, especially since the latter had carefully prepared for this last stand. At a meeting during the afternoon of November 8 in one of the rooms of Montecitorio, the elected officials of the PCdI did indeed decide that Ezio Riboldi would speak the next morning on their behalf. As the leader of the PCdI, Gramsci had no choice but to participate in this meeting. At this point, it would be unfair to his comrades and his party to hold them responsible for not choosing to get their leader out. In hindsight, exile surely would have saved Gramsci from Mussolini's clutches, but perhaps only to deliver him into the equally fearful clutches of Stalin. Flight from Italy had always been the solution they imagined. The first plan they devised was that Gramsci would cross the border with Jules Humbert-Droz after attending the meeting in Valpolcevera. But in the agitated atmosphere after Zamboni's attack, which led to a new wave of Fascist squads, Gramsci acted wisely by following the suggestion of a police commissioner who, after recognizing him at the Milan train station, advised him to return to Rome where his personal safety would be better guaranteed than it could be at a Milan police precinct.[5] Not able to reach the secret meeting in Valpolcevera, Gramsci meant to wage war in Montecitorio. The decision was certainly not motivated by a taste for sacrifice, whose hollow, inconsequential rhetoric he had always deplored—in prison, as we will see later on, he was scrupulously attached to making sure his meager rights were respected and didn't hesitate to demand favors. In this decisive moment, he wanted to fight beside his companions once more before setting off for the Soviet Union to join Julia and his two sons, the second of whom he still hadn't met, since he was born on August 31, 1926. Moreover, though he didn't have any illusions about the repressive nature of Fascism, he still hoped that his parliamentary immunity would protect him. He thought that if he was arrested, he would not be in prison long, and that the Fascists would let him go as they had done before when his comrades were arrested in February and March 1923 and freed a few months later.

The manacled man who was taken from his home to the Regina Coeli prison did not know that he was embarking on a long ordeal beset with physical suffering and mental distress.

Exile in Ustica

Within the walls of his Roman cell, Gramsci learned from the prison authorities that he had been condemned, on November 18, 1926, to five years of confined exile (*confino politico*) by virtue of article 184 of the consolidated text of public security laws.[6] A rumor circulated that his place of *confino* would be Italian Somalia, a colony that had been acquired, with difficulty, in 1889. The train was, in fact, heading south. After spending two nights in Carmine Prison in Naples, he was driven to Palermo in a paddy wagon, and from there he learned that his exile would take place on the island of Ustica.

As the former home of Circe, the sorceress, and now a diver's paradise, this little, three-and-a-half-square-mile island a bit more than forty miles northwest of Palermo had become a prison island under the Bourbons, and it maintained this sinister function until 1961. After Italian unity and the first halfhearted colonial undertakings by the Kingdom of Italy, several Abyssinian warlords were deported there. With his own eyes, Gramsci saw a colony of Bedouins from Cyrenaica, the eastern coast of Libya. In the 1920s and 1930s, the island continued to receive cohorts of prisoners from the colonies, and the inhabitants still remembered, in the 1960s, the Libyan chiefs who had lived there with their harem at the beginning of the 1930s. But, under Fascism, this island would mainly serve as a place of exile for many political prisoners. Gramsci was one of them.

He arrived in Ustica on December 7, 1926. Manacled, he disembarked from the Palermo-Ustica ferry *Lampedusa* and was driven to the police station, where he would stay in a cell for three days, the time it took to find him lodging. With ten of his Communist comrades, including Amadeo Bordiga, Gramsci lived in a hovel by the water. The ten men, who were fundamentally united by the same political faith and a shared hostility toward Fascism, swept their doctrinal divisions under the rug and came together as best they could to make their shared life bearable. Each one, in turn, was assigned a task. Gramsci prepared food and washed the plates, refusing a comrade's offer to take over for him. To pass the time, they played frenzied games of cards, particularly *scopa*, one of the most popular games in Italy. Bordiga proved to be a master at it, and he was soon matched by Gramsci. But this diversion was not enough for these men of action, who decided to create a cultural school. Gramsci obtained a small room from the *podestà*[7] of the island. Bordiga was responsible for teaching math and science, Gramsci taught history and literature. Thanks to the books he received from Piero Sraffa (see the next chapter), the Sardinian thinker was able to give four or five lessons, primarily devoted to ancient Egypt. Since his lectures were undoubtedly watched by the *carabinieri*, he had to choose subjects that would not immediately evoke any suspicion of political propaganda. He was happy to perform this teaching. Since Turin, a didactic dimension had been at the heart of his political culture, and it perfectly matched his frame of mind and his charisma. In his *Prison Notebooks*, his many reflections on the organization of culture and on intellectuals defined as "permanent persuaders"[8] were theoretical elaborations on a practice that was very much anchored in his actions. The method he used in his lessons resembled the one he had used in the different cultural circles he had started, with little success, after World War I. The lectures were followed by discussions before a synthesis emerged.[9]

These lessons, which were attended by the *carabinieri* and his companions in exile, were also attended by a few inhabitants of the island. They were a sign of the good relationships that developed between the *confinati* and the islanders. For this extremely poor population, the ten lire per prisoner they received was a blessing. But the relationship surpassed this simple monetary dimension. As Carlo Levi magnificently writes in his masterpiece *Christ Stopped at Eboli* (1945), confined exile was a painful life experience, but it was also the occasion for Italian intellectuals, and particularly those who lived in the north of the peninsula, to understand the southern reality physically, and, for the southerners, to begin a long process of acculturation. In contact with the political prisoners, these inhabitants of Ustica who had been forgotten by history discovered certain aspects of modernity like butter, toothpaste, and radios, but also new ideas. Incidentally, the islanders always knew how to distinguish between common criminals and the political prisoners, whom they treated with respect.

During his stay on the island, the Milan military tribunal delivered, on January 19, 1927, a warrant for Gramsci's arrest. He was required to come back to the capital of Lombardy to undergo interrogations for his trial. On January 20, 1927, manacled once again, Gramsci climbed aboard the *Lampedusa*. In the foam left on the wine-dark sea by the little steamer heading to Palermo, Gramsci watched the island of Ustica fading, along with the last days of a life lived under the sign of hope.

If his exile to the little Sicilian island can be considered the least unhappy period of his life as a prisoner, the trip from Palermo to the San Vittore prison in Milan was one of the worst ordeals: a Calvary of nineteen days and nineteen nights, whose stations were cells or dungeons in prisons or barracks in Palermo, Naples, Caianello (in the Caserta region), Isernia (Molise), Sulmona (in the L'Aquila region), Castellammare Adriatico, Caianello (Ancona), and, last, Bologna. In several letters, he describes this terrible journey in a watered-down, ironic way, so as not to frighten his correspondents too much and to avoid censorship (in vain). He described it for the first time, on February 12, 1927, in a letter addressed to his wife, Julia, and to his sister-in-law Tatiana, affectionately nicknamed Tania:

> Just imagine that an immense worm slithers from Palermo to Milan, a worm that continually breaks up and comes together again, leaving part of its rings in each prison, reforming new ones, tossing the same parts to right and left and then reincorporating the extractions. This worm has lairs in each prison, which accumulate the dirt and misery of generations, clotting them

together. You arrive tired, dirty, your wrists hurting because of long hours in manacles, and on your face a long stubble, your hair disheveled, eyes sunk deep and glittering both from the excitation of strained fatigue and sleeplessness; you fling yourself on to the pallets that are who knows how old, fully dressed so as not to come into contact with the filth, wrapping your face and hands in your towels, covering yourself with the skimpy blankets just to avoid freezing. Then you leave again dirtier and wearier for the next transit, and your wrists are even more bruised because of the cold irons and the weight of the chains and the effort of carrying, thus decked out, your own luggage . . .[10]

Two episodes particularly traumatized the detained Gramsci. The first was the leg from Palermo to Naples where, for fourteen long hours, he found himself in the hold of a ship, chained very close to an epileptic detainee who kept grimacing eerily. The journey across the Apennine Mountains, in a paddy wagon without heat, was still more painful for the Sardinian, who had suffered from cold all his life. In several letters, he straightforwardly writes that he thought several times he would die of cold, to the point that his poor bones kept the memory of those two nightmarish days. After these horrible days and terrifying nights, the bed in his cell in the judicial prison of San Vittore in Milan, where he was finally incarcerated on February 7, 1927, was a great comfort to him, especially since he could sleep there, wrapped in the coat that Tatiana had sent to him.

The Judge and the Prisoner

According to legal vocabulary, Gramsci had been moved from one prison to another by "ordinary transfer" (*traduzione ordinaria*), meaning without any privileges or convenience being afforded him. For Domenico Zucàro, whose pioneering study on the last decade of Gramsci's life remains essential,[11] it was a deliberate choice on the part of the police to make him more vulnerable and to facilitate introducing him to an informer. Though the police under Fascism clearly had no shame about humanitarian considerations when it came to detainees, whose will they tried to break, it makes sense to pause over a possible scheme hatched by the police.

In the cell where he was imprisoned in Bologna, Gramsci met Dante Romani, who introduced himself as an anarcho-syndicalist who had participated in the insurrection in Ancona in June 1920.[12] But Dante Romani was not a political militant. He was known by the authorities, who had arrested him several times for fraud. When he came across Gramsci, he was arriving from the prison in Portolongone, on the island of Elba, and was waiting to learn his place of exile, where he had to serve his five-year sentence for "fraud, forgery, and usage of forgeries and violence" according to the wording of his sentence from the Ancona court of appeals on April 25, 1922. It was likely by chance that he crossed paths with Gramsci, with whom he preferred to pose as a political prisoner for his own advantage. Several weeks later, he asked to become a police informer. In the letter he wrote to the prefect, he described himself as a former member of the secret police in "New Jorch" (*sic*), as someone who had infiltrated revolutionary ranks in Jesi, and above all, he was quick to mention his "friendship" with Gramsci. This last argument was baseless: he described the Sardinian thinker as the father of only one child and as having been detained in Lipari! Nonetheless, the police decided to play the Romani card. And so, though Gramsci had been put under the strictest isolation in the judicial prison of San Vittore, he was subsequently placed, day and night, in contact with Romani, who spent long hours in his cell and in the cell of Ezio Riboldi, offering to do favors for the two Communist deputies as soon as he was freed. Of course, neither Ezio nor Antonio fell for the trap, and the historian Zucàro put the affair to rest, emphasizing the lack of finesse and the crude methods used by the OVRA,[13] the Fascist political police.

In fact, the trap may have been subtler than it seemed. While Romani pursued his career as a crook and an informer—we will pick up his story in Gorizia in May 1932—Gramsci began to be questioned by Judge Enrico Macis (1897–1973), who would exploit this incident to gain a kind of respect in the eyes of the Communist prisoner.

Born in Cagliari, Enrico Macis belonged to the same generation as Antonio Gramsci, and, like the latter, he spent his childhood and adolescence in Sardinia. Though he was from Cagliari and came from more bourgeois and less rural circles than Gramsci, the two men shared a homeland as well as common feelings and experiences, since they had both spent time on the benches at Dettori high school and had both been influenced by Raffa Garzia, the Italian teacher who had initiated Gramsci into journalism (see chapter 1). With his law degree in hand, Macis joined the army at the start of the war. Diligent in his courses for student officers, he emerged from World War I with the rank of captain. He was wounded several times and was awarded the War Merit Cross and the Silver Medal for Valor (in 1923 and 1926, respectively). Though he failed the exam, on July 17, 1925, through a special procedure, he became a military lawyer and magistrate, third class, at the military tribunal in Milan, which would be attached to the Special Tribunal for the Defense of the State, presided over by another Sardinian, the general Carlo Sanna, who was the commander of the famous Sassari brigade during World War I. Named a knight of the Italian crown in May 1926, Macis was considered sufficiently reliable politically to be trusted with the delicate task of conducting the trial of the Communist deputies arrested in November 1926. His loyalty to the regime allowed him to climb through the ranks, to end up a colonel. Well regarded and noticed by his superiors and the Fascist bosses, in the 1930s he presided in Ethiopia and then in Slovenia, where he proved to have so much zeal at the Ljubljana military tribunal that the United Nations Commission put him on the list of war criminals. After the July 25, 1943, vote by the Grand Council of Fascism deposing Mussolini, he left Ljubljana and withdrew to Turin with his family. Refusing to participate in the bloody and desperate adventure that was the Italian Social Republic, he made useful contacts among the Resistance, which allowed him a political clean slate and the chance to resume his career normally after the war, though Yugoslavia still demanded his extradition as a war criminal. He died in Turin in March 1973.

When Macis was interviewed in the early fifties by Domenico Zucàro, he demonstrated a strange amnesia when it came to Gramsci, leading the historian to say that "Macis showed a certain openness toward a few of the accused in the mass trial when it came to their intellectual stature, but without compromising his career as a magistrate in the eyes of the Fascist regime."[14] This viewpoint owes a lot to Gramsci, who never sketched an unflattering portrait of the judge, even going so far as to describe him as one of those career officers who had not yet become insensitive to "traditional ideas of honor and dignity."[15] If this phrase reflects Gramscian thought, which had always distinguished two currents within Fascism, on the one hand the hardline wing, ready to radically break with the old legal system, and on the other the conservative wing that was still attached to safeguarding appearances as much as possible, it was clear that Gramsci placed his compatriot in this second category, ultimately thinking that Macis would do all he could, within the authorized limits and within the interests of his career, to improve the prisoner's position. Such an interpretation had much to do with the comfort of conversation between Sardinians, who never missed an opportunity to evoke their native island, awakening a whole world of memories for Antonio, a pleasure that was even more agreeable since he had been forced into isolation. Moreover, to get Gramsci on his good side, Macis pledged at every possible opportunity to improve the daily life of the defendant. He promised to make a request on his behalf for paper and pens. In fact, he did nothing. But most important, he knew how to cleverly take exception to the conditions under which the prisoner had been transferred and the so-called maneuvers by the police to trap him through an informer, first with Dante Romani, and then a second time, with a certain Corrado Melani. Gramsci complained about it directly in the long brief he addressed, in his own defense, to the president of the Special Tribunal. By declaring that the police were acting against the orders of the judge, Macis must have gained a certain amount of respectability in Gramsci's eyes.

Should we therefore make the Macis/Gramsci pair the key to understanding the Communist leader's behavior at San Vittore? In his 1991 essay[16] and in the work he edited in 1994, Giuseppe Fiori (the author of the first standard biography of Gramsci, published in 1966 and reissued five times) describes Judge Macis as "a hypocritical character, a zealous servant of the regime" who had mastered the double game and duped Gramsci, who was suffering "from an excess of ingenuousness unimaginable for a man who had experienced the spectral labyrinth of the Hotel Lux."[17] Was Gramsci a victim of Stockholm syndrome? Was he manipulated by a judge who was expert at tormenting him, whose perverse finesse became apparent with the "infamous Grieco letter" that would so trouble the last decade of Gramsci's life? To try to further answer this delicate question, which makes up one of the main historiographical tangles in Gramsci's life and legacy, it is worth pausing over the conditions of the latter's investigation and trial.

The Investigation of Gramsci and His Trial

At the end of August 1926, the Bologna police arrested two PCdI messengers, Bonaventura Gidoni and Giacomo Stefanini, who were carrying documents that allow us to reconstruct, in great detail, the last months of the PCdI's underground existence. Faced with the importance of the papers they had confiscated, the Bologna police decided they were outmatched and transmitted the dossier to Rome on November 10, 1926. After the passage of the Fascist laws, the investigation was relayed to the Special Tribunal for the Defense of the State since it concerned crimes of a political nature. And so, on December 18, 1926, the military bar in Rome transferred the case to the military tribunal of the Milan army corps, which functioned in tandem with the Special Tribunal, which hadn't yet set up its own branches in the provinces.

Made up of a president chosen from among the generals of different units of the army and the militia and five judges who also came from the militia, the Special Tribunal for the Defense of the State[18] judged according to the procedures that were used in military tribunals. All the same, it cannot be defined as a court martial in a strict sense, but more as a special court. And so, contrary to all modern legal traditions, its sentences were not subject to appeal. The trial of Gramsci and his comrades was the first big political trial held in this court, since up until then it had dealt only with individuals who had insulted the leader of the government.

On January 14, 1927, at the request of the military prosecutor from Milan, the presiding judge, Enrico Macis, issued his arrest warrants, one of which concerned the prisoner Antonio Gramsci. Contrary to the classic rules of penal procedure, Macis made no attempt to establish the precise guilt of each individual accused, but rather intended to expose the collective guilt of the PCdI leaders, accusing them of planning to topple the regime and replace it with a government of soviets. His reasoning was based on the documents confiscated from Gidoni and Stefanini and relied on reports from the prefecture of police in Rome, particularly those written by the commissioner, Guido Bellone, vice-prefect of Rome in charge of the political division. From the end of 1925 on, he had clearly been telling the minister of the interior that Gramsci was the general secretary of the PCdI. Thanks to his informer Silvestri (a pen name for the famous writer Ignazio Silone [1900–1978]),[19] it was once again Bellone who provided the most precise information about the organization of the party after the Lyons congress, insisting once again on the key role Gramsci played as "mastermind"[20] of this political family. Armed with all these pieces, which the tribunal would take for proof of guilt, Macis interrogated Antonio Gramsci three times: on February 9, 1927, only two days after he arrived at San Vittore prison; on March 20; and, a last time, on June 2, when he formally accused him of being a member of the CC of the PCdI and, as a result, of being guilty in the first degree of inciting a civil war, of calling for insurrection, and of propaganda to create havoc, plundering, and murder. Point by point, Gramsci denied all these accusations, of which none was substantiated by formal proof.[21] The accusations became heavier and heavier as Macis went through his dossier and received Bellone's reports. It is unlikely, but not impossible, that the "infamous letter" from Grieco may also have played a harmful role (see below). Whatever the case, once the investigation closed on July 16, 1927, the dossier passed to the military prosecutor for the Special Tribunal, which presented its indictment on February 20, 1928. After choosing Giovanni Ariis as his lawyer, Gramsci ordered a brief for his defense sent to the president of the Special Tribunal on April 3, 1928, in which he rigorously and methodically exposed the absence of proof and the irregularities of the procedure. On May 11, Antonio Gramsci left the prison in Milan, reaching the Regina Coeli prison the next day. This time he was accorded special transit (*traduzione straordinaria*).

On May 28, 1928, the mass trial (*processone*) began, which at first was set to decide the fate of fifty-five accused. Then the authorities decided to proceed in two stages to dampen the negative effect such an event could have in the eyes of the international press.[22] Gramsci was part of a group of thirty-seven leaders who were given priority (the figure was brought down to thirty-one, since six of them, including Grieco, were already condemned in absentia). The eighteen militants were tried in June 1929, and they were condemned to sentences that were just as harsh as those inflicted on their leaders.

Though Gramsci thought, after the fact, that his lawyer's defense had been "deficient, not to say negative and catastrophic,"[23] since Ariis did not plead Gramsci's innocence but limited himself to pointing out the lack of proof, it was clear the cards were marked in advance.

Though no archives exist for this *processone*, Domenico Zucàro has been able to reconstruct it through witness accounts, particularly those of Giuseppe Sardo, one of the defense lawyers. This trial can be summarized in three phrases:

You [the Fascists] have brought Italy to ruin, and it will be up to us [the Communists] to save it.

For twenty years, we must stop this brain from functioning.

The Tribunal has certainly understood: I am referring to the decision by the hearing committee along with the High Court of

Justice in the trial against General Emilio De Bono,[24] accused of conspiring to kill the deputy Matteotti, and absolved because of insufficient proof. Now I am asking you: is that jurisprudence valid in our case?[25]

The first phrase was the conclusion of the brief speech Gramsci addressed to the magistrates in a small voice that forced people to listen, as was his habit, a speech delivered from the cage where he remained with his companions. The second, famous phrase comes from the indictment pronounced against Gramsci on June 2 by Michele Isgrò, a representative of the prosecutor's office. The third phrase, less well-known, was mined from the declaration Umberto Terracini made to the judges of the Special Tribunal, forcefully emphasizing the illegality of such a trial, conducted through a so-called judicial body that respected neither precedent nor the appeals process. In the eyes of all those who observed this mass trial, Terracini was the judges' cleverest and most tenacious opponent. His mockeries of the president of the tribunal, General Saporiti, who couldn't beat this formidable adversary except by forbidding him to speak, earned Terracini the harshest punishment[26] imposed during this parody of a trial. He was sentenced to twenty-two years, nine months, and five days, in addition to three years of special surveillance by the police and a fine of 11,200 lire.

As the lawyer for the prosecution recommended, Gramsci was condemned to twenty years, four months, and five days in prison. The sentence was pronounced on June 4, 1928.

Though he was initially supposed to be imprisoned at the Portolongone penitentiary, which had a sinister reputation, Gramsci was eventually assigned to the special penal prison in Turi, after a doctor had established, at his sister Teresina's request, that he suffered from chronic uricemia. On July 8, 1928, he left Rome, and after a twelve-day journey (ordinary transport) with long stops in Caserta, Benevento, and Foggia, he reached his new prison on July 19, 1928. Registered as prisoner number 7047, he would remain in Turi until November 19, 1933.

The "Infamous Letter" from Grieco[27]

On February 10, 1928, Ruggero Grieco sent three letters from Basel, where he was living in exile. The letters were individually addressed to Terracini, Scoccimarro, and Gramsci while the three prisoners were waiting to stand trial. The three letters were sent to Moscow, where they were expedited to Milan with a Soviet stamp and seal, the latter bearing the date: February 29, 1928. After being intercepted by the prison police, the letter for Gramsci was handed over to Judge Macis. After reading it and making copies through the technical services of OVRA, Macis gave it to Gramsci, saying: "Honorable Gramsci, you have friends who certainly want you to remain in prison for a long time."[28] Though the three original letters were never found, Paolo Spriano located the photocopies[29] in the archives of the Fascist police and published them on August 9, 1968, in *Rinascità*, one of the main PCI magazines.[30]

A mere glance at the letter was enough to provoked Gramsci's anger and indignation. In a letter addressed to Julia on April 30, 1928, he wrote, "I have . . . recently received a strange letter signed Ruggero [Grieco], which requested an answer. Perhaps prison life has made me more distrustful than normal prudence would require; but the fact is that, despite its stamp and its postmark, this letter made me lose my temper."[31]

Less than two weeks later, on May 11, 1928, he mentioned it to Tatiana in even harsher terms while she was visiting him in prison. Three days after this meeting, she echoed her brother-in-law's words in a missive she wrote to her sister Julia: Gramsci lamented that certain comrades "wrote without understanding what would be harmful and what it is possible to do [and he asked her] to box the ears of those who decidedly did not seem to understand our situation here [in the Fascist jails]."[32] When he encountered Terracini at Regina Coeli while the two militants were waiting to stand trial, he spoke of Grieco's letter as "a deplorable act approaching a provocation."[33] This missive was once again at the center of the discussion he had in July

1930 with his brother Gennaro, who recorded Gramsci's analysis in a report[34] that he sent to Togliatti:

> During my stay at the prison in Milan, in the investigation period, Ruggero sent me a letter that was intercepted and photographed. The letter was conceived in such a way, and had in it such news, that the Giudice istruttore, in showing me the copy, said "Look carefully Mr. Gramsci—not everyone minds the fact that you stay in prison." I am convinced that this letter was for me the greatest charge. When one of us is on the inside, it is important to be careful because we all bear the consequences of it all.[35]

But it was mainly in his letter to Tatiana on December 5, 1932 that Gramsci was most precise about the consequences of this "criminal" letter:

> You remember that in 1928, when I was in the judiciary prison awaiting trial in Milan, I received a letter from a "friend" who was abroad. You remember that I told you about this very "strange" letter and I said that the pretrial judge, after having handed it to me, added these very words: "Honorable Gramsci, you have friends who undoubtedly want you to remain in prison for quite some time." You yourself reported to me another opinion about this same letter, an opinion that culminated in the adjective "criminal" . . . in reading some passages to me from the letter, the judge pointed out that (aside from everything else) it could be immediately catastrophic for me and it was not so only because they did not want to be excessively cruel, because they preferred to overlook it. Was this a wicked act or an act of irresponsible superficiality? It is hard to say which. Perhaps both at the same time; perhaps the person who wrote it was only irresponsibly stupid and someone else, less stupid, induced him to write. But there is no point in racking one's brain over such questions. There remains the objective fact that has its significance.

Dear Tania, I already told you that a third phase of my life as a prisoner has begun. The first phase ran from my arrest to the arrival of that infamous letter. . . . The second phase was from that moment to the beginning of last November. There still existed some possibilities . . . and they also were lost, I assure you, through no fault of mine, but because people refused to listen to what I had pointed out at the proper moment.[36]

Gramsci would come back to this letter several times, particularly in his conversations with his sister-in-law in January 1933, then in a letter he addressed to her on February 27, 1933. In a perhaps "less explicit"[37] way than in his December 5, 1932 letter, but more tragically because it implicated Julia, his spouse, he wrote:

The conclusion, to put it summarily, is this: I was sentenced on June 4, 1928 by the Special Tribunal, that is, by a specific collegium of men, which could nominally be by name, address, and profession in civilian life. But this is a mistake. Those who sentenced me belong to a much vaster organism, of which the Special Tribunal was only the external and material expression, which compiled the legal documents for the sentence. I must say that among these "sentencers" [*condannatori*] there was also Julca [Julia], I believe, indeed I'm firmly convinced she was there unconsciously, and then there is a series of less unconscious people. This at least is my conviction, but how irremoveably anchored in me because it is the only one that explains a series of facts that are successive and congruent with one another. I don't know whether I've done well to write to you about these things, I've thought about it many times, I've hesitated then I have decided in the affirmative. Don't even believe for a minute that my affection for Julca has diminished. From what I myself can judge, I would rather say that it has increased, at least in a certain sense. I know by experience the world in which she lives, her sensibility and the way in which a change might have taken place in her.[38]

Gramsci, still tormented by Grieco's letter, eventually asked Tatiana to shed some light on this affair, opening one of the major chapters in Gramsci's troubled posterity.[39] Though it is now out of the question that "the infamous letter" (*famigerata lettera*) was a fake, fabricated by OVRA to implicate Gramsci more easily, three hypotheses remain.

The first is that Macis introduced doubt, and then torment, into Gramsci's mind; the second is that it was an unfortunate but unintentional mistake on Grieco's part; the third, on the contrary, argues that the PCdI leadership was politically responsible. Before examining these three possible interpretations, let us first examine the letter at the heart of this political and historiographical storm.

The letter[40] was made up of three parts indicated by three line breaks: a first, brief personalized paragraph, a longer paragraph about politics, and a final, third part, as brief and personal as the first, concluding with warm greetings from Grieco and "cari saluti" from Fanny Jezierska, a German Communist who was then a Comintern functionary.

Based on a quick reading of this letter, nothing seems to explain Macis's interpretation or Gramsci's anger. Terracini and Scoccimarro, who had received nearly identical letters, the same day, did not display the slightest suspicion of Grieco. Questioned much later, Mauro Scoccimarro confirmed that he had even forgotten about its existence.

Was Gramsci troubled by the heart of the letter, its political analysis? Though it was written before the major shift at the Tenth Plenum of the Comintern (July 1929) that assimilated Fascism into social democracy, the political reasoning conveyed an unfailing support of Stalin, whose methods Gramsci had criticized in his two letters of October 1926. But although it bears remembering, it wasn't this point that provoked Gramsci's distress and ire. It was the last lines of the first paragraph, "Now we are told that you are not well, and we would like to know, for our peace of mind, what you are in need of and what we can do for you. Everything we have been asked for you we have done, always." Though these two sentences directly concerning Gramsci were not in the two other letters addressed to Terracini and Scoccimarro, the passage concerning the political analysis was practically identical. What significance did Judge Macis and prisoner Gramsci attribute to those two sentences?

In their eyes, these sentences indicated that the PCdI was acting—and would continue to act—on Gramsci's behalf, or, more precisely, against him, since this constituted proof that he was in fact an important member of this political organization since it was clearly supporting him body and soul ("Everything we have been asked to do for you we have done, always").[41] The Soviet stamp and seal were yet more proof that he was one of the central figures of the PCdI.

Of course, the letter came to him after the investigation was closed, but neither Grieco nor Gramsci could have known that the preparatory judicial procedure for the trial would completely wrap up on February 20, 1928. Gramsci's suspicions that this letter played a harmful role in his conviction are therefore not unfounded. Moreover, it was sent to the Special Tribunal for the Defense of the State and could have supported the accusations against the PCdI leader during the trial, even if the judges didn't explicitly mention it.

However, Gramsci's reaction becomes more understandable if we look at it from another angle: the "infamous letter" had aborted the attempt, between the Soviet and Fascist governments, to free the Communist leader imprisoned at San Vittore.

The First Attempt to Free Gramsci

There were three attempts to free Gramsci. The first and best documented, which interests us here, took place between the end of 1927 and the fall of 1928,[42] the second was in 1933 (at the moment when Gramsci referred again to the infamous letter in his February 27, 1933 letter to Tatiana, anxious that the mistake might repeat itself), and last, a final attempt, between June 1934 and January 1935, which we will examine in the epilogue.

Don Luigi Viganò initiated the first attempt, since the chaplain of the San Vittore prison hoped to organize a prisoner exchange between Italian Communists and ecclesiastical prisoners in the USSR. This priest, in close contact with the Holy See, did not formulate this offer until he was assured that the highest-ranking members in the Catholic hierarchy supported the idea. This was probably how he presented the situation to Gramsci. After being informed of it, the Comintern delegated Bukharin to see if the Soviet government could obtain, through the mediation of the Holy See, the liberation of a few Italian Communist leaders. Sacrificing Scoccimarro, who held a less important position within the PCdI, Egidio Gennari, a representative for the Italian Communists with the ECCI, asked this body to negotiate the liberation of Gramsci and Terracini. On September 29, 1927, the CPSU entrusted the affair to the vice-minister for foreign affairs, Maxime Litvinov (1876–1951), who tasked Nikolay Krestinsky, the Soviet ambassador to Berlin, with contacting Eugenio Pacelli, the future Pius XII, then the papal nuncio in the German capital. A brief note written in French specifies the Soviet diplomat's mission:

> The Italian Communists Gramsci and Terracini who are currently in prison in Italy are in danger of being *condemned to death*. The priest of the prison—so they claim—a person with some influence in the Vatican, has led Gramsci to believe that he and Terracini might be exchanged for Catholic priests who are imprisoned in the USSR. *Gramsci's friends* are under the impression that this proposition is known to the Vatican and to the Italian government. The Soviet government, which Gramsci's family and friends had reached out to, is eager to accept this proposition and expresses its consent to exchange Gramsci and Terracini for two Catholic priests, chosen by the Vatican, who are in prison in the USSR.[43]

On October 1, Krestinsky entrusted his chargé d'affaires, the diplomat Stefan Bratman-Brodowski, with making sure the Holy See had, in fact, received his offer. The documents kept at the Archivio

Segreto Vaticano demonstrate that this was the case, since Pacelli communicated the offer to Pietro Gasparri, the secretary of state. The Jesuit Pietro Tacchi Venturi (1861–1956), the main liaison between Pius XI and Mussolini, who was then in the midst of preparing the Lateran Treaty, took the trouble of informing the head of the Italian government of the Soviet authorities' offer. To substantiate his request, Tacchi Venturi attached, to the letter he sent to Mussolini on October 7, 1928, the note copied above that Bratman-Brodowski had written in French. This last bit of information, which recently came to light through Mauro Canali, is important in understanding Mussolini's negative reply. Moreover, in his letter, Tacchi Venturi indicated to the leader of the Italian government that the Holy See was very interested in this exchange, but that the plan did not originate there: "the impression of Gramsci's friends, with respect to the Vatican, does not correspond to reality, given that neither his Eminence the cardinal [Gasparri] nor others at the Holy See had any awareness of what they learned from the note delivered to the nuncio by the diplomat himself [Bratman-Brodowski]." Since he was careful to maintain the best possible relationship with the Holy See at the time, Mussolini gathered that it hadn't created this plan, on the one hand, and, on the other, that "Gramsci's friends," otherwise known as Italian Communists, were involved. Il Duce, who didn't intend to offend the Holy See or to appear to acquiesce to the desires of the PCdI, refused the exchange in his reply on October 15, 1927—the letter was signed by the undersecretary of the interior, Giacomo Suardo—arguing that he could not pardon the accused before they had been tried, but that he would try to accelerate their judicial procedure. Mussolini's response, which Tacchi Venturi communicated to Cardinal Gasparri on October 20, was therefore not a complete refusal. As Giuseppe Vacca concludes, Gramsci had reason to think that he could be liberated from the Fascist prison at any moment, as long as his liberation was the object of an exchange negotiated between the Italian and Soviet governments. But it was important that the PCdI stayed out of it.[44]

In this light, we must understand that Gramsci thought Grieco's letter was criminal because it scuttled his release, which in his mind could still have taken place as part of the planned meeting between Litvinov and Grandi in Germany. The fact that this meeting never took place, though it had been planned in 1928, does not mean that Gramsci exaggerated, but rather that he explicitly understood his case could be settled only within the framework of diplomatic relations between the two countries—Italy and the Soviet Union—without the direct involvement of the PCdI or the Comintern, since Mussolini would never agree to let his behavior be dictated by his Communist enemies, just as Gramsci never intended to ask Il Duce for pardon, since it would mean that he had bent to the dictator's will. As a political prisoner, Gramsci was faithful to this position, even after his health reached a critical point.

In the context of Gramsci's possible liberation, Grieco's letter can be seen as a major political and moral mistake. All the same, the failure of this first attempt to liberate Gramsci cannot be solely explained by Grieco's letter.

The attack on King Victor Emmanuel III on April 12, 1928, at the Milan fair certainly also played a role in the failure of this attempt. It also probably affected the harshness of the punishments dealt out at the end of the mass trial.

The press campaign orchestrated by Piero Sraffa in favor of Gramsci also worked against his liberation. In order to make the English public aware of Gramsci's situation, Sraffa entrusted Angelo Tasca with writing an article on the conditions of their friend's imprisonment, giving him specific recommendations:

> The letter should take the following elements into account: (a)
> Communism is very unpopular with liberal opinion over here
> [in England], and consequently the appeal should be purely
> sentimental, and should not stress the political aspect. English
> liberals are moved first of all by the life of an animal, then by the
> life of a man, and finally by that of a Communist; (b) they have
> already heard a lot about Fascist atrocities, and something special
> is thus necessary to awaken their consciences; that special thing,
> in our case, cannot be the personality of our friend, but rather his

physical condition and the ill-treatment which is being inflicted upon him.[45]

Translated into English by Sraffa and signed "An Italian in England," the article was published in the October 24, 1927 issue of the *Manchester Guardian*. The lede was that Gramsci risked a death sentence (an argument that also featured in the note entrusted to Bratman-Brodowski), giving Mussolini an excellent pretext for refusing to free Gramsci, since he had never meant for such a punishment to apply to the Communist leader.

It is equally possible that Moscow was not fully invested in this negotiation with the Holy See. At this same time, the master of the Kremlin conveyed an antireligious offensive with the deportation of Bishop Boļeslavs Sloskāns (1893–1981) to Siberia. Moreover, Moscow did not look at all favorably on the PCdI, or on Gramsci in particular, whose last public act had been to criticize the CPSU.

Last, the Holy See's insistence that this initiative had originated elsewhere clearly meant that Pius XI did not intend to prioritize this affair (or let it have the slightest impact on the process of aligning with the Fascist Italian state). It is also revealing that the Holy See did not follow up with Mussolini after his negative reply in October 1927 or even bother to inform the Soviet authorities.

Back to the Infamous Letter

Though it is true that Enrico Macis used this letter to mentally torture Gramsci, he didn't invent it, and his influence over the Communist leader was not so well established at this point that he would have known how to distort his judgment. The vast majority of historians theorize that "the role and the figure [of Judge Macis] conformed fully to Gramsci's perceptions,"[46] meaning those of a servant of the regime who still managed to maintain "the traditional ideas of honor and dignity," at least until he lost them in Ljubljana.

In a letter to Tatiana on September 18, 1937, Sraffa was the first to advance the idea that Grieco was at fault, but unintentionally so:

For me, reading it with a cool head, it's clear that this was a bit of casualness on the part of the author, but that there was no harm in it, and certainly not a diabolical plan. My opinion was confirmed by the fact that Nino [an affectionate nickname for Gramsci] said the pretrial judge planted this suspicion; and it's no secret that insinuating suspicions of this kind is part of the ABCs of a pretrial judge's job.[47]

This interpretation by Sraffa, whom the PCdI subsequently charged with ensuring Gramsci's legacy (his *Prison Notebooks*), is taken up and shared today by Angelo D'Orsi in his recent biography of Gramsci: "Grieco's letters do not seem to show an intention to harm Gramsci or the other detainees, but, rather, a thoughtlessness that all the same seems problematic for a leader of the first order as Grieco was."[48] Angelo D'Orsi's coherent and well-reasoned position nonetheless does not close the case, since the idea that the PCdI bears the political responsibility for Gramsci's fate is gaining more and more attention because it has garnered the most evidence.

Let's look at the case again.

Written in Basel, where Grieco had taken refuge after being condemned in absentia to seventeen years in prison, the letter was intentionally sent to the Soviet Union not only to mask where he was exiled, but also, in all likelihood, to receive the approval of the PCdI leadership and the Comintern. This would explain why Jezierska sent her best wishes to Gramsci, since she was a functionary within the Comintern whom Stalin had tasked with the PCdI at the time:

> her signature . . . implicated Stalin and that led to supposing that Grieco had sent the letter to Moscow with the goal of having it also signed by Fanny Jezierska, so as to confirm, through Stalin's authority, the allusions it contained about the imminent success of the negotiations to liberate Gramsci.[49]

Did Julia read this letter? Gramsci certainly thought so, since it occurred to him in his February 27, 1933 letter (see above) that she could be one of the people responsible for this missive. If that was not the case, how can we explain the fact that Julia never spoke of or even mentioned this letter in her correspondence with her husband? A deafening silence, and one that is shocking, at the very least.[50]

The different missives from the imprisoned Communist leader in which he speaks of the infamous letter not only have their own coherence but also agree with the accounts of Gennaro Gramsci, Tatiana Schucht, and Piero Sraffa, and they at last allow us to clarify a phrase that had long remained enigmatic in Grieco's letter to Terracini, written the same day he wrote to Gramsci. The historian Paolo Spriano was the first to draw attention to the following passage: "From Antonio's family, I had heard that his health had improved: but now I know there are *new facts*,"[51] the last two words underlined by the letter writer. Glancing at this letter, you could imagine that it concerned new information about Gramsci's health. But why underline this expression? And above all, what new information about his health could there be, considering that at the time, Gramsci's health was experiencing neither signs of improvement nor symptoms of significant deterioration? These new facts are therefore, in all likelihood, a reference to the ongoing negotiations to liberate him.

Togliatti and the leaders of the PCdI would therefore have unintentionally or knowingly sabotaged the attempts to liberate Gramsci. Several things work in favor of this hypothesis.

First of all, Gramsci believed it, and though he was certainly weakened by his precarious health and by prison, his lucidity remained intact, as shown by his plan to write down his thoughts "für ewig," as he puts it in a letter to his sister-in-law on March 19, 1927 (see the following chapter). During her third conversation with her brother-in-law in January 1933, Tatiana reports that he firmly refused the idea that "one can attribute the fact of having written this letter only to the imbecility of the one who wrote it, given that in this case his imbecility would have to transcend any and all limits, and there is no doubt that in the future, when this letter will be extracted from the archive, the one who wrote it will have a lot of work to do to justify it; actually, it's clear that he wouldn't be able to."[52] Another element that supports the hypothesis of the PCdI's guilt: unlike all his other letters, Gramsci believed his accusatory missive about the "infamous letter" was important enough to ask Tatiana not to copy it for Sraffa. Though he considered him a great friend, he did not trust Sraffa to withhold Gramsci's take from the leadership of his party. Gramsci expressly asked his sister-in-law to keep his own letter as a piece of evidence that he would bring to light once he was free. Tatiana did what he asked. She didn't give the letter to Sraffa, but when she eventually returned to Moscow in December 1938, she presented it to Stella Blagoeva, the Comintern agent charged with examining Togliatti's situation.[53]

Today, Gramsci's suspicions are shared by a number of historians. Gramsci's letter was absent from the first edition of the prison letters and was not published until 1965, a year after Togliatti's death. A simple coincidence? Proof that Gramsci's letter accused his party? Most specialists support the second hypothesis, including intellectuals who were party members or close to the Italian Communist Party. While refusing to admit that Togliatti was disloyal to Gramsci, Paolo Spriano is the first major Communist historian to connect Gramsci's barely veiled critiques of his comrade during their epistolary exchange in October 1926.[54] After research by Aldo Natoli,[55] a study by Silvio Pons,[56] and the discovery of the *Rapporto di Gennaro* [Gennaro's Report], Giuseppe Vacca, the current president of the Gramsci Foundation in Rome, who is also one of the intellectuals most concerned with emphasizing the solidity of the Gramsci/Togliatti duo, posits in one of his latest works that "there can be no doubt about the fact that at the end of 1932, Gramsci implicates Togliatti as the person who inspired Grieco's letter[57] [by making him] shoulder [along with the PCdI] the responsibility for having sabotaged the preceding attempts at liberation."[58]

All the same, Giuseppe Vacca does not connect, at least explicitly, this episode to the 1926 exchange of letters, even though, after the Valpolcevera meeting, Gramsci became the major absentee and major blind spot of the new pro-Stalin orientation of the Italian Communist Party under Togliatti's watch. During the Seventh

Plenum of the Comintern, which was held in Moscow in November 1926, Togliatti did not make any references to Gramsci, nor did he even mention his name.[59] Angelo D'Orsi is right to remind us that Togliatti was still the first to write a long theoretico-political article entirely devoted to Gramsci in 1927 in *Stato Operaio*, the PCdI's magazine in exile, titled "Antonio Gramsci, a Leader of the Working Class." The Turin historian sees this as proof that the PCdI intended to maintain a tie, though tenuous, with its imprisoned leader, all the while emphasizing that it also had to begin to construct "the architrave of the interpretation that would become canonical at the heart of the Italian Communist Party, keystone of the whole postwar 'Gramsci operation,'"[60] meaning the weaponizing of Gramsci within the fluctuations and wanderings of the PCI's ideological line.

Whatever the case, all those who specialize in the history of the PCdI agree that once Gramsci was imprisoned, the line of thinking developed in Lyons was abandoned, and that by aligning their party with Stalin's ideology, Togliatti and other Italian Communist leaders (including Grieco) didn't hesitate to politically sacrifice the man who had been the architect of the *Lyons Theses*. It is also significant that before he arrived at the special prison in Turi, Gramsci received no material help from his party, and Tatiana provided his main support.

Was it about the deep divide that would grow between Gramsci as he wrote his *Prison Notebooks* and the leaders of the PCdI who were faithful to Moscow? Or was it a strategic surrender by Togliatti and by the leadership of his party to safeguard their political organization from Stalin's fury, which had already been triggered by Gramsci's critiques of his brutal methods in October 1926? This issue is still contested to this day. Even if it is easy to judge the actions and the actors, ninety years later, we can't help but endorse a remark by historian Aldo Natoli, in reply to Giorgio Amendola,[61] lamenting the difficulties the PCdI went through because of Gramsci's polemic against the CPSU: "the international Communist movement and the PCI paid a much higher price for not having fought, from the start, as Gramsci intended, Stalin's drive toward absolute power."[62]

< 8 >

The Prisoner and the Philosopher
(July 19, 1928–November 19, 1933)

From San Vittore to Turi

Gramsci was a prisoner for ten years and two months. A fifth of his life, ticking away, second after second, first behind bars and barred windows, then in the room of a clinic, closely watched by the police. As soon as he was incarcerated in the judicial prison of San Vittore in Milan, he began to suffer from his situation as a detainee, especially when he compared it with the still-fresh experience of his four weeks of exile on the island of Ustica. All the same, he did his best to adapt to this new life that he hoped would be quite brief, at least until the infamous letter from Grieco arrived and the verdict was announced, sentencing him to twenty years, four months, and five days in prison. Hopeful that the Soviet and Fascist governments, under the auspices of the Vatican, would come to an agreement to liberate him, he poured all his efforts into preparing his defense before the Special Tribunal.

In order to relax, he always took advantage of the two hours of exercise that were allotted each morning. In contrast with the too-brief period he spent in Ustica, where he was exiled but authorized to receive books, he no longer benefited from that privilege at San Vittore. No longer able to order books through the account Piero Sraffa had opened for him at the Milan bookshop Sperling and

Kupfer, he had to content himself with borrowing those he found in the prison library. With a double subscription that allowed him to borrow eight books a week, in addition to six daily newspapers and several weeklies, Gramsci read and read, resuming his study of foreign languages (German, English, and Russian). To decorate his cell, he grew small plants there, a habit that came out of his Sardinian childhood and his sensitivity to nature. He kept it up in Turi, where he busied himself, as much as his physical condition allowed, with a small flowerbed seeded with flowers and herbs. Each day, he would feed the two little sparrows that came to perch on his windowsill. Did he think, then, of Giuseppe Mazzini, the apostle of Italian unity, facing, clear-eyed, the new direction his country had taken in the summer of 1860, a man who delighted in watching the two finches he allowed to fly freely through the Genovese attic where he hid?

Though Gramsci obtained paper and pens from the administration of the prison, the rules allowed him to write only two letters a week, and only to members of his family. At San Vittore, he got into the habit of dividing his letters into two parts: a first part intended for his family that Tatiana would copy for Julia or for Gramsci's mother, and a second, more impersonal part where he delivered his reflections on his reading. The brave, dedicated Tatiana would routinely make a copy for Sraffa, who would pass it on to the external center of the PCdI.[1] This habit of Gramsci's would become a real framework of thought when he began to write his *Prison Notebooks*.

At night, Gramsci's true torment began. When the lights went out at 7:30 p.m., it marked the start of a long night of insomnia, in which he would revisit the events of his day, mentally reorganize his thoughts, and dwell on his pain and suffering. Without questioning the lucidity of his analysis of Grieco's infamous letter, we must also keep in mind that life in prison fosters morbid rumination.

Along with his efforts to prepare as best he could for his defense, Gramsci also sought to reassure those he loved, with the exception of Tatiana, to whom he confessed his doubts and fears as directly as the guards' inspections would allow. Above all, he didn't want to worry his mother and lamented that his brother Mario, the Fascist of the Gramsci family, whom he still thought of as a "good guy,"[2] had alarmed Giuseppina about his situation. The poor woman had already suffered so much from her husband's imprisonment, and she should not be needlessly worried, especially since "in our villages it is difficult to understand that a man can go to prison without being a thief, crook, or murderer . . ."[3]

When he became inmate number 7047 at the Turi prison on July 19, 1928, Gramsci had already inhabited the universe of incarceration for eighteen months, so there was some continuity between his existence at San Vittore and the one he would come to know during more than five years at Turi. But there were also fault lines between them: his worsening health, the writing of his *Prison Notebooks*, and growing tensions with the Communist world, particularly the PCdI.

Antigone and Comrade Sraffa

Gramsci's sister-in-law Tatiana took uncontested pride of place in his prison life. While her family returned to Russia, which was becoming the Soviet Union, Tatiana remained in Italy, where she began a complicated romantic relationship with an Italian doctor. She began giving lessons in math and French and living at the Crandon Institute, a private school founded by American Methodists that was very popular among the Roman haute bourgeoisie. Tatiana gave up her studies in medicine but continued to frequent those circles, befriending two brothers, Giuseppe and Raffaele Bastianelli, who became Mussolini's doctors after 1926. (They were succeeded by one of their friends and disciples, Angelo Puccinelli.) Thanks to Tatiana, Puccinelli and Raffaele Bastianelli would play a decisive role in Gramsci's prison life (see the epilogue). Because she cut ties with her family after 1922, Gramsci struggled to find her. He and Tatiana didn't meet for the first time until February 2, 1925. They would continue to meet, first in an intermittent way at Turi, then more regularly in Formia, and uninterruptedly after 1935. A solid friendship quickly formed between them, a friendship that was probably tinged with platonic love as the years passed. Unsurprisingly, more than half of the letters Gramsci wrote in prison were addressed to her, making her his main correspondent.

She moved to Milan in May 1927 so she could be closer to her brother-in-law. But because she was immediately hospitalized, she didn't actually see him until September of that year. Despite her fragile health—she was hospitalized again between June and April 1928—she offered Antonio material and moral support as best she could. She arranged for a *trattoria* close to the prison to deliver meals to him. After exhausting her meager resources, she succeeded in convincing the innkeeper to give him credit for a time. After the latter demanded payment, she was fortunately able to count on the help of Pina, the wife of Enrico Tulli, a militant Communist incarcerated at San Vittore, to cook meals to supplement the ordinary prison fare. She also got to work putting together a network of monetary aid, asking Carlo Gramsci, who would start putting aside two hundred to two hundred and fifty lire each month from his wages, and her sister Julia, Gramsci's wife, who sent him thirty-five dollars at regular intervals starting in February 1928.

After her brother-in-law was imprisoned in Turi, Tatiana traveled to the small Apulian town as soon as she could. She met Gramsci there twice in December 1928, and then several more times between March and April of the following year. Her numerous absences cost her her job with the Soviet commercial delegation in Milan. In October 1929, she decided to leave the capital of Lombardy to return to live in Rome so she could be geographically closer to Gramsci. After working for the Soviet embassy for a time, she was finally hired by the NKVD to translate documents into Russian from the original French or Italian. Thanks to this work and the stable income it provided, she could devote much of her time and energy to her brother-in-law, so she remained in Turi for the whole first half of 1930.

Until she met Sraffa for the first time at the end of September 1928, she was Gramsci's unique link with the outside world. After this date, the Italian economist would be the only other person Gramsci could count on. It was significant that Gramsci's first letter from the island of Ustica was addressed to him on December 11,

1926, asking Sraffa to send him books and magazines. Sraffa replied immediately to this request, opening an account at the big Milan bookstore Sperling and Kupfer, which fed Gramsci's reading habit until he died. He also sent him money at the beginning of 1927. But after visiting him in San Vittore prison during the summer of 1927 and after organizing the press campaign in his favor in October (see chapter 7), he didn't appear again until September 1928. On that date, he decided, at his own initiative, to meet Tatiana. Informed by her direct account of Gramsci's particular situation, Sraffa would, from then on, serve as an intermediary between Tatiana and the PCdI, where he was probably already an important member, charged with delicate financial missions. After their meeting, it becomes difficult to distinguish between the help he gave Gramsci strictly out of friendship and what he did on orders from his party. Whatever the case, Piero Sraffa advocated for the PCdI to aid its imprisoned leader, whom they seemed to have forgotten. In a missive from December 26, 1928, to Alfonso Leonetti, he urged the PCdI to help Gramsci financially, by according him regular sums. This request was transmitted to Camilla Ravera (1889–1988), who was then the head of the PCdI in Italy. She met with Sraffa in Nice, and the two of them sent Antonio two hundred and fifty lire to cover his most urgent needs. Nonetheless, he still had to wait for more than a year for the PCdI to decide, on January 30, 1930, to organize a meeting specifically devoted to Gramsci's situation, during which the party decided to send three hundred lire a month to the man who officially remained their general secretary—three hundred lire, the equivalent of what the Fascist government gave to their exiles. This money came from International Red Aid (MOPR), which was tightly linked to the Comintern and whose Italian section was staffed by the PCdI.

Mauro Canali has shed light on the curious trajectory of the money sent to Gramsci, in which a figure called Lombardi the engineer played a pivotal role. For a long time, this person was wrongly identified as Tullo Tulli, the brother of Enrico, but it seems more likely that it was Riccardo Lombardi, whom the Communists nicknamed "l'inge" (short for *ingeniere*, engineer). Lombardi belonged to the left wing of the PPI and was the future leader of the Action Party[4] before becoming a key figure of the Socialist Party after World War II. At the time, Lombardi maintained ties to the PCdI, since he had become more aligned with it after the murder of Matteotti, to the point of being considered a fellow traveler of this political family from 1927 on. During his interrogation while he was briefly incarcerated in July 1930, the OVRA police were able to discover how money was being transferred to Gramsci: from the MOPR, the money went to his lawyer, Giovanni Ariis, who gave it to Lombardi, who transmitted it, at last, to Tatiana. More evidence of this complex system appears in the letters Sraffa addressed to the external center of the PCdI in which he condemned Lombardi's negligence and even mentioned that he was starting to have some suspicions about his honesty. Whatever the case may be, the question remains: why this distrust of "l'inge" on Sraffa's part? Did the PCdI investigate after Sraffa shared his suspicions? Why did neither the PCdI nor Sraffa ever explain themselves on this point? Last, why did the external center of the PCdI give so little financial support to its leader and entrust its transport to a fellow traveler? Was it out of concern to act prudently? Or was it proof that the new leadership of the PCdI had forgotten its general secretary?

Above all, Gramsci had to count on comrade Sraffa, whose loyalty to the party never completely stifled his friendship with Antonio, and on Tatiana, the new Antigone,[5] who never hesitated to stand up to the powerful, whether Fascist or Communist, to help her brother-in-law. But as devoted as she was to Antonio's cause, Tatiana could not feel all the pain he was experiencing; she could not experience his daily battles against illness, against the torments of political struggle, and against the vexations and difficulties that life in prison imposed.

Turi: Place of Torments

Known for the mildness of its climate, Turi is a large agricultural town surrounded by vines, olive trees, peaches, and almonds, about twelve miles south of Bari. After Italian unity, the large monastery complex constructed at the start of the nineteenth century to house the monks of the Scolopi order[6] was turned into a prison—a function it serves to this day. Though its exact designation is *Casa penale speciale per condannati sofferenti di mali fisici e psichici*, the Turi prison met none of the appropriate criteria for a medical prison facility.

On July 19, 1928, after traveling for twelve days (less nightmarish, but almost as trying as the nineteen days spent between Ustica and Milan), Gramsci finally reached this sad place, which he would inhabit for more than five years. After arriving in the company of five other prisoners, he was assigned to a cell where there were already four other prisoners suffering from tuberculosis. Exhausted from the transfer from Milan and Turin, he was suffering from purulent herpes in addition to the uricemia diagnosed by the doctor at San Vittore, who got him out of going to the Portolongone Prison. A few days after his arrival in Turi, he asked his brother Carlo to write to their mother. He wanted her to send a letter to the head of the government requesting that he get his own cell so that he could take better care of himself and "undertake a few literary works and study languages."[7] On August 25, 1928, Giuseppina wrote a letter to Mussolini, and Il Duce's secretary immediately sent a favorable reply.

Five months later, the prison administration also allowed him to receive books and to write in his cell. These two advantages were not privileges, since they came from the *General Prison Rules* of June 13, 1891, and, more important, from the discretionary power of the director. Giovanni Parmegiani, who held that post at the Turi prison when Gramsci was transferred there, had no sympathies toward the Communist leader, but he had to follow Mussolini's wishes. However, he proved hostile to the imprisoned Gramsci, refusing to allow Tatiana to visit him until the Prefecture of Rome sent over the proof of Julia and Antonio's marriage as evidence of Tatiana's rights as a close relative. His successor, Vincenzo Azzariti, was no less hostile to Gramsci, who was mainly fighting to be able to sleep without being woken by the guards. Gramsci's cell was one of the noisiest in the whole prison, situated across from the stairs, where all the guard tours had to pass. Some guards, day and night, made as much noise as possible on purpose, slamming doors and gates, letting their keys drag across the bars, and banging on walls to find hiding places. The cells were inspected five times a day, including twice at night. Though some of the guards were aware of Gramsci's physical distress,[8] others were indifferent to his fate, and a few took malicious pleasure in tormenting him and preventing him from sleeping. Gramsci reacted by writing to Giovanni Novelli, the general director of prisons:

> The daily and nightly visits were made like military exercises and were akin to the assaults of soldiers in the trenches or those of the *squadristi* against social gatherings. The doors (which each weighed about a ton) were opened and closed as though to mimic the rhythms of firecrackers; after the noise made by the bolts themselves, there would follow the roar of the doors opening, striking the side of the wall, and then the violent closing of the doors, which would resound like a shot from a cannon (a ton of wood to which is administered a rapid, violent rotation of almost 180 degrees). . . . Nor did things improve during the intervals between one visit and the next; at every moment there were either doors being slammed, steel boots running in the halls, loud arguments like you'd hear at a rowdy bar, tables being dragged, or keys being struck against the prison bars to the tune of an opera or a popular song. And all this happened even if someone was gravely ill or approaching death.[9]

Unlike the town doctors assigned to the Turi prison in rotation (Giuseppe Resta, who was strikingly ineffective, and Francesco Cisternino,[10] a notorious Fascist), a new director tried to remedy the situation after he was hired in March 1933. Pietro Sorrentino acted as much out of humanity—Gramsci considered him the best director he had dealt with—as out of concern that the circumstances Gramsci criticized would mar Fascism's image as a rule of law and order. This concern went far enough that the letter Gramsci sent on June 27, 1933, immediately provoked the regime to send an inspector to Turi, who confirmed Gramsci's observations and demanded that the necessary measures be taken to alleviate these shortcomings. Antonio was then assigned to a more isolated cell, but it was draftier. Despite the sympathy the director showed toward Gramsci's plight, the director also had to deal with his guards:

> Concerning the noises, [Gramsci] said that last night, the director himself did the rounds to take note of the facts, and that the staff made noise expressly to show that it was impossible to do otherwise, while when the deputy director demands silence, he successfully makes it completely quiet. It's a question of bad faith, of sabotage. The guards have already asked if he [Gramsci] was the one in charge of the prison, and he understands very well that these noises must be the consequences for him of a punishment that will be inflicted by the director. . . . Only trouble will come out of all this, nothing else; he said that here, like in all other environments elsewhere, certain elements are terrible, ready to do anything.[11]

These remarks on the forced insomnia that Antonio guessed was responsible for "ninety percent of [his] discomfort"[12] raise the question whether Gramsci was slowly killed by Fascism. Legitimately worried, no doubt, about distancing themselves from the portrayal of Gramsci as a heroic figure and a martyr of Fascism, which led to his thinking and actions being used and distorted after 1945, Angelo Rossi and Giuseppe Vacca estimate:

> The vulgate of the "slow assassination of Gramsci" does not seem to have an adequate documentary foundation. Each time that Gramsci sustained abuses and excessive force, as with the transfers from one prison to another that he would denounce as traumatic and putting his life at risk, they were not a demonstration of homicidal plans, but rather the product of the prison environment, which was peopled with individuals who were characterized by a mix of brutality and ignorance.[13]

Though it is true that Gramsci was neither beaten nor starved, and though it is also correct to remember that the Fascist prison was less harsh than Stalin's gulag or the Nazi concentration camps, it is nonetheless important not to soften the suffering Gramsci faced or to attribute it only to his health, which was steadily failing. Preventing someone from sleeping is physical torture, pure and simple. The absence of care and food adapted for his general state are also forms of mistreatment. Fascism did not assassinate Gramsci in the proper sense of the term, but it did nothing to slow the collapse of his health. The idea that Mussolini tried to keep him alive for the prestige of his regime or as a bargaining chip should be strongly tempered. In Turi, Gramsci was a prisoner like all the others, a prisoner who was permitted to write and read in his cell as the rules stated. Gramsci did not benefit from any particular privileges except an individual cell. If some of his fellow prisoners accused him of enjoying special treatment, we must place that accusation within the world of incarceration, which exacerbates the smallest differences between prisoners. For example, when food arrived, Gramsci's was warm, while the prisoners secluded at the end of the hall got their food cold. The latter complained about this situation so the order of the rotation was reversed, and it was Gramsci's turn to eat cold food.

Of the small daily humiliations that accumulated into great suffering, only a feeble echo made it into the letters he sent to Tania, not only because he had to account for censorship—all his letters were read—but also because he didn't intend to fall into self-pity. In Turi, he wanted to remain, through and against it all, the activist intellectual he had always been.

The Lessons of Turi and the "Broken Ties" with the PCdI

In the Turi prison, the political detainees and the common criminals lived separately. Each group had its quarters and its own courtyard for exercise. When his health permitted, Gramsci never missed a chance to take advantage of the hours of fresh air, a moment when he could unwind. Several accounts describe him joking and laughing while he was enjoying the sun or a refreshing light rain, allowing him momentarily to forget the barred windows of his cell. These windows *a bocca di lupo* (wolf's mouth) prevented him from seeing outside, bringing him so much melancholy that he complained about them countless times in his letters.

But the moments intended for exercise were also those when he could speak with his comrades. Antonio once again became the pedagogue he'd never really ceased to be. Wishing to create "organic intellectuals,"[14] meaning militants who had the capacity to give force and life to Communist ideas, he practiced in the prison courtyard in Turin the Socratic method that he had honed in Turin and that he had also used in Ustica: a few detainees would read a book and then present the principal ideas to the other prisoners before engaging in a general discussion. Though some of his companions griped, calling the work a *pensum* (schoolwork assigned as a punishment) and complaining about Gramsci's stubbornness when it came to working with seriousness and rigor, most of the "students" remembered being moved by this extremely focused man whose eyes were noticeable for their "alertness and uncommon depth."[15] This peripatetic school (the detainees conversed while walking to avoid, in vain, attracting the suspicions of the guards) was attended by a number of Communist comrades, some anarchists, and a young Socialist militant who would have a grand destiny: Alessandro (known as Sandro) Pertini (1896–1990). This man would become the most beloved president of the Italian Republic, and he was strongly influenced by Gramsci's personality and intellectual vitality. In a collection of memoirs published in the 1960s, he remembered how he met Gramsci:

> I went up to him and introduced himself. I told him I came from Santo Stefano and that I was honored to make his acquaintance. I spoke to him in a formal register and called him "Honorable Gramsci." He started to laugh: "Why are you being so formal? We are both anti-Fascists, both victims of the Special Tribunal." But I reminded him that, for the Communists, we were "social traitors." He told me to abandon this pathetic polemic.[16]

These two men, confronting their political conceptions, would very quickly learn to value and respect each other:

> Another day, Gramsci said to me, "We have to start a conversation that will last two months."... I understood immediately that he wanted to persuade me to join the Communist Party. He couldn't understand that a man like me, with the vision I had of struggle, with my temperament, could side with the Socialists. But when I told him, "I cannot leave my party, I'm devoted to it. I can dissent from some of its positions, but I remain a part of it," he respected my position. At the time, for Communists, we, the Socialists, were "Social Fascists." Not for Gramsci, because he foresaw that one day there would be an alliance between Socialists, Communists, and all anti-Fascist forces.[17]

From Pertini's portrait of Gramsci, we can infer personal qualities such as his sharp intelligence and open-mindedness. We can also glean a clear political position that rejected the line of class against class endorsed by the Sixth Congress of the Comintern in summer 1928 and that the PCdI adopted wholeheartedly as its platform during its Fourth Congress in Cologne in April 1931.

The conversations with the other prisoners on themes such as the role of the Church in social life or on Fascism and the social structure of Italy were not only a way for Gramsci to test the validity of the concepts he was developing in his *Prison Notebooks*, but also a chance to defend his political convictions as openly as the world of incarceration would allow, particularly the idea that the battle against Fascism would be long and would not translate directly into a Communist society, and that they therefore had to think of an intermediate phase, in which the fight would gather all anti-Fascists around the idea of a constituent assembly that was democratic and republican. This idea, which he advanced explicitly as early as October 1930, was not an individual act of rebellion but a critique of the official line of the PCdI, provoking a response from the party. This official line is probably why Gramsci's argument caused immediate consternation within the Italian Communist family. In a letter from November 2, 1931, that managed to secretly reach the external center of his party, Umberto Terracini wrote:

> The rumour that Antonio radically disagrees with the line of the party is current and growing stronger in our groups in prison, with repercussions you can imagine. He's settled for a Coalition, say the most impressionable and least capable elements [in the party]. I haven't yet been able to meet anyone who spoke directly with Antonio: so I can't specifically say what he is thinking, which you perhaps already know. Nonetheless, it is certain that on the theme of upcoming prospects Antonio came up against the comrades in Turi, particularly on the eventuality of a transition period. He doesn't rule it out (I even think he accepts it). This is the central point of endless discussions in all the prisons.[18]

It would be an understatement to say that Antonio's position clashed with that of his comrades who were imprisoned in Turi. Though some among them, then in the minority, were on his side (for example Mario Garuglieri, who proved to truly admire the man he called his mentor), others, in the majority, were furious that this man who remained general secretary of the PCdI was arguing for unorthodox positions. They decided to form an anti-constituent bloc under the aegis of two prisoners, Athos Lisa and Bruno Tosin. In a report that he sent to Togliatti in February 1933, the Communist Athos Lisa, who had participated in the lessons in Turi, confirmed that there was a strong sense of antipathy, if not hostility, toward Gramsci at the time. Some prisoners tried to denounce him to his party, while others were quick to insult him. Some even tried to harass the man they considered a pariah and a traitor. Sandro Pertini, who stuck by Gramsci during these dramatic days, reports that one day, when the detainees had a snowball fight, Gramsci became the main target. He took refuge in a corner of the prison courtyard, a snowball barely missed his face, and when it crashed into the wall, a stone emerged.[19]

In October 1932, taking advantage of the amnesty provided by the tenth anniversary of the March on Rome, Giuseppe Ceresa went to Moscow in 1933 to present the brief that Gramsci had tasked him with writing as a way to communicate Gramsci's positions to his comrades who had remained in the USSR. Ceresa, a militant Communist close to Gramsci, got this unequivocal reply from two Comintern functionaries he met for the first time, one Italian and the other Russian:

> The Italian said to him, "What are those papers?" Ceresa, shocked, replied, "Didn't you read them? That's the memo Gramsci charged me with delivering to you." But he didn't let me finish, and exclaimed in an ironic tone: "What can he know in prison between those four walls about what's going on in the world! He must know that in his situation, the rule is to keep quiet, to be serious. Constituent assembly, hegemony are just prisoner's fantasies. . . . You shouldn't talk to anybody about those things, since its harmful for your party."[20]

This episode reveals how difficult the relationship between Gramsci and his party had become. The Sixth Congress of the Comintern (July 1928), the lessons in Turi (autumn 1930), and the Fourth Congress of the PCdI (April 1931) all broke ties between Gramsci and his political family. "It seems to me that every day a new thread is broken in my bonds with the world of the past and that it becomes ever more difficult to retie so many torn threads," he wrote to Tania on July 13, 1933.[21] These broken ties included his relationship with Julia, but also with Togliatti, who, a year later, didn't even mention Gramsci's name in the biographical note he wrote for the Cadres Section of the Comintern. In January 1930, Togliatti nonetheless published Gramsci's essay on the southern question. A few months later, he also published his essay "Introduction to the First Course of the Party School" for the internal school of the party. But he had no intention of resisting the Comintern's pressure to erase the strategy put in place by the Lyons congress. In Cologne, Togliatti aligned the PCdI policies completely with the Comintern's, and therefore with the policies Stalin wanted, unequivocally condemning any form of constituent assembly that would delay establishing a dictatorship of the proletariat after the collapse of Fascism, which was supposedly imminent. At the same time, he tried to establish the iconic figure of Gramsci as a martyr to Fascism. Was it a way of embalming him to signify his political death? A clever strategy for quieting his comrade's critics and protecting him from Moscow's fury? Undoubtedly both were true!

Turi, Workshop of Creation: The Material Conditions for Writing the Prison Notebooks

Though the prison in Turi was a place of suffering, a closed universe in which Gramsci became aware of his political and emotional solitude, it was also a place where he wrote down the insights that have marked the history of political thought since the 1950s.

In a letter to Tatiana on March 19, 1927, while he was incarcerated in San Vittore awaiting his sentence, he wrote:

> My life still goes by always with the same monotony. Studying too is much more difficult than it might seem. I've received some books and I actually read a lot (more than a book a day, besides the newspapers), but this is not what I'm referring to. I'm talking about something else. I am obsessed (this is a phenomenon typical of people in jail, I think) by this idea: that I should do something *für ewig*.[22] . . . In short, in keeping with a preestablished program, I would like to concentrate intensely and systematically on some subject that would absorb and provide a center to my inner life. Up until now I've thought of four subjects . . . (1) a study of the formation and the public spirit of Italy during the past century; in other words, a study of Italian intellectuals and their origins . . . (2) A study of comparative linguistics! . . . (3) A study of Pirandello's theater and of the transformation of Italian theatrical taste that Pirandello represented and helped to form . . . (4) An essay on the serial novel and popular taste in literature.[23]

Beyond the plan he laid out for his research,[24] three elements seem important in this missive. First of all, writing was a way to fight against imprisonment and against the ravages of illness. Moreover, though he was used to working as a journalist and a teacher, Gramsci had to give up the polemic vein and dialectical method when he was in prison (the Turi lessons lasted only a few months, from the end of 1930 to the beginning of 1931),[25] and he had to find a new way to transmit his thought. His unfinished essay on the southern question shows that he was already in the right frame of mind to write *für ewig* (for posterity). All the same, and this is the third element, Goethe's phrase should not be interpreted in an unequivocal way. Though it displays a distant perspective on the political events of the moment, it was not at all about shutting himself away in an ivory tower. Contrary to what he mistakenly believed to be Julien Benda's wish,[26] Gramsci remained an activist intellectual, whose detours into theory allowed him to better respond to the challenges of the moment. If *für ewig* was a way of making the censors believe that Gramsci was interested only in cultural questions, renouncing political involvement, the expression also indicates a philosophical engagement that could tackle the problems of his moment. And so, to limit ourselves to an example to which we will return, his interest in comparative linguistics was not simply erudite research but a reflection on the relationship between socialism as it was developed in the Soviet Union and as it had to be translated, i.e., adapted, for different Western nations.

But before we analyze the principal themes developed by the Sardinian thinker, let us pause on the material conditions in which he wrote the famous *Prison Notebooks*.

Notebooks. Why notebooks? Since leaving school, Antonio hadn't written in this medium. When he asked for loose sheets of paper, the prison authorities gave him notebooks, which were easier to control, especially since each one was marked with the stamp of the prison, receiving an authorization from the director, and each page was also numbered, to prevent any pages from being ripped out and escaping the surveillance of the guards.

From August 1928 on, Gramsci had his own cell, and from February 1929 on, he was allowed to write in prison. He was also permitted to keep a few books in his cell during the day. These were not privileges but rather measures specifically given in the *General Prison Rules* of June 13, 1891, confirmed by the new *Rules* put out on June 27, 1931. Nonetheless, the two rulebooks left much of the discretionary power up to the director. Article 140 of the 1931 rules specifies that "the director decides what books the detainees can read and if the reading must be done within the library or the cells, or even in other places." Gramsci could keep only four books at a time in his cell, along with his two notebooks. When he finished using a volume, he had to bring it to the storeroom where his things were kept to be able to take another, never having more than four books on the little table in his cell. Every evening, a guard, usually Vito Semerano, would take the books and notebooks to the prison storeroom. At any moment, the latter could be read and photocopied by OVRA agents. Several converging indications allow us to confirm that Mussolini had read, or at least partially read, Gramsci's *Prison Notebooks*.

Though Gramsci intended to write from March 1927 on, he still had to wait almost two years to obtain a pen and paper. The first notebook was dated February 8, 1929. This date written in Gramsci's hand clearly indicates the beginning of his experience writing the *Prison Notebooks*, and it is recognized and accepted by all specialists in his work. On the other hand, the debate continues about whether Gramsci stopped writing at the end of the first half of 1935 or if he continued to take his notes until the beginning of 1937, the last year of his life.[27] In light of the worsening condition of his health, we agree with the majority opinion, estimating that the Sardinian philosopher was suffering too much in the last two years of his life to continue to carry on this intense and trying intellectual work.

Strictly speaking, the *Prison Notebooks* were not all written behind bars, since some of them were written when Gramsci was secluded in a room at the Formia clinic. All the same, he was still a prisoner. It is also important to keep in mind that the *Notebooks* are not books, as the first edition might have us believe, comprising six thematic volumes, edited between 1948 and 1951 by Felice Platone and Palmiro Togliatti. The edition compiled by Valentino Gerratana in 1975 has given the notebooks back their form of prison writings, while the ongoing undertaking by the Institute for the Italian Encyclopedia endeavors to re-create, as closely as possible, the *work in progress* dimension of Gramsci's writing.[28] This is a labor of love. In fact, with the exception of ten allusions to dates, Gramsci never dated his notes or numbered his notebooks himself, except during a brief period in 1932. They can still be dated by looking at several signs (stamps from the prison, signatures of directors, tax stamps on the notebooks, the development of the handwriting, references to recently published works, etc.).[29] We can distinguish two main periods in the writing of the *Prison Notebooks*: 1–17 are the Turi notebooks, with the addition of four translation notebooks, then 18–29 are the Formia notebooks, devoid of any external signs, unlike those from Turi. We must also be aware of the fact that notebooks 10, 14, 16, and 17 were finished at Formia.

According to Gianni Francioni, one of the supervisors of the ongoing project to publish the *Notebooks* in eighteen volumes, it is possible to distinguish four types of notebooks:

> The contents of the manuscripts allow us, in fact, to define, as a first approximation, three types: in the first place, there is the notebook containing only translations (notebooks A, B, C, D were intended only for translations; notebooks 7 and 9 were also, at the start, given this function, but Gramsci used them later for writing notes). Furthermore, the miscellaneous notebook, containing all kinds of notes on various subjects (almost all distinguished by a section title, which allowed Gramsci to find them quickly); last, the special notebook, in which many of these same notes were resumed and revised. . . . All the same, there are other specifics within the manuscripts: notebooks 1–3, 5, 6, 14, 15, 17 (which exclusively gather paragraphs devoted to subjects that Gramsci had defined in his plans for the work) present differences from

notebooks 4, 7, 8, and 9. In fact, the latter form a fourth type of notebook, which I've called mixed to denote, in this way, each manuscript where Gramsci gathered different undertakings: for example, the notebooks that contain, in addition to various notes, blocks of paragraphs that are thematically similar, gathered under specific titles . . . or notebooks of various notes, thematic blocs, and translations.[30]

From February 8, 1929, to the first half of 1932, Gramsci kept notebooks of translations from German, English, and Russian, all the while taking notes on various subjects. In the first half of 1932, the translation project was abandoned, and Gramsci began to write special notebooks, continuing to take notes on different subjects: "From 1932 on, the map of the notebooks became simpler: these series of homogeneous notes disappeared and what was left were mixed notebooks next to monographic notebooks. This would become the final structure of Gramsci's work until his writing was cut short."[31]

Today, we know, with relative precision, how Gramsci worked in Turi. Gustavo Trombetti, a militant Communist incarcerated in June 1932 who was very close to Gramsci, assisted him with daily tasks so that he didn't overtire himself. According to Trombetti, Gramsci would pace in his cell, "absorbed by his thoughts, then, suddenly, he would stop and write another few lines before going back to pacing."[32] He worked on several notebooks simultaneously, after picking up this habit by writing two letters on the same sheet of paper. When he worked on his special notebooks, he would revise and elaborate on notes that he had already written, crossing things out with a diagonal strike of the pen that usually doesn't prevent us from reading them. This palimpsest is precious in understanding the Gramscian method of writing and in dating the different fragments of the *Prison Notebooks*.

How many notebooks did Gramsci write? The vast majority of critics argue that thirty-three notebooks exist: twenty-nine mixed notebooks, both special and miscellaneous, and four translation notebooks. In a work published in 2012 in Italy, the linguist Franco

Lo Piparo theorizes, through arguments that deserve to be taken into consideration, that a thirty-fourth notebook exists with twenty-six pages: "Did it contain opinions of Fascism that were impossible to make public? Did it contain references to Togliatti and his role in the affair of Grieco's sadly famous letter that were too personal? Or did it contain an explicit critique of Soviet Communism? These are only guesses. We'll have to wait to read it. Provided we ever do."[33]

The Aesopian Writing of the Prison Notebooks

For Gramsci, the *Prison Notebooks* were the main way of intervening in a specific historical situation, namely, the first half of the 1930s, a decade dominated by Americanism, Fascism, and Stalinism. Like Machiavelli when he was writing *The Prince*, a book that was constantly on Gramsci's mind while he was in prison, Gramsci wanted to respond to the challenges of the present by proceeding undercover. If we consider that Gramsci continued to consider himself the leader of the PCdI, and that his writing from prison had a political content, a first, serious question arises: how could he elude censorship? To avoid it, Gramsci would become a master of the art of "Aesopian" writing.

This term shows up in a letter Tatiana wrote to her sister Julia on May 5, 1937, a few days after Antonio's death, "He [Gramsci] has managed to keep them [the notebooks] by writing in an Aesopian language."[34] This adjective, which refers to Aesop's fables, takes on a very specific connotation in this letter written in Russian, given that "since Pushkin, Aesopic signifies the literary form (the hallmark) of covering up a purposefully political content."[35]

One of the principal modes of Aesopian writing in Gramsci's hands was to resort to a coded language.[36] A good example of this technique can be found in his analysis of canto 10 of Dante's *Inferno*.[37] Since Gramsci knew of the major decisions from the Cologne congress, which were copied out for him in invisible ink on an English magazine in May 1931, he intended to make his opposition known to Togliatti by convincing him that he remained a militant Communist, ready to continue to fight for the ideas he had put forward in Lyons. He therefore refused to be a sanctified hero, for whom political action was forbidden. In Aesopian language: he didn't want to assume the role of Farinata, he wanted to keep the role of Cavalcante, someone who, according to his analysis of canto 10 of *Inferno*, still belonged to history—with his doubts, his need to understand, and his thirst for action:

> Traditionally, the tenth canto is Farinata's canto. . . . I maintain that two dramas are played out in the tenth canto: Farinata's and Cavalcante's. . . . We can see here the difference between Cavalcante and Farinata. When the latter hears Florentine spoken, he becomes a partisan again, the Ghibelline hero, while Cavalcante thinks only of Guido and on hearing Florentine spoken rises up to find out whether Guido is alive or dead at that moment.[38]

As with all his letters, Tatiana copied this one for Sraffa, who did not fail to communicate it to the PCdI. A subsequent passage in the *Prison Notebooks* confirms this reading:

> What is the position of Cavalcante? What is his torment? Cavalcante sees into the past and into the future, but he does not see the present: that is, he does not see within a specific zone of the past and the future that comprises the present. In the past, Guido is alive; in the future Guido is dead. But in the present? Is he dead or alive? This is Cavalcante's torment, his affliction, his sole dominant thought. When he speaks, he asks about his son; when he hears "he had"—the verb in the past tense—he persists in his questioning. As the answer is delayed, he no longer doubts: his son is dead. He disappears into the fiery tomb.[39]

Another aspect of Aesopian writing was the recourse to metaphorical language, language that could avoid precise terms that might alert the censors. For example, Gramsci didn't write "Marxism" but rather "philosophy of praxis." But the border between literal and metaphorical usage was not always that traceable, and the challenges of detection were often very difficult, and sometimes impossible. Moreover, though the expression "philosophy of praxis" could be interpreted as an equivalent to Marxism, it also conveyed Gramsci's conception of Marxism as opposed to the theorists who saw it as static, reduced to a materialist economic determinism. In particular, Gramsci was thinking of Bukharin's work *Historical Materialism: A System of Sociology*, published in 1921 in Russia, and he owned the French edition that came out in 1927. A large part of notebook 11 (June–December 1932) is devoted to his critique of this work.

The effort behind Gramsci's writing was directed not only at avoiding Fascist censorship but also at proposing his own hermeneutic for the political challenges facing the Italian Communists in that moment. As the leader he still considered himself to be, he had convinced them of the ideological line established at Lyons, an ideological line that had been rejected during the Cologne congress, whose decisions strictly followed those of the Sixth Congress of the Comintern. He therefore condemned abandoning the united front strategy in favor of the slogan "class against class," which he thought was a fatal move.

The most recent investigations into his works are right to focus on the linguistic theory he developed. Given that he was a very promising student in this discipline (see chapter 2),[40] it is significant that his first *Prison Notebooks* were filled with translations. We must not see these as mere preliminary exercises, as a warming up of the mind, but as a real intellectual project, in which the notion of translation is central and fundamental. Romain Descendre and Jean-Claude Zancarini have pertinently shown that the notion of "translation/translatability" is a "leitmotif"[41] that runs through all of Gramsci's works, from his student research to the writing of the *Prison Notebooks*. Translation can be interpreted in two ways: to make the original language heard, as in the approach theorized by Walter Benjamin, or to transcribe the original faithfully into the target language. Gramsci was definitely a follower of the second approach, which illustrated his historicist vision of the world. Along those lines, his condemnation of Esperanto is significant. The supposedly international language invented by L. L. Zamenhof was, in his eyes, an artificial, antihistoric language since each civilization, and therefore each national culture, had its own corresponding language, a way of understanding history and the world *sui generis*. Consequently, the Comintern should not become a kind of "philosophical Esperanto [like] the positivist and materialist Marxism of Bukharin."[42] Contrary to the way doctrine was becoming more rigid in the USSR, which was apparent in Moscow's drive to impose maxims that were not workable beyond the USSR, Gramsci thought they should undertake the project of translating Communist internationalism into each nation's own language. A successful political translation of the Bolshevik Revolution and of Leninism in Italy would happen through a serious awareness of Fascism and the ways it could be fought.

Fascism, Hegemony, War of Position

Before the March on Rome, the Gramscian perception of Fascism as the "spiritual offspring of Giovanni Giolitti"[43] was cursory and conformed to the canon of the brand new Third International. After 1923–24, his interpretation would develop, becoming subtler and more original, before coming into its own in the *Prison Notebooks*. There, he approaches Fascism from three complementary perspectives. It is first of all interpreted as the expression of Italy's social structure—the reader will remember this was one of the themes of his Turi lessons. The structural fragility of Italian political and civil society is analyzed within a sociological frame as the result of the weakness of the bourgeoisie and the subordinate classes. From this, the old-fashioned manifestation of class conflict in the country ensued: Gramsci summed up this phenomenon with the term "subversive" (*sovversismo*):

> The characteristically Italian concept of "subversive" can be explained thus: a negative rather than positive class position; the "people" feel that they have enemies and identify them only

empirically as the so-called signori. (The concept of "signore" contains much of the old antipathy of the country toward the city, and dress is a basic element of distinction. There is also a dislike for the bureaucracy, which is their sole perception of the state. The peasant, as well as the small landowner, hates the "bureaucrat"—not the state, which he does not comprehend—and regards him as the "signore," even though the peasant is better off economically; hence the apparent contradiction whereby the peasant often considers the signore a "starveling.") This is not so much a modern as a semifeudal kind of "generic" hatred, and it cannot be advanced as evidence of class consciousness: it is barely its first glimmer; indeed, it is only the negative and hostile rudimentary position. Not only do the "people" have no precise consciousness of their own historical identity, but neither are they conscious of the historical identity and exact limits of their enemy. (The lower classes, being historically on the defensive, cannot acquire self-consciousness except through negations, through a consciousness of the identity and class boundaries of their enemy, but it is precisely this process that has yet to dawn, at least on a national scale.)[44]

On this foundation of immature class relations, the economic and social modernization of Italy introduced a new historical subject: the petite bourgeoisie who would form the majority of Fascist militants and cadres.[45] Contrary to the thesis upheld by the Comintern, Fascism was therefore not the agent of big financial capital, and its historic function was not limited to defending the latter's interests. Fascism could not be classified as simply the sword arm of the economic and social elite, preventing the proletarian revolution from forming. It was also the expression of the leading role that the middle classes began to play as they became strong enough to impose their power and political choices on that former elite, creating a new state that no longer belonged to Giolitti's or Salandra's time.

This analysis is corroborated by Gramsci's interpretation of Fascism as a new form of command and domination. Even though the Sardinian thinker did not theorize on the modern techniques of communication put in place by this regime, he nonetheless understood the totalitarian nature of Fascism, which tried to fundamentally change each person to create social conformity:

> There are always cases of individuals belonging to more than one private association, and often they belong to associations that are essentially in conflict with one another. A totalitarian policy in fact attempts: (1) to ensure that the members of a particular party find in that one party all the satisfactions that they had previously found in a multiplicity of organizations, that is, to sever all ties these members have with extraneous cultural organisms; (2) to destroy all other organizations or to incorporate them into a system regulated solely by the party. This occurs: (1) when the party in question is the bearer of a new culture—this is a progressive phase; (2) when the party in question wants to prevent another force, bearer of a new culture, from becoming itself "totalitarian"—this is a regressive and objectively reactionary phase, even if the reaction (as always) does not admit it and tries to create the impression that it is itself the bearer of a new culture.[46]

From these lines, it is obvious that totalitarian politics existed in Italy as it existed in the USSR.[47]

As the social expression and politics of the middle class, and the translation of a new form of command, Fascism was still a passive revolution in Gramsci's analysis. Though it has become common in historiography to refer to Fascism as a revolutionary movement, it was certainly not the case during the time the *Prison Notebooks* were written. Unlike the Bolshevik Revolution of 1917, the Fascist revolution was a passive revolution, and the adjective plays just as important a role as the noun. Theorized for the first time in the forty-fourth paragraph of the first of the *Prison Notebooks* between February and March 1929, and revisited in paragraph 24 of notebook 19 between July 1934 and February 1935, the concept of passive revolution was taken from the *Historical Essay on the Neapolitan Revolution of 1799,* published in 1801 by the writer and philosopher Vincenzo Cuoco (1770–1823), which reads:

> It makes no difference whether a revolution has one symbol or another, but it does have to have one that people understand and want.... Active revolutions are always more effective, because the people on their own direct themselves immediately towards what affects them most closely. In a passive revolution, the government's agent has to try to guess the mind of the people and present them with what they want but would not be able to procure on their own.[48]

Fascism is a passive revolution, insofar as it is a response to the revolutionary threat carried by the workers' movement during the *biennio rosso*. But Fascism is also a passive revolution because it is "the Italian variety of the passive global revolution" aiming for a social structure based on the model at work in the United States (which Gramsci refers to with the term "Americanism" in notebook 1):

> a project founded, on the one hand, on an extension of the factory model [Taylorism] to all of society, and, on the other, on the activation of mechanisms of integration and broadening of the social bases of capitalism, which is concretized especially in the system of mass production, in high salaries, and the diffusion of consumerism [Fordism].[49]

Though Fascist Italy had not yet reached this degree of organization, it did not keep this fundamental mutation at bay, as demonstrated by its willingness to put a corporatist[50] politics in place. Gramsci thought that the creation of the Instituto Mobiliare Italiano (November 1931), the Institute for Industrial Reconstruction (January 1933), and the nationalization of the major banks were the basis for a mixed economy and constituted a possible step[51] toward the organization of a "planned economy" that found its most successful expression in Roosevelt's America, having overcome the crisis of Black Thursday on Wall Street.

This hermeneutic of Fascism developed by Gramsci in several of his *Prison Notebooks* is incompatible with the one imposed by the Comintern, in which Fascism was the symptom of the crisis of capitalism. The strategy of class against class, which rested on the idea of the irreversible and imminent collapse of Fascism and its replacement by the revolutionary way, with a corollary that characterized the non-Communist anti-Fascists as "Social Fascists," was totally maladapted for fighting the regime Mussolini had established. Though Fascism was the form modern capitalism took in Italy, the fight had to be conducted over the long term, following strategies different from the ones that were used in the economically and socially backward Russia of 1917. The Bolshevik Revolution was the last episode in the War of Maneuver, which had to be followed by a War of Position (Gramsci of course borrowed these two concepts from the military events of World War I).[52] During this War of Position, it was not the anti-Fascists' aim to come into power, but to conquer the political hegemony of civil society conceived as "a social terrain on which rivalries and struggles of a cultural and ideological nature are played out and decided among individuals and social groups."[53] This fight could not be waged except within a national framework—additional proof that Gramsci was never a supporter of Trotsky's permanent revolution. In contrast to the years 1923–24, the problem was no longer adapting the strategy of the Comintern to Italian particularities, but initiating a long-term plan to transform the political culture of Italy. Gramsci's strategy in favor of a constituent assembly, which he had stubbornly defended in the courtyard of the Turi prison, was therefore no simple reprisal of the goal of the Republican Constituent Assembly developed after the Matteotti crisis; rather it is conceived as a "unified platform of all the anti-Fascist parties to develop the struggle against the Fascism in power. For this simple reason alone, the Constituent Assembly must have been unpalatable, at least for the comrades with the most elementary political culture within the Turi collective."[54] And to conclude with Giuseppe Vacca: "The link between war of position and hegemony encapsulates a conception of the struggle for power that was finally liberated from the Bolshevik model."[55]

Epilogue
(November 19, 1933–April 27, 1937)

The Throes of Illness

I certify the following: Antonio Gramsci, prisoner in the Turi prison, is affected by serious kyphoscoliosis [abnormal curvature of the spinal column leading to a hunch] due to Pott's disease [tuberculosis spondylitis], from which he has suffered since he was a child. He has tubercular lesions in the upper lobe of the right lung, which have provoked two bouts of hemotypsis [bloody expectorations], one of which was accompanied by a bout of serious fever lasting several days. He also suffers from arteriosclerosis with an aortic hypertension (190/110). He has been subject (in March 1933) to fainting spells with protracted loss of consciousness, following which he experienced paraphasia [difficulty speaking] lasting a few days. He shows signs of a precocious senility, he has lost several teeth [he probably suffered from scurvy and one of its symptoms, acute hallucinations], as a result of which he cannot chew properly and suffers from bad digestion. Since October 1932, he has lost 7 kilograms; he is plagued by prolonged, agitated insomnia. Given these afflictions, he is no longer capable of sitting at his desk and writing, as he did in the past. In conclusion: I believe that in light of his maladies, Gramsci will not be able to survive very long in his present conditions, and I thus believe it necessary for his health that he be transferred to a public hospital or a clinic, at least if it is not possible to grant him conditional freedom. Signed Professor Umberto Arcangeli, Rome hospital, March 25, 1933.[1]

Since his childhood, Gramsci had suffered from tuberculosis in the bone (Pott's disease), which was finally diagnosed correctly by Arcangeli, professor of medicine, and a member of the team led by the Bastianelli brothers. Like all other forms of tuberculosis, this disease was incurable at the time. All the same, Gramsci's living conditions had surely accelerated the deterioration of his health. The insomnia he suffered from all his life worsened in prison, though it had improved during his hospitalization at the Serebryany Bor sanitarium in Moscow. With age, he increasingly suffered from arteriosclerosis. Despite his serious illnesses, he displayed an astonishing resistance. In exile at Ustica, he was in relatively good health. His health truly began to decline with the fearsome journey from the Sicilian island to Milan. It is understandable that afterward he was nervous to leave Turi. When the possibility of his hospitalization in a clinic in Formia materialized, he had a somatic reaction, breaking out in pus-filled herpes.

Though the medical exam he underwent at San Vittore got him out of harsh treatment at the fearsome Portolongone Prison—the diagnosis recognized that he was suffering from uricemia (a high concentration of uric acid in the blood, gout, also accompanied by kidney stones, his tuberculosis of the bone probably having migrated to his kidney), leading to distension and peritonitis (infection of the peritoneum due to a tear in an abdominal organ, whose symptoms can include fever and vomiting, as well as renal colic), and from nervous exhaustion—the sixty-four months he spent at Turi saw his already precarious health deteriorate irremediably. In fact, though the penal institution in Turi was classified as a medical prison by the penitentiary administration, it did not follow the existing norms for a hospital or even those of basic hygiene. The tubercular prisoners were not isolated from the other detainees, whom they visited at the canteen or even at the barber.

At first, Gramsci did not receive any special care. It was only after his health crisis on August 3, 1931, during which he lost around 300 milliliters of blood, which he spat out in clots in a series of coughing fits, that Cisternino, the doctor, finally decided to examine him. In his summary of August 5, he confirmed that "Gramsci has not been suffering from pulmonary tuberculosis, [he is suffering] only from gouty polyarthritis with consecutive endocarditis [inflammation of the interior portion of the heart]; because of this last illness, he had a one-time bronchorragea by venous stasis [hemorrhage of the bronchi] in the short circulation [the flow of blood from the heart to the lungs]." He prescribed calcium chloride (which could be restorative for people suffering from malnutrition) and adrenaline dosed at one part per thousand (which could have had positive effects on his kidney and especially on his heart). Though it wasn't blatantly incorrect, Cisternino's diagnosis was an attempt to minimize the gravity of inmate 7047's general state, since he should have been hospitalized on the spot.

Through force of will, Antonio still managed to regain some of his strength, but he remained very much weakened. In his letters, he complained more and more about the physical pain that crippled him and eventually had a serious impact on his morale. He wrote frankly to Tania: "I have reached a point where my powers of resistance are near to complete collapse. I don't know what the result will be. These last few days I've felt more ill than ever before in my life; for more than eight days now I have not slept more than three quarters of an hour a night, and sometimes I haven't closed my eyes."[2] What kind of prison for the sick would keep its patients from resting?

Under such conditions, it's not surprising that Gramsci fell victim to a second serious crisis at Turi, on March 7, 1933. In the morning, while trying to get up, he collapsed. Luckily, Gustavo Trombetti was able to help him immediately and managed to lay him on his bed. In the days that followed, Gramsci suffered from hallucinations and became incapable of walking. Tatiana got permission from the authorities for him to be examined by Doctor Arcangeli. It was done on March 25, 1933. After seeing the results of Gramsci's examination, Tatiana was so worried that on March 26 she wrote to Giovanni

Novelli, the general director of prisons, to ask him to take "the necessary measures to save Gramsci's life, meaning that he would benefit from a conditional release . . . [and in the meantime, to order] his transfer to a private clinic, under the surveillance of the authorities."[3] Novelli immediately informed Piero Sraffa's maternal uncle, Senator Mariano D'Amelio (1871–1943), who was then the first president of the court of appeals, that Novelli had launched an investigation to gather, as fast as possible, some useful information that would clarify the prisoner Gramsci's situation. After his own examination of Gramsci on August 10, 1933, the health inspector Filippo Saporito estimated that

> the concerns raised over his health seem to be attributable more to the past crises he has overcome than to his present conditions. The measures that have been recommended in favor of moving him to a public hospital or even freeing him altogether do not seem absolutely indispensable in light of the nature and origin of his illness, which does not occasion a broader therapeutic action than the one already undertaken. That said, we do not exclude that attenuating his condition or bringing an end to his state of detention could bring an indirect benefit in terms of raising his spirits, which could have a physical effect as well.[4]

In accordance with this diagnosis, which was much less worrisome[5] than Umberto Arcangeli's, the authorities contented themselves, at first, with moving Gramsci to a quieter cell, on the first floor, prescribing Angioxil syrup (a medicine, new at the time, to treat hypertension), and above all, getting another detainee to help him with daily tasks. This role unsurprisingly fell to Gustavo Trombetti, who was immediately willing. Though Doctor Cisternino, one of two doctors in Turi, observed shortly afterward that inmate 7047 was suffering from "expulsive gingivitis" (in other words, he was losing his teeth), he would allow him the shots of caffeine and camphor he had been prescribed to fight his tiredness and lower his tension only once he had paid for them with his own money—and it was the same with chicken broth, one of the only foods he could tolerate after losing twelve teeth. This horrible example shows that Gramsci had to fight an indifferent bureaucracy on a daily basis. The reader will remember that it was through his own initiative, by writing directly to Novelli, that he obtained a minor improvement in the guards' behavior.

After Arcangeli's visit on March 25, 1933, he would have to wait more than eight months before being transferred to a clinic, and more than a year and a half before he received a conditional release. This wait was not only due to the slowness of the administration. Mussolini was already prepared to show clemency to Gramsci if he asked him for it. But for the leader of the Communist Party, this gesture was impossible. Nothing spells out the psychological significance of this unequivocal refusal better than the letter Sandro Pertini wrote to his mother after she demanded Mussolini's pardon:

> In what state of mind could you do this? ... How can anyone think that I, even for the sake of being freed, would be willing to turn against my faith? And without faith, what would I care for freedom? My freedom, this precious good that is so dear to humankind, becomes a dirty rag to throw away once it has been bought at the price of this betrayal that you have dared propose to me. ... Tell me, Mother, how could you embrace your son if he returned to you with the mark of this base betrayal? How could I live near you after having sold my faith, which you have always so greatly admired?[6]

Once asking for a pardon was unimaginable, only two solutions remained: to obtain his complete freedom through a prisoner exchange, what Tania called "the great attempt" in the letters she sent to Piero Sraffa,[7] or barring that, to gain his conditional freedom through moving him to a clinic, what we'll call "the small attempt."

Gramsci's Impossible Liberation

Since the summer of 1932, a rumor had been circulating through the prisons that there would be general amnesty for the tenth anniversary of the March on Rome. Worried that the PCdI would intervene once more, as they had done at the end of the 1920s with consequences that he had found drastic, Gramsci was particularly irritable in the letters he wrote to Tatiana. While the latter endeavored to get professor of medicine Vittorio Puccinelli, whom she knew personally through the Bastianelli brothers, to pay a medical visit to her brother-in-law, she attracted the ire of Antonio, doubtless afraid to relive the horror of his transfer from Ustica and Milan. Gramsci reproached her for taking the initiative without informing him:

> The idea that I am like a soccer ball that anonymous feet can kick from one end of Italy to the other, as has happened in the past, that for four years and four months I have been prisoner number 7047 who is not allowed to have a will of his own and does not enjoy a citizen's rights (few though they are), has still not entered your head, and therefore you are not at all troubled when the chance arises to add your kick to that ball and remind me that for you too I am only a number.[8]

We can easily imagine how much such a letter might have hurt Tania, who was so devoted to Antonio. She apologized afterward for getting carried away. But if he proved to be particularly touchy with his sister-in-law, it was because he absolutely wanted the PCdI to stay out of it while he played the card of Senator D'Amelio, who was a very influential person even though he wasn't a Fascist. The latter was in fact working to obtain prisoner 7047's freedom, complete if possible, and if not, conditional. Antonio explained this clearly to Tatiana, who made it known to Piero Sraffa, asking him to act with discretion. But not only did the latter inform Togliatti, but he also passed Arcangeli's diagnosis on to the external center of his party.

Did the publication of this document in *L'Humanité* on May 8, 1933, scuttle the second attempt at liberating him? That was Angelo Sraffa's impression in the letter he wrote to his son Piero:

> The PG [Procurer General] promised Mario [D'Amelio] to come back soon to bring him the request for the reexamination

[of Gramsci's situation] and that the response would certainly be favorable.

Only . . . crash! . . . at the last moment news arrived that *L'Humanité* had published Arcangeli's report, to the fury of the chief of police and everyone else, targeting Novelli, who went terror-stricken to Mario, who was not happy about it. They want to know how Arcangeli's report could have gone out of Italy and who it is who could be to blame. They think it is some Paris refugee, but they want to find who is responsible for the publication. Now they have their eyes fixed on Arcangeli, who is supposed to have exaggerated in the prisoner's favor, and are carrying out an intense scrutiny of letters from abroad, especially from Paris, hoping to trace the a(uthor) of the publication. But now poor G. will no longer see a favorable disposition as was hoped up to Friday.[9]

As for Gramsci, he was furious that Tatiana had not scrupulously followed the instructions that had been orally transmitted to her:

To the degree that it is possible, under the conditions of physical and moral lethargy in which I find myself, I've been exasperated at learning from you that once again my instructions with regard to the handling of matters that concern my very physiological existence have been foolishly and capriciously neglected and scorned, without any reason, plausible or of any other kind. I am profoundly convinced that in a different form, but with equal levity, you have repeated the same series of blunders that took place in 1927–28 in regard to which the pretrial judge [Enrico Macis, see chapter 7] was right to say that it really seemed as though my friends were collaborating to keep me in prison as long as possible. Such statements will displease you, but I cannot refrain from making them. When, last January, I spoke to you during our visit, I begged you with all the strength I had to adhere scrupulously to my instructions.[10]

According to Mauro Canali, Togliatti had done nothing to prevent the publication of Arcangeli's diagnosis. He began to express some scruples only on May 9, the day after it was published, scruples that did not prevent the publication of two other articles, both in *L'Humanité* on May 9 and 11, in which Gramsci was also presented as at death's door.[11] Though Togliatti admitted, some time later, that this publication was "a grave error," he nonetheless enjoyed the success of this media operation whose "repercussions have been very noteworthy and favorable to the growth of the campaign [against Fascism] in all areas."[12]

The publication of Arcangeli's medical summary certainly hurt Gramsci, but is it necessary to see it as an ill-intentioned or cynical act on the part of the PCdI? Let us take up the case. We must understand, first of all, that the press campaign for Gramsci went beyond the goal of his possible release. After the lessons of Turi, Gramsci's name disappeared from speeches by the leaders of the Comintern and the PCdI for almost two years, from the end of 1930 to 1932. Even the MOPR no longer undertook anything on his behalf. During this time, Gramsci hoped that the Soviet and Italian governments would continue to think of releasing him as part of a prisoner exchange. But alongside "the great attempt," he continued to work toward "the small attempt," especially since after March 1932 (the date his prison sentence was reduced to twelve years and four months) he hoped to benefit from the measure, laid out in article 176 of the new *Penal Code*, developed under the aegis of Alfredo Rocco and passed in 1931, granting conditional release to any detainee who had served half his sentence. This was the case for Gramsci, since he had been behind bars for six years since his incarceration on November 8, 1926. Also, to get all the odds in his favor, he asked his friend Piero Sraffa to ask his uncle, Mariano D'Amelio, to use his influence.

To avoid repeating the terrible mistake of 1928 and Grieco's letter, Gramsci intended to keep the PCdI in the dark about the steps he was taking. But this plan became difficult, not only because Piero informed the external committee of his party, but also because the anti-Fascist, non-Communist newspaper *La Liberté* announced that Gramsci had died in prison. *L'Humanité* had to react, unable to abandon the fight for the man who was still the official leader of the PCdI to anti-Fascists who weren't Communists. In four articles on March 26, 27, 30, and April 2, 1933, the daily for the PCF called for pulling Gramsci out of the prison that was killing him. *Avanti!*, the newspaper for the PSI, and *La Liberté* (once again) followed in *L'Humanité*'s footsteps, launching a press campaign for Antonio Gramsci's liberation. This was nonetheless abruptly halted in mid-April. At that time, all the efforts of the Comintern and its satellite organizations like the MOPR were focused on arranging the release of Ernst Thälmann, the German leader of the KPD, arrested on March 3, 1933. He was never released and would be executed after eleven years in prison, on August 8, 1944, at the Buchenwald concentration camp. Denouncing Italian Fascism was no longer the order of the day. This silence was not due to the concern for disrupting the plans in progress to transfer Gramsci to a clinic, but rather followed the will of Moscow, which was then in the midst of a reconciliation with Rome, a diplomatic move that would lead to the signing of a pact of friendship between the two countries a few months later, on September 2, 1933. Though the press campaign in favor of Gramsci's release continued on May 8, 1933, with the publication of Professor Arcangeli's brief in *L'Humanité*, it was once again because neither the PCdI nor the Comintern could leave this fight in the hands of their opponents, with the aggravating circumstance that these opponents were Trotskyites: on April 21, 1933, the Trotskyite newspaper *La Verité* published an article in French in favor of the liberation of the Sardinian thinker. Moreover, Angelo Tasca, Ignazio Silone, and Amadeo Bordiga, who had been kicked out of the PCdI in 1929, had called for a big demonstration of all anti-Fascists on behalf of the political prisoners, and Gramsci's name was first among them.

Togliatti did not want to hamper this media uproar in the Communist press, which he thought, as we have seen in the letter to Piero Sraffa in May 24, 1933, would have beneficial political effects. According to a very thorough study by Claudio Natoli, Togliatti did nothing to suspend the campaign on Gramsci's behalf. It only grew during the month of May. In this way, more than seven thousand demonstrators, a significant number of whom were Italian workers, gathered on May 28, 1933, before the Mur des Fédérés in Paris to demand the liberation of Thälmann, Georgi Mikhailov Dimitrov,[13] and Gramsci. Nonetheless, despite the creation, on May 23, 1933, of a committee for Gramsci's liberation led by the writers Romain Rolland and Henri Barbusse, the Moscow authorities, who were then in the phase of finalizing the nonaggression pact with Rome, demanded that all the critiques of Fascism be silenced to keep the emphasis on the danger represented by National Socialism. The rhythm of the press campaign (after it was launched at the end of March, it was stopped in April and then began again at the beginning of May, before being sharply curtailed at the end of that same month) seemed to be dictated entirely by Moscow, whose orders the PCdI relayed without any margin for action. In this sense, more than Togliatti's moral accountability, it's important to highlight his political accountability.

It is still not certain that this campaign prevented his liberation, as Angelo Sraffa and Gramsci himself thought. The reconciliation in course between the Kingdom of Italy and the USSR actually played a positive role, especially since Mussolini's regime could be satisfied that Moscow would hold its troops and impose silence about Fascism among its sister parties, so they could concentrate their critiques on National Socialism, which Il Duce regarded, at the time, in a negative light. Elsewhere, far from the challenges of this party of dupes, the international campaign triggered a wave of critiques: the Austrian, Danish, French, and Estonian embassies in Rome denounced the conditions of Gramsci's imprisonment. The leader of the Italian government could not ignore it. Releasing Gramsci was unimaginable, since it would mean submitting to the will of the Communists, while on the other hand, hospitalizing him and granting his conditional release could pass for gestures of clemency rather than weakness.

"The small attempt" would still take some time to materialize. Carlo Gramsci had to address two requests to the head of the Italian government, a first, on July 27, 1933, which did not come to fruition, and then another, on August 23, 1933, which worked. Mussolini accepted

Carlo's request on Gramsci's behalf for his gravely ill brother to be hospitalized in a clinic. It would still take three months (during which Antonio, losing all hope, feared a new transfer so much that he preferred to die in Turi)[14] for the services of the minister of the interior to find a care facility that could be secured to avoid any escape attempts by Gramsci. The prefects of Viterbo, Terni, Rieti, Frosinone, and Rome were mobilized. The choice finally came down to Doctor Giuseppe Cusumano's clinic in Formia, a small maritime city a few miles north of Gaeta. This care facility fulfilled the criteria demanded by the OVRA agents since it already housed a famous prisoner, General Luigi Capello (1859–1941), implicated in the planning of an assassination attempt against Mussolini in November 1925. All that remained was to find the 120 lire per day it cost to take care of the patient. Despite the sale of a little house in Ghilarza, Carlo and Tatiana could not afford such an expense, which represented roughly three hundred dollars a month. After many hesitations and negotiations, the MOPR, the PCdI, and the Comintern—the latter agreeing to do its part only after the direct intervention of Togliatti and Nadezhda Krupskaya, a friend of the Schucht family (see chapter 4)—finally managed to assemble the sum. The OVRA agents had trouble establishing the route the money took. It likely traveled this way: the MOPR gave the bills to a member of the PCdI, who left them at the Hotel Lux in Moscow, where they were picked up by Eugenia Schucht, who took them to the NKVD, who transferred them to the Soviet embassy in Rome, where Tatiana went to get them.

On November 16, 1933, the director of the prison in Turi received Giovanni Novelli's orders to authorize Gramsci's special, direct transfer to the prison in Civitavecchia. With a very heavy escort, Gramsci left Turi on November 9, 1933, for the Civitavecchia prison infirmary, which he reached that evening. Through the windows of the vehicle, he could see passing fields, trees, the sky, birds, kids playing, "the vast world had continued to exist"[15] while he saw, day in and day out, for six years, the same roofs and the same walls that were imbued with sadness. But this dizzy freedom was still only the faraway foretaste of a freedom he would experience only for a few hours.

In the infirmary of the Civitavecchia prison, having become prisoner 6589, Gramsci spent most of his time resting. Though he was not pampered, he could finally have a bit of quiet. Neither the guards nor his cellmate made noise. When he was not in bed, sleeping a little at last, he was allowed to walk alone, including outside of the hours that were designated for that activity. Scoccimarro and Terracini, who were also in transit to Civitavecchia then, tried to see him. In vain. During the seventeen days that he remained in this little town on the seaside, he received only one visit, from the faithful Tatiana.

On December 7, 1933, he left Civitavecchia for Doctor Cusumano's clinic in Formia. The OVRA agents had established, down to the smallest details, that his room was secure, and, more generally, they had put in place the drastic security measures the authorities demanded for Gramsci's stay.

Formia (December 7, 1933–August 24, 1935)

In this long-standing care facility run by Doctor Cusumano, Gramsci was still a closely surveilled prisoner: Mussolini had given explicit orders on the subject to Arturo Bocchini, the chief of police. In particular, the *carabinieri* in Formia (who were later compensated for the seriousness with which they had carried out their task) and the OVRA functionaries watched the beach, where they feared well-armed commandos would disembark to free Gramsci.[16]

During her first visit with Gramsci in Formia, Tatiana found her brother-in-law even thinner than he had been at Civitavecchia. By then, Antonio was fully aware that his health had declined irreversibly, but he wanted to continue to resist, until the end. His principal concern was that his books, and especially his notebooks, would arrive as fast as possible. They reached him a few days after he was hospitalized in Formia, and the prison administration probably did not create any obstacles to their delivery.[17] To avoid offending the old Neapolitan aristocrats who visited General Capello, Gramsci was excused from wearing a prisoner's uniform. Between two *carabinieri*, he was allowed to walk in the garden of the clinic. But, even more than at Turi, Gramsci suffered from the constant presence of the guards. Though they did not make noise, their omnipresence, even in the hallways outside his room, was torture for his already strained nerves. His struggles with insomnia returned, particularly after the OVRA agents increased the random checks of his room, day and night. And so, despite very comforting support from Tatiana, who had obtained permission to visit him weekly, and though he still had the capacity and the will to read and to work on his *Notebooks*—he was then working on several special notebooks—his main goal was to obtain his freedom.

He had not given up on "the great attempt." This development seemed, for a while, to be taking shape. Since Gramsci's wife and children were Soviet citizens, the diplomatic services in Moscow seemed favorable to an exchange that would, once again, be carried out under the auspices of the Holy See, trading him for a Russian princess, Antoinette Urusova, who had been accused of spying and deported to Siberia in 1924. The deputy director of the Third Department of the People's Commissariat for Foreign Affairs, Chaïm Vejnberg, and the advisor to the ambassador Vincenzo Berardis endeavored to move the negotiation forward. Fulvio Suvich, the undersecretary of foreign affairs for the Fascist government, and Bernardo Attolico, the Italian ambassador to Moscow, were also involved in favor of this exchange. But the plan was vetoed by Mussolini, who wouldn't agree to Gramsci's expatriation. Mussolini made this very clear to Potemkin, the Soviet ambassador, on November 25, 1934, when Potemkin spoke with him before moving on to another posting.

The third and last press campaign was organized by the Communist Giovanni Germanetto, and it put the Sardinian thinker at a disadvantage, as it had in 1933. The documents kept at the Central Archives of the State furnish damning proof: "the efforts by Attolico and the embassy staff to obtain a favorable solution to the Gramsci question have been made futile by interventions like that of Germanetto at the congress of Soviet writers,[18] in which he declared that Gramsci is the leader of the Italian Communist Party."[19] Beyond the negative effects this had on Gramsci's fate, this last, brief press campaign merits study[20] because it is emblematic of the relationship the Comintern cultivated with the Sardinian thinker.

This campaign took place during a period marked by tension within the ranks of the Comintern, tension that was still implicit but that would become more explicit, between the old guard, who remained faithful to the program of class against class (which was still the official doctrine reaffirmed at the Thirteenth Congress of the Comintern Bureau, which was held in Moscow in November 1933) and those who supported the strategy of popular fronts, meaning an alliance between all anti-Fascist forces. The latter position found a powerful outlet in the writings and speeches of Willi Münzenberg (1889–1940), a sort of "clandestine minister of propaganda for the Comintern across the world and especially in Western Europe."[21] In this way, the first group interpreted the liberation of Dimitrov from the Nazi jails as the triumph of the vigorous Bolshevik campaign against the delays of Social Democracy (the Social Fascists), while the second saw it as a victory in the fight for law and truth. Whatever the case, Moscow still set the tone according to its own diplomatic interests. In the autumn of 1934, the USSR, which had just been admitted to the League of Nations, wanted to align with France, all the while consolidating its ties with Fascist Italy. Under these conditions, we can understand why the Soviet authorities did not go out of their way to get involved with Gramsci's liberation and his expatriation to the USSR, as soon as Mussolini opposed it. This situation has led historian Massimo Mastrogregori to compare, with the necessary adjustments, Gramsci's situation to that of Aldo Moro, both victims of the bad faith of two parties who did not intend to find a common ground.[22] Moscow prevented all significant action on Gramsci's behalf, on the part of both the MOPR and the PCdI.

The great article by Romain Rolland, titled "Pour ceux qui meurent dans les prisons de Mussolini: Antonio Gramsci" [For Those Who Perish in Mussolini's Prisons: Antonio Gramsci], published in Paris in September 1934, appeared as a rather isolated account in support of Gramsci, and unfortunately one that was counterproductive. The French writer's essay is nonetheless interesting, since it puts the Führer and Il Duce on the same level,[23] comparing Gramsci's agony to the murder of Matteotti,[24] and recalling the idealist origins of this thinker and his actions during the era of *L'ON*. He ultimately traces a portrait of Gramsci through the *Quaderni di "Giustizia e Libertà"* of Carlo and Nello Rosselli, famous militant anti-Fascist brothers who were not Communists, but who were in exile in Paris after Carlo's July 1929 escape from the Lipari Islands, where he was exiled. The spectacular nature of Carlo's escape was one main reason why the Fascist authorities were worried that a commando unit would rescue Gramsci.

The assassination of Kirov on December 1, 1934, marked an ideological toughening that reinforced, for a time, the conservative camp within the Comintern that resisted the line of approach Dimitrov and Münzenberg represented. The one-year delay of the Seventh Congress of the Comintern (planned for summer 1934, it finally took place in Moscow from July 25 to August 21, 1935) bears witness to this ideological freeze. After the publication of Romain Rolland's article, Gramsci disappeared once more from the Comintern and PCdI radar, only to reappear after his death. Without knowing the ins and outs of the situation, the imprisoned Antonio Gramsci understood that the only card he could still play was "the small attempt."

On September 24, 1934, he requested his conditional release from Mussolini:

> I ask Your Excellency to please intervene so that I may be allowed conditions of existence which permit me the possibility of alleviating, if not completely negating, the more acute forms of my illness, which for four years has destroyed my nervous system and made life a continuous torture. Parole, internal, exile, or treatment as an internal exile [*confino di polizia*],[25] what I ask you to please allow me is the end of my conditions of confinement in the strict sense, with its forms of arrest and surveillance day and night, at all times, which prevents peace and rest, in my case necessary to stop the progressive and tormenting destruction of my physical and mental constitution.... Antonio Gramsci, Formia, Cusumano clinic, September 24, 1934.[26]

Mussolini was aware that he had won his terrible power struggle with Gramsci, but he was also anxious to avoid letting the latter die in prison. Mussolini was well aware, from doctors Raffaele Bastianelli and Vittorio Puccinelli, who were involved thanks to Tatiana's interest in Gramsci's case, of the very sorry state of the Communist leader's health. Still, Il Duce demanded that the prisoner write and sign by his own hand, in the presence of the police inspector Antonio Valenti, a declaration that he would no longer make any political propaganda in Italy or outside the country. Gramsci signed it on October 14, 1934:

> I thank you for the news you have brought me regarding the acceptance of the request to His Excellence the Head of the Government that I be granted conditional freedom. For the moment I would like to remain in Formia. If, in the future, on the advice of trusted doctors I have not yet had the chance to consult, I should choose a different residence, then I will notify you with no delay. I am of the opinion that the benefit that is about to be granted to me is not attributable to political causes, and as far as I am concerned, I assure you that I will not take advantage of this situation to advance propaganda within Italy or abroad. With my respects, Antonio Gramsci. [On this document, Chief of Police Arturo Bocchini added in his own hand]: "By the order of His Excellence the Head of the Government: It is fine. Grant him conditional freedom."[27]

This declaration should not be interpreted as an act of cowardice, but rather as the gesture of a very sick man, whose nerves were exhausted, who was distanced from his political family after losing his faith in it. Gramsci was not the martyr to Fascism that the Communist and non-Communist hagiographers of the postwar era made him out to be—so heroic that he was no longer human.

On October 25, 1934, the decree granting him conditional release was finally approved. According to the list of restrictions given with this type of measure,[28] Gramsci remained a closely monitored

prisoner. His correspondence was systematically read. Piero Sraffa and Tatiana were constantly followed. When he received a letter from New York, the OVRA services immediately opened an investigation to see if an escape plan was being financed from abroad. The harbormasters in Gaeta and Formia were put on alert. More than a hundred photos of Gramsci were distributed to all the police precincts (*carabinieri*, police, railroad police, customs officers) in Rome and Naples. This little hunchback with an unquestionably powerful brain still frightened Mussolini, despite the fact that consensus around him still continued to strengthen.

Aware that he was not sufficiently well cared for in Formia, Gramsci asked, in March 1935, to be transferred to a center for specialized care. He was thinking of the Poggio Sereno clinic in Fiesole. But the Fascist authorities refused, arguing that this establishment did not conform to adequate security parameters. In June 1935, his health brutally deteriorated. The effects of his tuberculosis made themselves forcefully felt, and he suffered several attacks of hyperesthesia (pathological sensitivity) of his hands and feet that made writing and walking difficult. Hypertension, his other major illness, also worsened during this time. He also suffered from insomnia, attacks of gout, and the discovery of an inguinal hernia.

Gramsci was a physically broken man, "an invalid suffering from serious ailments,"[29] who was beginning a slow and agonizing death that would take another two years. Agony—the word is fitting here, for Gramsci continued to fight until his last breath. In August 1935, he finally obtained permission to be hospitalized at the Roman clinic Quisisana ("qui si sana," literally, "here one gets healthy"), a clinic that still exists to this day.

Quisisana (August 24, 1935–April 27, 1937)

On August 24, 1935, Gramsci left Formia for the Quisisana clinic, which was directed by Professor Puccinelli. He accompanied Gramsci during his journey, which took place, once again, under tight surveillance. As soon as he took possession of his room, number 26, on the top floor, he was exhausted. He was no longer capable of working on his *Notebooks*, but he still had the strength and desire to read. Through his window, without bars or gates, he could see the Tiber, the fat, lazy lizard snaking across the Roman countryside. Tatiana was allowed to visit him each day. Piero Sraffa, who came to see him from time to time, remembered him as a man "calm, resigned, almost content. He had no more desire to live, he was at the end of all his physical and moral suffering, and the disagreement with the party."[30] His letter of February 27, 1933 (examined in chapter 7), which, you will remember, was not published until after Togliatti's death, could be interpreted in an Aesopian way as Gramsci's break with the Communist world—not with the ideal of this world, but as it presented itself concretely before his eyes. And so it was not surprising that his last fight would be to obtain his release so that he could withdraw to his Sardinian shell. On May 8, 1936, in a letter she addressed to Teresina Gramsci, Antonio's favorite little sister, Tatiana wrote:

> What I write to you is of an extremely confidential nature. Nino [Antonio Gramsci's nickname] begs you not to divulge anything and not even to write to Carlo. This is what it concerns: Nino would like to return to Sardinia, to Santulussurgiu. . . . Naturally, he will have to make a request to the minister to do so. And if his request is granted, he will have to be able to go immediately to the location he indicated beforehand in his request, and, as a consequence, find somewhere to stay there that is adapted for the conditions of his health. And so my request to you is as follows: Nino would like a member of the family to look into the possibility of renting a few rooms in Santulussurgiu, in a house situated on the street called "la costa." . . . In looking for this house, it is of course not necessary to make any mention of Nino, nor to actually rent it. They should simply say that they are looking for a house for someone who is ill and needs a lot of quiet. . . . For a long time now, he has been thinking about going back to the place where he spent his adolescence.[31]

Why this secret if it was not to hide his decision from the PCdI? How else to understand why Carlo, a brother he valued, should be kept in the dark? Antonio told another story to his friend Piero Sraffa, allowing him to understand, in a hush-hush way, that he didn't intend to end his days in Sardinia, but that it would be easier for him to flee from his native island. For Franco Lo Piparo, this strategy had "two objectives: (I) reassuring the Communist establishment about the instrumental nature of Gramsci's plan to withdraw into his Sardinian shell . . . (II) reduce the pressure from Sraffa and the party for Gramsci to sign the request for expatriation to the Soviet Union."[32]

Gramsci did not intend to renounce his political ideals, but the contemporary Communist world was, from then on, strange and hostile to him, and he wanted to free himself from it definitively, as he had already done theoretically in the *Prison Notebooks*. We are aware that this is only a theory, but it is a plausible theory that is corroborated by a series of elements. Though the need to return to one's native land is doubtless experienced by anyone who feels their death approaching, in Gramsci's case the return to his origins also signified the collapse of an internationalism whose derailment he had witnessed. To avoid living through this collapse, he would have had to die, a gesture as vain as it was heroic, like the death of Jacques Thibault, one of the two heroes of the eponymous masterpiece by Roger Martin du Gard (*The Thibaults*, published in several volumes between 1922 and 1940).

The last letters Antonio wrote were mainly addressed to his two sons, Giuliano, whom he had never met, and Delio, whom he had known so little, as well as his wife, Julia, whom he had never really understood. The militant gave way before the individual, who had been deprived of love from his wife and sons owing to his personal choices and the turn his fate had taken. But to end his life on his own terms, in the place where he had been born, he still had to obtain his freedom.

Near noon on April 25, which would become, in an ironic historical wink, the day celebrating Italy's liberation from Fascism,[33] the faithful Tania returned from the Tribunal of Rome with the declaration, duly signed by a judge, certifying that Gramsci was a free citizen from that day in 1937 on. She let him savor this happy decision and recover from his understandable emotion. She came back to see him at 5:30 that evening. They discussed the next French lesson she had to give—Tatiana was once again making a living by giving private lessons. Together, they searched for the precise definition of several terms in the *Larousse* dictionary. After dining frugally on soup, cooked fruit, and a little *pan di Spagna*, an Italian specialty made with lemon and sugar, he collapsed in the bathroom. He lost the use of the left side of his body and spoke with difficulty. Since he was in the middle of an urgent operation, Professor Puccinelli could not immediately come to Gramsci's bedside, and the physician on duty who examined him decided not to do anything. Around nine at night, Puccinelli ordered them to bleed him. Gramsci's health progressively declined during the night. He lost his ability to speak, breathing with increasing difficulty. He remained in this state for nearly forty-eight hours, after which he vomited and breathed more harshly until there "emerged the silence without remedy."[34] This was on April 27, 1937. It was 4:10 in the morning.[35]

Arriving on the scene, Carlo went to the trouble of finding a photographer to take a picture of his brother's remains, which were already laid out at the morgue. The Fascist bureaucrats insisted on a private funeral. On April 28 or 29—sources differ—his remains were collected by the employees of the Campo Verano cemetery in Rome. They were cremated there on May 5, 1937. The urn that held his ashes remained at the Verano cemetery until August 30, 1938 (not 1945, as you still sometimes read), when it was transferred to the Roman cemetery for non-Catholics, which is next to the Pyramid of Cestius, commonly called the "English" cemetery, since many British citizens are buried there, including the poets Keats and Shelley.

Why cremation? Why this choice of an English cemetery? Why a service organized by the pastor Emanuele Sbaffi, a Freemason close to the Methodists who officiated at the Waldensian Church in Rome?[36] Since Gramsci didn't leave instructions in his will—at least no trace of any remain—this was undoubtedly Tatiana's doing, since she had personal ties to these Methodist cultural circles from her time teaching at the Crandon Institute (see chapter 4).

It is more interesting to note her refusal, conscious or unconscious, to have her brother-in-law's ashes transferred to Moscow. Did she mean to jealously watch over the memory of the man she had accompanied since 1926? Was she respecting Antonio's wishes to be buried in Italy, his native land? Was she symbolically demonstrating the political separation between Gramsci and so-called real communism, as it was in the midst of being disfigured by the USSR? Did she intend to keep the PCdI at a distance, as she would vainly try to do after her return to Moscow, on August 30, 1938, the fate of the *Prison Notebooks*, the main inheritance her brother-in-law had explicitly entrusted her with? This intellectual heritage concerns us all to this day.

English Editions
of Gramsci's Writings

The Antonio Gramsci Reader: Selected Writings, 1916–1935. Edited by David
Forgacs. Introduction by Eric Hobsbawm. New York: New York University
Press, 2000.

Further Selections from the Prison Notebooks. Edited and translated by Derek
Boothman. Minneapolis: University of Minnesota Press, 1995.

A Great and Terrible World: The Pre-prison Letters, 1908–1926. Edited and translated by Derek Boothman. London: Lawrence and Wishart, 2014.

History, Philosophy and Culture in the Young Gramsci. Edited by Pedro
Cavalcanti and Paul Piccone. Candor, NY: Telos Press, 1975.

Letters from Prison. Edited by Frank Rosengarten. Translated by Raymond
Rosenthal. 2 vols. New York: Columbia University Press, 1993–94.

The Modern Prince and Other Writings. Translated by Louis Marks. New York:
International Publishers, 1957.

Pre-prison Writings. Edited by Richard Bellamy. Translated by Virginia Cox.
Cambridge: Cambridge University Press, 1994.

Prison Notebooks. Edited and translated by Joseph Buttigieg. 3 vols. New York:
Columbia University Press, 1991–2011.

Selections from Cultural Writings. Edited by David Forgacs and Geoffrey Nowell-
Smith. Translated by William Boelhower. London: Lawrence and Wishart,
1985.

Selections from Political Writings. Edited by Quintin Hoare. Translated by John
Matthews. 2 vols. London: Lawrence and Wishart, 1977.

Selections from the Prison Notebooks. Edited and translated by Quintin Hoare
and Geoffrey Nowell-Smith. London: Lawrence and Wishart, 1989.

The Southern Question. Introduced and translated by Pasquale Verdicchio.
Toronto: Guernica, 2005 [1995].

Selected Chronology
of Gramsci's Life

January 22, 1981: Birth of Antonio Gramsci at Ales in Sardinia.

August 14, 1892: Founding of the Party of Italian Workers, which became the Italian Socialist Party (PSI) in 1895.

1901–1914: Italian political life is dominated by Giovanni Giolitti.

June 16–18, 1901: Founding congress of the Federazione impiegati operai metallurgici (FIOM).

September 4, 1904: Miners' strike in Buggerru (Cagliari).

September 29, 1906: Founding congress of the Confederazione generale del lavoro (CGL).

1908–1911: Gramsci is a student at the Dettori school in Cagliari.

November 1911: Gramsci registers at the Faculty of Letters at the University of Turin.

July 7, 1912: Thirteenth Congress of the PSI—control of the party taken over by the revolutionary wing led by Costantino Lazzari and Benito Mussolini.

June 7–14, 1914: The Red Week.

August 3, 1914: Italy declares itself neutral in the conflict enveloping Europe.

October 18, 1914: publication of an article by Mussolini in favor of Italy's intervention in the war on the side of the Entente powers.

October 31, 1914: "Neutralità attiva ed operante."

November 15, 1914: First issue of *Il Popolo d'Italia*.

November 24, 1914: Mussolini expelled from the PSI.

May 23, 1915: Italy declares war on Austria.

September 5–8, 1915: Zimmerwald Conference.

December 10, 1915: Gramsci joins the Turin editorial staff of *Avanti!*

February 11, 1917: He publishes the single issue of *La Città Futura*.

December 24, 1917: *La rivoluzione contro il Capitale.*

November 11, 1918: Signing of the Armistice that marks the end of World War I.

1919–1920: *Biennio rosso.*

March 1919: First Congress of the Comintern.

May 1, 1919: Publication of the first issue of *L'Ordine Nuovo.*

June 21, 1919: *Democrazia operaia.*

October 5, 1919: Sixteenth Congress of the PSI, ratifying its membership in the Third International.

March 22, 1920: Strike "of the clock hands" in Turin.

May 8, 1920: *Per un rinnovamento del Partito socialista.*

July 19–August 7, 1920: Second Congress of the Comintern that adopted the Twenty-One Conditions.

August 31, 1920: Beginning of the movement to occupy the factories and to put workers councils in place in Italy.

November 28–29, 1920: Formation of the Communist fraction of the PSI.

December 24, 1920: Last issue of the first run of *L'Ordine Nuovo.*

January 21, 1921: Founding of the Communist Party of Italy (PCdI).

May 15, 1921: Gramsci is not elected as a candidate for the Turin province in the legislative elections.

November 7, 1921: Founding of the Partito Nazionale Fascista (PNF).

March 20–24, 1922: Second Congress of the PCdI, held in Rome.

May 26, 1922: Gramsci leaves Turin for Moscow, arriving June 3.

June 7–11, 1922: Gramsci attends the Second Conference of the Enlarged ECCI.

June 11, 1922: Gramsci's hospitalization at the Serebryany Bor (silver forest) sanitarium, where he meets Eugenia Schucht and then Julia Schucht, who becomes his companion and the mother of his two sons.

October 28, 1922: Fascist March on Rome.

November 16, 1922: Mussolini obtains the full powers of Parliament.

December 3, 1923: Gramsci is in Vienna (Austria) as a Comintern representative.

February 12, 1924: First issue of *L'Unità*, led by Gramsci.

March 1, 1924: First issue of the third run of *L'Ordine Nuovo.*

March 15, 1924: *Contro il pessimismo.*

April 6, 1924: Gramsci is elected as a deputy in the Veneto.

May 12, 1924: Gramsci returns to Italy.

June 10, 1924: Assassination of Matteotti.

June 17–July 8, 1924: Fifth Congress of the Comintern (the bolshevization congress).

June 27, 1924: The Aventine Secession.

August 10, 1924: Birth of Delio, Gramsci's first son.

January 3, 1925: Mussolini's speech in the Chamber of Deputies.

February 2, 1925: First meeting with Tatiana Schucht, Gramsci's sister-in-law.

May 16, 1925: Gramsci's only speech in the Chamber of Deputies.

1926: *Leggi Fascistissime* (Fascist laws).

January 23–26, 1926: Third Congress of the PCdI, secretly held in Lyons. Gramsci becomes its leader.

August 31, 1926: Birth of Giuliano Gramsci, Julia and Antonio's second son.

October 14–26, 1926: Exchange of letters between Gramsci and Togliatti.

November 1–3, 1926: Meeting in Valpolcevera.

November 8, 1926: Gramsci's arrest.

December 7, 1926: Exile on the island of Ustica.

January 4, 1927: The Special Tribunal for the Defense of the State begins to operate.

February 7, 1927: Gramsci is incarcerated at the San Vittore judicial prison in Milan.

September 1927–end of 1928: First attempt to liberate Gramsci.

February 10, 1928: Grieco writes his infamous letter.

May 28, 1928: Beginning of the mass trial of the Communist leaders.

June 4, 1928: Gramsci is condemned by the Special Tribunal for the Defense of the State to twenty years, four months, and five days in prison.

July 19, 1928: Gramsci is incarcerated in the Turi prison (in the Bari region).

July–August 1928: Sixth Congress of the Comintern, officially marking the end of the United Front strategy in favor of the struggle of class against class.

February 8, 1929: Gramsci begins to write his *Prison Notebooks*.

February 11, 1929: Signing of the Lateran Treaty between Mussolini and the Holy See.

April 14–21, 1931: Fourth Congress of the PCdI in Cologne.

August 3, 1931: Significant worsening of Gramsci's health.

November 1932: Gramsci's sentence is shortened to twelve years and four months.

Spring 1933: Second attempt to liberate Gramsci.

March 7, 1933: Gramsci can no longer walk or stand up on his own; the effects of this collapse will be felt until November.

March 20, 1933: Professor of medicine Umberto Arcangeli examines Gramsci and judges that his days are numbered if he isn't transferred to a clinic.

March 26, 1933: Beginning of the international press campaign for the liberation of Gramsci, with the publication of the article "Mussolini assassine Gramsci dans la prison de Turi" in *L'Humanité*.

April 18, 1933: Professor of medicine and health inspector Filippo Saporito examines Gramsci as well.

May 8, 1933: *L'Humanité* publishes Umberto Arcangeli's medical diagnosis.

May 23, 1933: A committee for the liberation of Gramsci forms in Paris under the aegis of Romain Rolland and Henri Barbusse.

May 26, 1933: PCF and PCdI campaign to liberate Dimitrov, Gramsci, and Thälmann.

September 2, 1933: Signing of the Pact of Friendship between Rome and Moscow.

November 19, 1933: Gramsci leaves the Turi prison for the infirmary of the Civitavecchia prison.

December 7, 1933: Still a prisoner, Gramsci is hospitalized in Formia in Dr. Cusumano's clinic.

January 1934–January 1935: Third and final attempt to liberate Gramsci.

July 12, 1934: Professor of medicine Vittorio Puccinelli examines Gramsci.

September 1934: Publication of "Pour ceux qui meurent dans les prisons de Mussolini. Antonio Gramsci," by Romain Rolland.

September–October 1934: A new international press campaign in favor of Gramsci's release.

September 24, 1934: Gramsci sends a request to Mussolini to obtain conditional release.

October 14, 1934: Gramsci promises in writing to no longer create political propaganda.

October 25, 1934: Publication of the decree granting Gramsci conditional release.

June 1935: Worsening of Gramsci's health and the end of his work on the *Prison Notebooks*.

July 25, 1935: Seventh Congress of the Comintern, which puts in place the policy of Popular Fronts.

August 24, 1935: Gramsci leaves Formia to be hospitalized that same day at the Quisisana clinic in Rome, run by Professor Puccinelli.

April 25, 1937: The end of conditional release. Gramsci becomes a free citizen.

April 25, 1937: Gramsci likely suffers a stroke.

April 27, 1937: Gramsci dies at 4:10 in the morning.

Appendix A
Family Tree of the Schucht Family

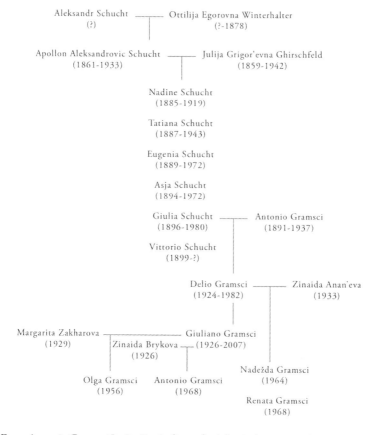

Aleksandr Schucht — Ottilija Egorovna Winterhalter
(?)   (?-1878)

Apollon Aleksandrovic Schucht — Julija Grigor'evna Ghirschfeld
(1861-1933)   (1859-1942)

Nadine Schucht
(1885-1919)

Tatiana Schucht
(1887-1943)

Eugenia Schucht
(1889-1972)

Asja Schucht
(1894-1972)

Giulia Schucht — Antonio Gramsci
(1896-1980)   (1891-1937)

Vittorio Schucht
(1899-?)

Delio Gramsci — Zinaida Anan'eva
(1924-1982)   (1933)

Margarita Zakharova — Giuliano Gramsci
(1929)   (1926-2007)
Zinaida Brykova
(1926)

Olga Gramsci   Antonio Gramsci   Nadežda Gramsci
(1956)   (1968)   (1964)

Renata Gramsci
(1968)

From Antonio Gramsci Jr., *La Storia di una famiglia rivoluzionaria. Antonio Gramsci e gli Schucht tra la Russia e l'Italia* (Rome: Editori Riuniti, 2014), 27.
  NB: *The Schuchts were Gramsci's family by marriage.*

Appendix B

Overview of Gramsci's Visits and Visitors between May 1927 and His Death in April 1937

Place and Time	Tatiana	Carlo	Gennaro	Sraffa	Others
Milan, May 1927	Came to live in Milan				
Summer				1 visit	Mario
September 1927– January 1928	Frequent visits				
Trial	1 visit				
Turi 1928					Priest (several visits)
December	A few visits				
April 1929	1 visit				
November		1 visit			
December	Moved to Turi				
1930	Several visits				
June	1 visit		1 visit		
July			1 visit		
October		1 visit			
March 1931		1 visit			
August		1 visit		Attempted visit	
May 1932		1 visit			

(continued)

(*continued*)

Place and Time	Tatiana	Carlo	Gennaro	Sraffa	Others
January 1933	In Turin until the summer				Dr. Arcangeli (March)
August	Several visits	Several visits			
Civitavecchia November	1 visit				
Formia	1 visit per week	A few visits		A few visits	
Rome 1935–1937	Uninterrupted presence	Several visits		Several visits	

From Antonio Gramsci, *Cahiers de prison 1, 2, 3, 4 et 5*, ed. Robert Paris (Paris: Gallimard, 1996), 67.

Notes

Chapter One

1. Manlio Brigaglia, "Il sogno dell'autonomia," in *Storia della Sardegna: Dal Settecento a oggi*, vol. 2, ed. Manlio Brigaglia, Attilio Mastino, and Gian Giacomo Ortu (Rome-Bari: Laterza, 2006), 112.

2. Gennaro was born in Ghilarza in 1884. Grazietta (1887), Emma (1889), and Antonio (January 22, 1891) were all born in Ales. Mario (1893), Teresina (1895), and Carlo (1897) were born in Sorgono. After Carlo was born, the family decided to return to live in Ghilarza.

3. Antonio Gramsci to his mother, Giuseppina Marcias, June 15, 1931, *Letters from Prison*, ed. Frank Rosengarten, trans. Raymond Rosenthal, 2 vols. (New York: Columbia University Press, 1994), 2:40 (hereafter *LFP*). Unless otherwise specified, the original Italian versions of Gramsci's letters can be found in Giuseppe Fiori, *Antonio Gramsci. Vita attraverso le lettere* (Turin: Einaudi, 1994).

4. Antonio Gramsci to his father, Francesco Gramsci, May 24, 1910, in Antonio Gramsci, *A Great and Terrible World: The Pre-prison Letters, 1908–1926*, trans. Derek Boothman (London: Lawrence and Wishart, 2014), 73.

5. Antonio Gramsci to his father, February 10, 1910, ibid., 72.

6. The expression *padre-padrone* (father and boss) was used by Antonio Gramsci in a letter addressed to his father on November 15, 1911: "Fathers should not be fathers for nothing, but we know you're the boss and not the father." Cited in Fiori, *Vita attraverso*, 23.

7. Antonio Gramsci to Tatiana Schucht, January 30, 1933, in *LFP*, 2:261–62. For the Italian, see Aurelio Lepre, *Il prigioniero: Vita di Antonio Gramsci* (Rome-Bari: Laterza, 1998), 3–4.

8. Palmiro Togliatti, *Gramsci* (Florence: Patenti Editore, 1955), 47–48.

9. The reader will forgive this neologism translated directly from the Italian.

10. Antonio Gramsci, *Quaderni del carcere*, vol. 3 (Turin: Einaudi, 1964), notebook 23, §54.

11. Jean-Yves Frétigné, "Une réponse scientifique et politique à la thèse de Niceforo sur l'infériorité des méridionaux," in *Bolletino Bibliografico e rassegna archivistica e di studi storici della Sardegna e delle comunità sarde fuori dell'isola* 1 (2001): 45–62.

12. For more on Arturo Labriola and Antonio Labriola, see chapters 2 and 3.

13. Piero Gobetti, *On Liberal Revolution*, trans. William McCuaig (New Haven: Yale University Press, 2008), 20.

Chapter Two

1. Antonio Gramsci to his father, November 15, 1911, in Giuseppe Fiori, *Antonio Gramsci. Vita attraverso le lettere* (Turin: Einaudi, 1994), 23.

2. Jules Vallès, dedication to *Le Bachelier* (Paris: Georges Charpentier, 1881).

3. Cited in Giuseppe Fiori, *Antonio Gramsci: Life of a Revolutionary* (New York: Dutton, 1971), 98. For the Italian, see *Vita di Antonio Gramsci* (Bari-Rome: Laterza, 2008), 106.

4. Antonio Gramsci to his sister, Grazietta Gramsci, 1916, in Antonio Gramsci, *A Great and Terrible World: The Pre-prison Letters, 1908–1926*, trans. Derek Boothman (London: Lawrence and Wishart, 2014), 95. For the Italian, see Fiori, *Vita attraverso*. [English translation adapted slightly to match author's original. —Trans.]

5. Antonio Gramsci, *Quaderni del carcere*, vol. 2 (Turin: Einaudi, 1964), notebook 15, §19.

6. Antonio Gramsci to his mother, Giuseppina Marcias, January 13, 1913, *Great and Terrible World*, 87. For the Italian, see Fiori, *Vita attraverso*, 29.

7. Antonio Gramsci to Tatiana Schucht, March 19, 1927, *Letters from Prison*, ed. Frank Rosengarten, trans. Raymond Rosenthal, 2 vols. (New York: Columbia University Press, 1994), 1:84. For the Italian, see Fiori, *Vita attraverso*, 162.

8. G. Schirru, "Linguistique et philosophie de la praxis chez Gramsci," in *Gramsci da un secolo all'altro*, ed. R. Descendre and F. Frosini, *Laboratoire italien* 18 (2016).

9. Gramsci to Tatiana Schucht, February 23, 1931, *LFP*, 2:15. In November 1920, Gramsci had written an article titled "True Words for a Bourgeois" that had been published in *Avanti!* in which he attacked Cosmo's political positions in an extremely violent tone that had shocked his former professor, to the point that he supposedly stayed home weeping for an entire day. Above all, Cosmo was profoundly saddened by the last sentence of the article: "Frankly, we say to him [Cosmo] that all the respect and all the affection his students had for him have turned into great pity and profound scorn."

10. Geoffrey Hunt, "Did Annibale Pastore Influence Gramsci?" *Thesis Eleven* 8, no. 1 (February 1984): 133–39.

11. Jean-Yves Frétigné, "De la traduction comme effort pour préciser les concepts: L'exemple des notions de liberismo/liberalismo et de questione meridionale/meridionalismo," in *Histoire et pratiques de la traduction*, ed. S. Crogiez-Pétrequin and P. Pasteur (Rouen: PURH, 2010), 73–85.

12. Gramsci, "Contro il feudalismo economico" (Against Economic Feudalism), *Il Grido del Popolo*, August 19, 1916.

13. Gramsci, "Socialism and Actualist Philosophy," *Il Grido del Popolo*, February 9, 1918, included in *Pre-prison Writings*, ed. Richard Bellamy, trans. Virginia Cox (Cambridge: Cambridge University Press, 1994), 50.

14. On this book as representative of Gentilian thought, see Jean-Yves Frétigné, *Les conceptions éducatives de Giovanni Gentile. Entre élitisme et Fascisme* (Paris: L'Harmattan, 2006).

15. On this point, see in particular the works of Domenico Losurdo.

16. Benedetto Croce, *A History of Italy, 1871–1915* (New York: Russell & Russell, 1963), 237.

17. Named for the deputy Ottorino Gentiloni, president of the Catholic Voters Union.

18. The title of a famous pamphlet that Salvemini published in 1910.

19. Giuseppe Bevione was the first Italian journalist to be recognized as a special envoy.

20. Not to be confused with the newspaper of the same name founded by Gramsci in 1924; see chapter 6.

21. This statement would have been made to Salvemini by Ottavio Pastore when Pastore met him in Florence to convince him to participate in the Turin election. Statement reported by Gramsci in "Some Aspects of the Southern Question" (October 1926), in *The Antonio Gramsci Reader: Selected Writings, 1916–1935*, ed. David Forgacs (New York: New York University Press, 2000), 171.

22. Ivanoe Bonomi (1873–1951) and Leonida Bissolati (1857–1920) then founded the Italian Socialist Reformist Party.

23. Article published May 27, 1913, and cited in Paolo Spriano, *Storia di Torino operaia e socialista* (Turin: Einaudi, 1972), 233.

24. Cited in ibid., 225.

25. Palmiro Togliatti, *Gramsci* (Florence: Patenti Editore, 1955), 117.

26. Like Gramsci, all three of them were scholarship students. On the other hand, unlike the young Sardinian, all three of them earned their *Laurea*, Togliatti in political economy in 1915, Tasca in letters in 1917, and Terracini, the youngest of them, in financial sciences in 1919.

27. *Critica Sociale* was the bimonthly review of reformist socialism founded in 1891 by Turati and his companion Anna Kuliscioff on the model of Karl Kautsky's *Die Neue Zeit*.

28. Cited in Spriano, *Storia di Torino*, 253.

29. In Turin three of the five deputies were Socialists.

30. P. Milza, *Mussolini* (Paris: Fayard, 1999), 174.

31. A. D'Orsi, *Gramsciana. Saggi su Antonio Gramsci* (Modena: Mucchi Editore, 2014), 106.

32. Ibid., 107.

33. The Italian Communist organization was not called the Italian Communist Party (PCI) until 1943. Before that, it was the Communist Party of Italy (PCdI).

Chapter Three

1. It concerns a series of articles that were published, for the first time, in August and September 1935 in the review *Il Mondo*.

2. Cited in Robert Paris, "Introduction," Antonio Gramsci, *Écrits politiques 1914–1920*, vol. 1 (Paris: Gallimard, 1981), 20.

3. The Antonelliana building is one of the largest masonry buildings in Europe. Opened in 1889, it was named after the architect Alessandro Antonelli (1798–1888). It was originally intended as a synagogue before the city bought it and made it into the public Museum of the Risorgimento in 1908. As a symbol of the city of Turin, the Antonelliana dome has been the home of the extraordinary Museum of Cinema since July 2000.

4. He had studied Gentile's pedagogy along with his professor Annibale Pastore (see chapter 2).

5. Gramsci was referring to the very negative reception of *A Doll's House*, a play he wrote about in several articles and spoke about in a lecture to militant Socialists. Antonio Gramsci, "Morality and Standards (Ibsen's *A Doll's House* at the Carignano)," *Avanti!*, Turin edition, March 22, 1917, included in *Selections from Cultural Writings*, trans. William Boelhower (London: Lawrence and Wishart, 1985), 71.

6. *Ardito* was the Italian term for elite combatants during World War I, such as Captain Conan in the eponymous novel by Roger Vercel. These combatants infiltrated enemy lines in order to pull off spectacular actions.

7. Aurelio Lepre, *Il prigioniero: Vita di Antonio Gramsci* (Rome-Bari: Laterza, 1998), 18.

8. Giuseppe Fiori, *Vita di Antonio Gramsci* (Bari: Laterza, 1965), 121.

9. Antonio Gramsci, "Three Principles, Three Orders," *La Città Futura*, February 11, 1917, in *History, Philosophy and Culture in the Young Gramsci*, ed. Pedro Cavalcanti and Paul Piccone (Candor, NY: Telos Press, 1975), 70.

10. Ibid., 75.

11. We have borrowed this typology from Leonardo Rapone's 2011 monograph, suggestively titled *Cinque anni che paiono secoli. A. Gramsci dal socialismo*

al comunismo (1914–1919) [Five Years That Seemed like Centuries: Antonio Gramsci, from Socialism to Communism (1914–1919)] (Rome: Carocci, 2011).

12. The latter two themes—the Bolshevik Revolution and the one hoped for in Italy—are examined in the last section of the chapter.

13. Antonio Gramsci, "Il paese di Pulchinella," in the Piedmont edition of *Avanti!*, January 30, 1919.

14. Antonio Gramsci, "The Italian Catholics," *Avanti!*, Piedmont edition, December 22, 1918, in *History, Philosophy and Culture in the Young Gramsci*, 113.

15. Antonio Gramsci, "Torino città di provincia," *Avanti!*, August 7, 1918.

16. Antonio Gramsci, "Astrattismo e intransigenza," *Il Grido del Popolo*, May 11, 1918.

17. B. Croce, "Per bene intenderci," *La Critica*, January 20, 1916.

18. Antonio Gramsci, "La Lega delle nazioni," *Il Grido del Popolo*, January 19, 1918.

19. Antonio Gramsci, "Vita politica internazionale," *L'Ordine Nuovo*, May 15, 1919.

20. A term used to designate a refusal to join the reformist fight for minimum gains, in favor of revolutionary action to create radical changes.

21. It cost 7.50 lire to feed a household in 1917, as opposed to only 3.50 in 1914.

22. The Sassari brigade, exclusively made up of soldiers from Sardinia, distinguished itself during World War I on the Asiago Plateau. The absurdity of the war, along with the despair and heroism of these men, was immortalized in the novelistic account of Emilio Lussu (1890–1975), *Un anno sull'altipiano* (1938). This book was twice adapted for film: *Gli uomini contro* by Francesco Rosi in 1970 and *Torneranno i prati* by Ermanno Olmi in 2014.

23. Antonio Gramsci, "La dittatura democratica," *Il Grido del Popolo*, October 19, 1918.

24. Account cited in Paolo Spriano, *Storia di Torino operaia e socialista* (Turin: Einaudi, 1972), 460.

25. Director of *Il Resto del Carlino*, the oldest daily newspaper in Bologna, before heading up *Il Secolo*, the main newspaper among radical and republican circles.

26. Antonio Gramsci, "Il Sillabo ed Hegel," *Il Grido del Popolo*, January 15, 1916, cited in Gramsci, *Scritti giovanili* (Turin: Einaudi, 1975), 15.

27. Antonio Gramsci, "The *Syllabus* and Hegel," cited in Dante Germino, *Antonio Gramsci: Architect of a New Politics* (Baton Rouge: Louisiana State University Press, 1990), 37–38.

28. On this relationship between antipositivism and anti-Giolittism, see Jean-Yves Frétigné, "La leçon des faits ou la fuite en avant. L'opposition entre les

intellectuels giolittiens et les intellectuels anti-giolittiens en Italie (1903–1913)," *Storiografia* 15 (2011): 271–78.

29. Rapone, *Cinque anni che paiono secoli*, 272.

30. Antonio Gramsci, "Notes on the Russian Revolution," *Il Grido del Popolo*, April 29, 1917, from *Selections from Political Writings*, vol. 1, (1910–1920), ed. Quintin Hoare, trans. John Matthews (London: Lawrence and Wishart, 1977), 28.

31. Ibid., 1:29.

32. Ibid.

33. Socialist journalist, onetime director of *Avanti!*, eminent representative of the reformist camp, Oddino Morgari was considered the diplomat of the PSI.

34. Antonio Gramsci, "The Revolution against 'Capital,'" *Avanti!*, December 24, 1917, from *Selections from Political Writings*, 1:35.

35. Antonio Gramsci, "The Russian Maximalists," *Il Grido del Popolo*, July 28, 1917, *Selections from Political Writings*, 1:31.

36. Ibid., 1:32.

37. Cited in Spriano, *Storia di Torino*, 460.

38. Antonio Gramsci, "Revolution against 'Capital,'" 34.

39. Ibid.

40. Ibid., 36.

41. Claudio Treves, "Lénine, Martov e . . . noi," *Critica Sociale*, January 1–15, 1918.

42. Amadeo Bordiga, "Gli insegnamenti della nuova storia," *Avanti!*, February 16, 1918.

43. Antonio Gramsci, "The Constitutional Assembly and the Soviets," *Il Grido del Popolo*, January 26, 1918, in *History, Philosophy and Culture in the Young Gramsci*, 146.

Chapter Four

1. On *La Voce*, see chapter 3.

2. Paolo Spriano, *L'Ordine Nuovo e i consigli di fabbrica* (Turin: Einaudi, 1971), 35.

3. It's hard to see Togliatti's choice to sign his articles with the name Empedocle as anything other than a homage to Giovanni Gentile, another Sicilian philosopher.

4. Antonio Gramsci, "On the *L'Ordine Nuovo* Program," *L'Ordine Nuovo*, August 14, 1920, in *Selections from Political Writings*, vol. 1, (1910–1920), ed. Quintin Hoare, trans. John Matthews (London: Lawrence and Wishart, 1977), 293.

5. Sergio Soave, "Angelo Tasca Communista," *Studi storici*, July–September 2007, cited in Catherine Rançon, *Angelo Tasca. Biographie intellectuelle*, thesis, University of Paris 1 and Università degli Studi della Tuscia di Viterbo, 2011, 106.

6. Gramsci, "On the *L'Ordine Nuovo* Program," 292.

7. Gramsci, "Workers' Democracy," *L'Ordine Nuovo*, June 21, 1919, *Selections from Political Writings*, 1:66.

8. Piero Gobetti, "Storia dei comunisti torinesi scritta da un liberale," *Rivoluzione Liberale*, 1922.

9. All the quotations in this paragraph are from Gramsci's article "Workers' Democracy," *L'Ordine Nuovo*, June 21, 1919, *Selections from Political Writings*, 1:65–68.

10. See chapter 2.

11. Antonio Gramsci, *Écrits politiques*, vol. 1, ed. Robert Paris (Paris: Gallimard, 1974), 434. This quotation is Paris's own commentary.

12. John Reed, *The Weekly People*, May 11, 1918, cited in Henry Kuhn, "Reminiscences of Daniel De Leon," in *Daniel De Leon, The Man and His Work, a Symposium* (New York: Socialist Labor Party, 1920), 81.

13. See chapter 3.

14. Antonio Gramsci, "Cronico," *L'Ordine Nuovo*, October 11, 1919.

15. Cited in Spriano, *L'Ordine Nuovo*, 84.

16. Cited in ibid.

17. Amadeo Bordiga, "Per la costituzione dei Consigli operai in Italia," *Il Soviet*, January 4, 1920.

18. Armando Borghi, "I Consigli di fabbrica e noi," *Guerra di Classe*, December 6, 1919.

19. Rançon, *Angelo Tasca*, 110.

20. Angelo Tasca, "I valori politici e sindacali dei consigli di fabbrica" (Turin: Tipografia Alleanza, 1920), 5 (short eighteen-page essay reproduced in *L'Ordine Nuovo* on May 29, 1920).

21. Gramsci, "Some Aspects of the Southern Question," *Pre-prison Writings*, ed. Richard Bellamy, trans. Virginia Cox (Cambridge: Cambridge University Press, 1994), 314.

22. Gramsci, "On the *L'Ordine Nuovo* Program," *Selections from Political Writings*, 1:292–93.

23. Historians estimate that more than five hundred thousand people participated in the April 1920 struggle.

24. This expression, which comes from Tasca's book *The Rise of Italian Fascism, 1918–1922*, first published in 1938, summarizes the actions of the Fascists from summer 1920 on, when the squads terrorized militants and Socialist and Communist elected officials, with the passive and sometimes active support of the bourgeoisie, who feared a revolution that never took place.

25. Cited in Spriano, *L'Ordine Nuovo*, 100–101 n. 4.

26. Antonio Gramsci, "Towards a Renewal of the Socialist Party," *L'Ordine Nuovo*, May 8, 1920, in *Selections from Political Writings*, 1:190–94.

27. Lenin, *Lenin's Collected Works*, vol. 31, trans. Julius Katzer (Moscow: Progress Publishers, 1965), 184–201.

28. Born in 1895, Mauro Scoccimarro joined the PSI in 1917 before becoming one of the principal leaders of the PCdI. Like Gramsci, he was arrested in 1926. Released in 1943, he participated in the Resistance. He served as minister of finance from 1945 to 1947, after which he became a regularly elected senator.

29. Antonio Gramsci to Mauro Scoccimarro, January 5, 1924, in Antonio Gramsci, *A Great and Terrible World: The Pre-prison Letters, 1908–1926*, trans. Derek Boothman (London: Lawrence and Wishart, 2014), 199.

30. Antonio Gramsci, "The Occupation," *Avanti!*, Piedmont edition, September 20, 1920, in *Selections from Political Writings*, 1:327.

31. Antonio Gramsci, "Men of Flesh and Blood," *L'Ordine Nuovo*, May 8, 1921, available online at https://www.marxists.org/archive/gramsci/1921/05/flesh-blood.htm.

32. The seventh condition explicitly mentioned the necessity of expelling Turati and Modigliani.

33. Spriano, *L'Ordine Nuovo*, 126.

34. The centrists were militants who held the majority at the time and who supported the Third International without wanting to abandon the PSI.

35. Antonio Gramsci and Palmiro Togliatti, "The Lyons Theses," *Selections from Political Writings*, vol. 2, *(1921–1926)*, ed. and trans. Quintin Hoare (London: Lawrence and Wishart, 1978), section 30.

36. Guido Liguori and Pasquale Voza, eds., *Dizionario Gramsciano, 1926–1937* (Rome: Carocci, 2009), 597–98.

37. Antonio Gramsci, "Einaudi, or the Liberal Utopia," *Avanti!*, May 25, 1919.

38. Ibid.

39. Antonio Gramsci, "Il compagno G. M. Serrati e le generazioni del socialismo italiano," *L'Unità*, May 14, 1926.

40. Cain Haller was born in Poland in 1881. In Italy, where he completed his studies, he took the name Chiarini. As a representative of the Comintern, he was present for the first meeting of the Communist Fraction of the PSI in Imola.

41. Lenin probably learned of Gramsci's text from Degott, a Comintern agent who was active in France and Italy in 1919 and 1920. A copy of the article was given to him by Riedel, another Comintern agent. This episode demonstrates Gramsci's early ties to the Third International.

42. Grigori Zinoviev, *Le Lotte dell' Internazionale comunista* (Rome: Libreria editrice del PCdI, 1921), 30.

43. Cited in Paolo Spriano, *Storia del Partito comunista italiano*, vol. 1 (Turin: Einaudi, 1967), 116.

44. This was a real increase compared with his former salaries, but it is important to take account of the marked inflation in the immediate postwar period.

45. Cited in Giuseppe Fiori, *Antonio Gramsci: Life of a Revolutionary*, trans. Tom Nairn (London: Verso, 1990), 151.

46. Following the initiative of two ex-lieutenants, Argo Secondari and Umberto Beer, the Arditi del Popolo movement came together in March 1920 to organize armed resistance to Fascist violence. *L'Ordine Nuovo* demonstrated interest and sympathy for this movement, which had several thousand followers organized into hundred-man units. This initiative also interested the Comintern, which lamented the sectarianism of the PCdI with respect to it. Ruggero Grieco's flimsy analysis criticized the Arditi del Popolo for being manipulated by Nitti and Giolitti got him this devastating response from a member of the Comintern who remains anonymous but was surely eminent: "For our movement, it is always more advantageous to make mistakes with the masses than to keep our distance from them." Cited in Spriano, *Storia del Partito comunista italiano*, 1:151.

47. The PCdI had its own militia.

48. Cited in Spriano, *Storia del Partito comunista italiano*, 1:158.

49. This phrase is reported by Gramsci in "Cinque anni di vita del partito," *L'Unità*, February 24, 1926. On this date, as we will see later on, Gramsci lamented that the PCdI had not followed this strategy.

50. Montagnana to Togliatti, July 14, 1923, cited in Spriano, *Storia del Partito comunista italiano*, 1:190 n. 2.

Chapter Five

1. A letter (August 24, 1924) that Gramsci and Ambrogi sent to the PCdI leadership reads: "taking steps toward Serrati means making the International make a right turn that would discredit all the work the PCdI has been doing."

2. Angelo Tasca, "Schema di tesi della minoranza del Comitato Centrale del PCD'I," *Lo Stato Operaio*, May 15, 1924.

3. In 1912, only a minority of reformists who supported the war in Libya had chosen to break away, under the leadership of Leonida Bissolati and Ivanoe Bonomi, forming the Italian Reformist Socialist Party.

4. [I have chosen to use the first names of the Schucht family members as they are transliterated by the International Gramsci Society. —Trans.]

5. See the family tree in appendix A.

6. Acronym for the Soviet political police that succeeded the Cheka in February 1922. It would be absorbed by the NKVD in 1934.

7. Antonio Gramsci to Julia Schucht, December 16, 1923, in Antonio Gramsci, *A Great and Terrible World: The Pre-prison Letters, 1908–1926*, trans. Derek Boothman (London: Lawrence and Wishart, 2014), 187. For the Italian, see Giuseppe Fiori, *Antonio Gramsci. Vita attraverso le lettere* (Turin: Einaudi, 1994), 48.

8. Gramsci to Julia, January 13, 1924, *Great and Terrible World*, 208. For the Italian, see Fiori, *Vita attraverso*, 50.

9. Gramsci to Julia, March 15, 1924, *Great and Terrible World*, 250. For the Italian, see Fiori, *Vita attraverso*, 60.

10. A letter of June 15, 1931, cited in Antonio A. Santucci, ed., *Antonio Gramsci. Lettere, 1908–1926* (Turin: Einaudi, 1992), 426.

11. Antonio's letters to Delio and Giuliano were published in Italy in 1966 by Editori Riuniti, and a French anthology was also published by Éditions Messidoe-La Farandole in 1987 titled *L'Arbre du hérisson* [The Hedgehog's Tree].

12. Antonio Gramsci Jr., *La Storia di una famiglia rivoluzionaria. Antonio Gramsci e gli Schucht tra la Russia e l'Italia* (Rome: Editori Riuniti University Press, 2014), 135. Delio became an officer in the Soviet army, Giuliano—the father of the author of this work—became a music professor. They took several trips to Italy for commemorations in their father's honor, but they kept their distance from any attempts by the PCdI to use their name.

13. On this point, see J.-P. Potier, *Les lectures italiennes de Marx, 1883–1983* (Lyon: Presses universitaires de Lyon, 1986), 113–30. To Graziadei, the Marxist theory of value was wrong, but that of surplus labor remained valid.

14. Beyond Tasca and Graziadei, this minority included the deputy Nicola Bombacci; Giuseppe Berti, the secretary of the Italian Communist Youth Federation; Smeraldo Presutti, secretary of the Chamber of Labor of Castellamare Adriatico; Giovanni Roveda, secretary of the Turin Chamber of Labor; Giuseppe Vota, secretary of the League of Woodworkers; and the journalists Ottavio Pastore et Nicola Cilla. They were all present at the Fourth Congress of the Comintern.

15. Cited by Paolo Spriano, *Storia del Partito comunista italiano*, vol. 1 (Turin: Einaudi, 1967), 250.

16. Character from the commedia dell'arte who has given his name to the most famous of Piedmontese sweets.

17. Excerpt from the summary of the Comintern meeting, cited in Spriano, *Storia del Partito comunista italiano*, 1:250.

18. Ibid., 1:252.

19. There were 5,361 votes for the Nenni-Vella antifusionist motion compared with 3,968 for the one proposed by Constantino Lazzari in favor of fusion with the PCdI.

20. Excerpt from the speech Zinoviev gave during the Enlarged ECCI meeting on June 1923, reproduced in *Lo Stato Operaio*, April 24, 1924.

21. Ruggero Grieco, "Bordiga," *Il Lavoratore*, March 7, 1923.

22. Bianco, Bordiga, Gennari, Parodi, Ravera, Tasca, Terracini, Scoccimarro.

23. "Anguilleggiato," the neologism for "undulating like an eel," can be found in the letter Gramsci sent to Togliatti and Scoccimarro on March 1, 1924.

24. Gramsci to Togliatti, January 27, 1924.

25. A note from Gramsci (June 1923) to the Comintern, cited in Spriano, *Storia del Partito comunista italiano*, 1:293.

26. Ibid., 1:279.

27. The principal figures in the *terzini* group were Malatesta, Maffi, Riboldi, and Serrati.

28. Gramsci to the PCdI leadership, September 12, 1923. See *Great and Terrible World*, 170.

29. Ibid., 171.

30. It disappeared in 1930 and was replaced with the International Agrarian Bureau.

31. Though Scoccimarro was not one of *L'ON*'s founders, he was one of its editors when it became a daily in 1921.

32. Was this decision the result of an act of clemency on the part of the government to celebrate the first anniversary of the March on Rome and/or a concern on the part of the judiciary to affirm its independence (for the last time)?

33. This third run of *L'ON* was published between March 1924 and April 1925.

34. Antonio Gramsci, *Écrits politiques*, vol. 3, ed. Robert Paris (Paris: Gallimard, 1980), 367n.

35. The *Listone*, literally "big lists," was a national bloc that called for populists and liberals prepared to collaborate with the Fascist majority to merge. Two former prime ministers, Vittorio Emanuele Orlando and Antonio Salandra, were part of the *Listone*.

36. The PCdI came out with more votes and more elected officials than the old Italian Republican Party, the constitutional oppositions, or Amendola's group, but it did worse than the PPI, the PSU, and the PSI, which had 39, 24, and 22 representatives, respectively.

37. Gramsci to Zino Zini, April 2, 1924. See *Great and Terrible World*, 271.

38. Antonio Gramsci, "Against Pessimism," *L'ON*, March 15, 1924, in *Pre-prison Writings*, ed. Richard Bellamy, trans. Virginia Cox (Cambridge: Cambridge University Press, 1994), 257–58.

39. Ibid., 258.

40. Ibid., 259.

41. Gramsci to Togliatti, Scoccimarro, and Leonetti, March 21, 1924. See *Great and Terrible World*, 253.

42. Jean-Pierre Potier, *Piero Sraffa: Unorthodox Economist (1898–1983)* (London: Routledge, 1991), 21.

43. Ibid.

44. Ibid., 22.

45. Spriano, *Storia del Partito comunista italiano*, 1:357.

46. Quoted in Potier, *Piero Sraffa*, 22. In the letter of March 21, 1924, to Leonetti, Togliatti, and Scoccimarro, which we have already cited, the Sardinian thinker was more nuanced, judging that Piero Sraffa was still a Marxist, and

that they should keep in contact with him "to straighten him out and make him an active element of our Party, to which he will be useful in many ways, now as well as later."

47. Ibid.

48. Antonio Gramsci, "Problems of Today and Tomorrow," *Selections from Political Writings*, vol. 2, *(1921–1926)*, ed. and trans. Quintin Hoare (London: Lawrence and Wishart, 1978), 235.

49. Antonio Gramsci, "The Mezzogiorno and Fascism," *Pre-prison Writings*, 260.

50. Ibid., 262.

51. Ibid.

52. Ibid., 263–64.

Chapter Six

1. Gramsci to Julia, July 21, 1924, in Antonio Gramsci, *A Great and Terrible World: The Pre-prison Letters, 1908–1926*, trans. Derek Boothman (London: Lawrence and Wishart, 2014), 316.

2. Cited in Paolo Spriano, *Storia del Partito comunista italiano*, vol. 1 (Turin: Einaudi, 1967), 358.

3. Ibid., 1:377.

4. Unlike Buozzi, who was resolutely anti-Fascist, D'Aragona and Colombino were ready to give in to the siren call of Fascism.

5. M. Ostenc, *Mussolini. Une histoire du fascisme italien* (Paris: Ellipses, 2013), 80.

6. Laws against associations (May 1, 1925); law purifying the administration (June 19, 1925); Mussolini was no longer responsible to parliament but only to the sovereign, he could enact decrees without the input of the Chamber (December 2, 1925); suppression of the Mayor's duties and replacement by a *podestà* (February 4, 1926); recognizing only the one Fascist union and outlawing the right to strike (April 3, 1926); forbidding all political parties except for the PNF (November 5, 1926); forfeiture of the parliamentary mandate for all deputies of opposing parties and establishment of the Special Tribunal for the Defense of the State (November 26, 1926).

7. Cited in Spriano, *Storia del Partito comunista italiano*, 1:398.

8. After World War II, G. Li Causi would become one of the prominent figures of Sicilian Communism and a hero in the fight against the Mafia. See Jean-Yves Frétigné, *Histoire de la Sicile des origines à nos jours* (Paris: Fayard, 2009), 418–44.

9. Cited in Giuseppe Fiori, *Antonio Gramsci: Life of a Revolutionary*, trans. Tom Nairn (New York: Verso, 1990), 185.

10. Jean-Yves Frétigné, "Le Panthéon des Italiens," in *L'Italie contemporaine de 1945 à nos jours*, ed. M. Lazar (Paris: Fayard, 2009), 68–81.

11. Spriano, *Storia del Partito comunista italiano*, 1:434.

12. A real occasion for Comintern leadership and decision-making, the meetings, still referred to as congresses, of the Enlarged Executive Committee of the Comintern marked all the decisive moments during the first years of the Comintern. The first congress was held in February 1921, the second in June of the same year, the third, which we have studied in detail, in June 1923, the fourth in June 1925, and the fifth in March and April 1925.

13. The article would be published nonetheless in the pages of *L'Unità* on July 4, 1925.

14. Antonio Gramsci, *La situazione interna del Partito e i compiti del prossimo congresso*, May 11, 1925, cited in Spriano, *Storia del Partito comunista italiano*, 1:451.

15. Ibid.

16. Gramsci to Julia, May 1925, *Great and Terrible World*, 341–42.

17. Spriano, *Storia del Partito comunista italiano*, 1:453.

18. When he was one of the main figures of the maximalist wing of the PSI, he had managed, at the Ancona congress (1912) to exclude Freemasons from the Socialist movement.

19. Antonio Gramsci, *Contro la legge sulle associazioni segrete*, speech before the Italian Parliament (Chamber of Deputies), May 16, 1925, trans. Michael Carley, https://www.marxists.org/archive/gramsci/1925/05/speech.htm. We have not included the notations indicating the reactions of Fascist deputies. It should be noted that this speech was reproduced in *L'Unità* on May 23, 1925, and was considered a pertinent analysis of Italian Freemasonry, and to that end has been studied by the principal specialists of its history: Aldo A. Mola, *Storia della Massoneria italiana dalle origini ai nostri giorni* (Milan: Bompiani, 1993), 542–47, and Fulvio Conti, *Massoneria italiana dal Risorgimento al fascismo* (Bologna: Il Mulino, 2003), 315–22.

20. Antonio Gramsci, "Comunicato del comitato esecutivo: Il partito combatterà con energia ogni ritorno alle concezioni organizzative della socialdemocrazia," *L'Unità*, June 7, 1925, included in "Gramsci tra Marxismo e idealismo," https://www.marxists.org/italiano/damen/gramsci/5.htm#p2e. Cain Haller, alias A. Chiarini, the Comintern's representative in Italy, would emphasize "the beneficial nature" of this article in a text that was published in *La Correspondance Internationale* on August 19, 1925.

21. Spriano, *Storia del Partito comunista italiano*, 1:490.

22. Ibid., 1:497.

23. Maffi and Serrati, also members of the CC, were quick to rally to Gramsci's motion.

24. As we mentioned in the previous chapter, Bordiga was part of the executive body of the international organization at the time.

25. Ruggero Grieco, "I lavori del VI Plenum del CE della Internazionale comunista," in *L'Unità*, June 27, 1926, cited in Paolo Spriano, *Storia del Partito comunista italiano*, vol. 2 (Turin: Einaudi, 1969), 17.

26. Antonio Gramsci, "Some Aspects of the Southern Question," *Selections from Political Writings*, vol. 2, *(1921–1926)*, ed. and trans. Quintin Hoare (London: Lawrence and Wishart, 1978), 445.

27. Ibid.

28. On Salvemini and the significance of this southern intellectual's candidacy in one of the workers' electoral colleges in Turin in 1914, see chapter 2.

29. Gramsci, "Some Aspects of the Southern Question," 447.

30. Here Gramsci takes up his analysis of the two solutions the Italian bourgeoisie used to accomplish the unification of Italy, Giolitti's solution and Salandra's solution, an analysis he had already developed in several articles and his one speech in the Chamber of Deputies.

31. Gramsci, "Some Aspects of the Southern Question," 457.

32. Ibid., 462.

33. Spriano, *Storia del Partito comunista italiano*, 2:38.

34. The first tendency, represented by Rocco, "wants to liquidate the Fascist Party as a political organism and to incorporate into the State apparatus the bourgeois position of strength created by Fascism in its struggles against all the other parties." The second, represented by Farinacci, "sees the Party as its instrument of defense, its Parliament, its democracy. It seeks to put pressure on the government through the Party, to prevent itself from being crushed by Capitalism." Antonio Gramsci, "A Study of the Italian Situation," paper delivered at the meeting of the executive of the PCdI, August 2–3, 1926, in *Pre-prison Writings*, ed. Richard Bellamy, trans. Virginia Cox (Cambridge: Cambridge University Press, 1994), 292.

35. Law on the creation of the Opera nazionale Dopolavoro to organize the leisure activities of adults (May 1, 1925); the signing of the Pact of the Vidoni Palace formalizing the monopoly of the Fascist union and forbidding strikes and lockouts (October 2, 1925); creation of the Opera Nazionale Balilla, charged with indoctrinating young Italians from ages eight to eighteen (April 3, 1926).

36. Gramsci, "We and the Republican Concentration," *L'Unità*, October 13, 1926, in *Selections from Political Writings*, 2:425.

37. "I tre rivali," in *La Stampa*, August 25, 1926, cited in Spriano, *Storia del Partito comunista italiano*, 2:46.

38. Cited in the introduction to Antonio Gramsci, *Selections from the Prison Notebooks*, trans. and ed. Quintin Hoare and Geoffrey Nowell Smith (London: Lawrence and Wishart, 1989), lxxxv.

39. Antonio Gramsci, "On the Situation in the Bolshevik Party," in *Selections from Political Writings*, 2:426.

40. Ibid., 2:427.

41. [From this point on, the Communist Party in the Soviet Union is interchangeably referred to by the acronyms RCP (Russian Communist Party) and CPSU (Communist Party of the Soviet Union). Though the Soviet Union was established in 1922, the name CPSU did not become the official party name until 1952, though it was used by Gramsci and others long before that date. —Trans.]

42. Antonio Gramsci, "On the Situation in the Bolshevik Party," in *Selections from Political Writings*, 2:428.

43. Ibid., 2:428–29.

44. Ibid., 2:430.

45. Ibid., 2:431.

46. Ibid., 2:432.

47. Ibid.

48. Togliatti to Gramsci, October 18, 1926, in *Selections from Political Writings*, 2:432.

49. Ibid., 2:322.

50. Ibid., 2:233.

51. Ibid.

52. Gramsci to Togliatti, October 26, 1926, *Great and Terrible World*, 378.

53. Ibid., 378–79.

54. Ibid., 379.

55. Ibid., 381.

56. Mauro Canali, *Il tradimento. Gramsci, Togliatti e la verità negata* (Venice: Marsilio, 2013), 82.

Chapter Seven

1. It's possible to consult the original *Verbale di perquisizione domiciliare nell'alloggio di Gramsci* in Domenico Zucàro, *Vita del carcere di Antonio Gramsci* (Milan-Rome: Edizioni Avanti!, 1954), 105–6.

2. Carmine Senise was particularly tasked with the sector of general and restricted affairs concerning the people on file at the Casellario Politico Centrale (the central files of the police who gathered information on people who were being surveilled for their political or unionist opinions). In this way, he played an important role during the very last year of Gramsci's life.

3. From 1923–25 on, the adjective "totalitarian" appeared in speeches by the anti-Fascist liberals, Democrats, and Christian Democrats, who were aware of the fact that Fascism constituted a break with the liberal system and sought to destroy it. See Olivier Forlin, *Le Fascisme. Historiographie et enjeux mémoriels* (Paris: La Découverte, 2013), 45 and passim.

4. Giuseppe Fiori, *Vita di Antonio Gramsci* (Rome: L'Unità, 1991), 254.

5. From the actual state of the documentation, a certain and final reconstruction of this episode is not possible, and the explanation we've provided is the one agreed upon by the vast majority of historians.

6. The original *Proposta di assegnazione al confino di A. Gramsci* can be consulted in Zucàro, *Vita del carcere*, 106–7.

7. The name given at the time to the chief magistrate of a city-state, named by the prefect, after the Fascist suppression of local elections.

8. Antonio Gramsci, notebook 8, *Selections from the Prison Notebooks*, ed. and trans. Quintin Hoare and Geoffrey Nowell-Smith (New York: International Publishers, 1972), 10.

9. After Gramsci left, Bordiga didn't pursue the adventure, but it was taken up by another militant Communist, Giuseppe Berti, before finally being banned by the authorities in October 1927.

10. Gramsci to Julia and Tatiana Schucht, February 12, 1927, *Letters from Prison*, ed. Frank Rosengarten, trans. Raymond Rosenthal, 2 vols. (New York: Columbia University Press, 1994), 1:70–71 (hereafter *LFP*).

11. See the first note in this chapter.

12. Not to be confused with the Red Week of June 1914, the June 1920 insurrection began with the refusal of soldiers who were garrisoned in the Adriatic city to be sent to fight in Albania.

13. An acronym that has several interpretations: Opera Volontaria per la Repressione dell'Antifascismo (Volunteer work for the repression of anti-Fascism), Organizzazione di Vigilanza e Repressione dell'Antifascismo (Organization for surveillance and repression of anti-Fascism), or Organo di Vigilanza dei Reati Antistatali (Authority for the surveillance of crimes against the state).

14. Dominico Zucàro to Luciano Canfora, February 16, 1989, in Canfora, *Spie, URSS, antifascismo, 1926–1937* (Rome: Salerno Editrice, 2012), 282. Thanks to Ruggero Giacomini, author of *Il Giudice e il prigioniero* (Rome: Castelvecchi, 2014), we have the first well-documented analysis of the figure of Enrico Macis.

15. Antonio Gramsci, *Memoriale di A. Gramsci al Presidente del Tribunale Speciale*, reproduced in Zucàro, *Vita del carcere*, 118.

16. Giuseppe Fiori, *Gramsci, Togliatti, Stalin* (Rome-Bari: Laterza, 1991).

17. The Moscow hotel where the members of the Comintern stayed. *Antonio Gramsci: Cronaca di un verdetto annunciato*, ed. Giuseppe Fiori (Rome: I Libri dell'Unità, 1994), 11.

18. Charged with judging offenses against the legal entity of the State, this tribunal functioned from 1927 to 1943. It judged 5,619 people, 5,496 of whom were condemned to a total of 27,735 years in prison or exile; 42 were condemned to death and 31 were executed.

19. Dario Bocca and Mauro Canali, *L'informatore: Silone, i comunisti e la polizia* (Milan-Trento: Luni, 2000).

20. Cited by Mauro Canali, *Il tradimento. Gramsci, Togliatti e la verità negata* (Venice: Marsilio, 2013), 63.

21. The summaries of Gramsci's three interrogations were published by Domenico Zucàro, *Vita del carcere*, 123–31.

22. The trial was covered by a foreign correspondent for the *Manchester Guardian*, a journalist for the *Petit Parisien*, as well as by a representative of the TASS Soviet news agency (the last one arrived only on the third day of the trial).

23. Gramsci to Tatiana Schucht, April 23, 1933, *LFP*, 2:289.

24. Emilio De Bono (1866–1944) was a general who joined the PNF in 1922. He was one of the organizers of the March on Rome. General director of security and head of the Milice, he was considered one of those responsible for the assassination of Matteotti. Then he made a career as governor of Tripolitania, then as minister of the colonies. As a marshal of Italy, he didn't play more than a supporting role within the regime. He voted for Grandi's motion to overthrow Mussolini. Arrested in October 1943 by the partisans of the Italian Social Republic, he was executed by firing squad on January 11, 1944.

25. These three quotations are cited in Zucàro, *Vita del carcere*, 51, 53, 133.

26. The harshness of Terracini's sentence was not only due to his tenacity during the trial but also because he was perceived as the best organizer in the PCdI. He would remain in prison, then in exile, until 1943.

27. The quoted phrase comes from a letter Tatiana Schucht addressed to Piero Sraffa on February 11, 1933.

28. Quoted in a letter from Gramsci to Tatiana Schucht, December 5, 1932, *LFP*, 2:237.

29. Much ink has been spilled about this "discovery," with some researchers having supported, without proof, the idea that Spriano had surreptitiously slipped these three documents, which had been in the PCI's possession, in an envelope from the archives of the Fascist police so he could cut short the polemics surrounding the publication of the incomplete *Prison Letters*. On this episode, see Canali, *Il tradimento*, 84–85.

30. After World War II, the PCdI became the PCI.

31. Gramsci to Julia Schucht, April 30, 1928, *LFP*, 1:201.

32. Tatiana Schucht to Julia Schucht, May 14, 1924, in Tatiana Schucht, *Lettere ai familiari* (Rome: Editori Riuniti, 1991), 40.

33. Cited in Canali, *Il tradimento*, 87.

34. This report is composed of two typed documents, respectively titled "Rapporto Gennaro" and "Riservata da Gennaro." It was discovered in the Comintern archives in July 2003 by historian Silvio Pons.

35. Cited in Angelo Rossi and Giuseppe Vacca, *Gramsci tra Mussolini e Stalin* (Rome: Fazi, 2007), 214.

36. Gramsci to Tatiana, December 5, 1932, *LFP*, 2:237–38.

37. Canali, *Il tradimento*, 90.

38. Gramsci to Tatiana, February 27, 1933, *LFP*, 2:276.

39. For a good summary of Tatiana Schucht's attempts to shed light on this affair and, in particular, to clarify the role Palmiro Togliatti played, see Canali, *Il tradimento*, 165–81, and Silvio Pons, "L'affare Gramsci-Togliatti' a Mosca (1938–1941)," *Studi storici*, no. 45-1 (2004): 83–117, as well as Franco Lo Piparo, *I due carceri di Gramsci: La prigione fascista e il labirinto comunista* (Rome: Donzelli, 2012).

40. On this theory, see Piparo, *I due carceri di Gramsci*, 16.

41. Italics ours. The insertion of the adverb "always" (*sempre*) at the end of the sentence reinforces the sentiment of dedication to Gramsci.

42. In 1988, Gorbachev would consign these documents to Alessandro Natta, who was the leader of the PCI at the time, during a visit to the USSR. Without questioning the authenticity of these archives, Paolo Spriano, who examined them first, just before his death, was perplexed by the fact that these texts were translated into Italian, and that a trip to the USSR was necessary to verify the originals. As I write this (in May 2017), I am unaware of whether this step has been taken. To the best of my knowledge, it has not.

43. Document reprinted by Canali in *Il tradimento*, 249. Italics ours.

44. This exchange could have taken place after the Soviet icebreaker *Krassine* had found, in July 1928, the survivors of the dirigible *Italia*, the victim of a tragic accident above the North Pole. At the time, Togliatti and Grieco asked Bukharin to work toward the development of a plan to liberate Gramsci, but the Bolshevik leader's disgrace, in autumn 1928, nipped theses plans in the bud.

45. Piero Sraffa to Angelo Tasca, October 2, 1927, cited in Jean-Pierre Potier, *Piero Sraffa: Unorthodox Economist (1898–1983)* (London: Routledge, 1991), 25.

46. G. Vacca, *Vita e pensieri di Antonio Gramsci, 1926–1937* (Turin: Einaudi, 2014), 79.

47. Piero Sraffa to Tatiana Schucht, September 18, 1937, reprinted in Gramsci, *Lettere dal carcere* (Turin: Einaudi, 1947), 646.

48. Angelo D'Orsi, *Gramsci. Una nuova biografia* (Milan: Feltrinelli, 2017), 248.

49. Vacca, *Vita e pensieri*, 385.

50. This is the case unless we see Julia as a metaphor for Soviet Russia and for the reality of communism, which Gramsci intended to disavow on both philosophical and political levels—this is the hypothesis put forward by Franco Lo Piparo in his book *I due carceri di Gramsci* [Gramsci's Two Prisons].

51. Cited in Paolo Spriano, *Antonio Gramsci and the Party: The Prison Years*, trans. John Fraser (London: Lawrence and Wishart, 1979), 161.

52. Tatiana Schucht to Piero Sraffa, February 11, 1933, cited in Canali, *Il tradimento*, 90.

53. On this episode, which we can't justify presenting in full in a biography of Gramsci, see note 39 of this chapter. Let us simply remember that *the*

infamous letter is a key element in the investigation ordered by the Comintern, under the care of Stella Blagoeva, against Togliatti's wishes. Excluded from the governing body of the Comintern, Togliatti was sent under Dimitrov's orders to Oufa, before returning to Italy in spring 1943.

54. Paolo Spriano, *Gramsci in carcere e il partito* (Rome: Editori Riuniti, 1977), 23–34.

55. Aldo Natoli, "Gramsci in carcere, il partito, il Comintern," *Belfagor* 13 (March 31, 1988): 167–88, and Natoli, *Antigone e il prigioniero* (Turin: Einaudi, 1990).

56. See note 39 of this chapter.

57. Another reading, which is very much in the minority and strongly contested, is the one proposed by Luciano Canfora, who sees Piero Sraffa as "*the only source* for Gramsci's suspicions against Togliatti," in Canfora, *Spie, URSS, antifascismo*, 121. Italics in original.

58. Rossi and Vacca, *Gramsci tra Mussolini e Stalin*, 164.

59. Aldo Agosti, *Palmiro Togliatti* (Turin: Einaudi, 1996), 91 and passim.

60. D'Orsi, *Gramsci. Una nuova biografia*, 229.

61. Giorgio Amendola (1907–80), the son of Giovanni Amendola, leader of the Aventine Secession, became a member of the PCdI in 1929. A militant anti-Fascist, he was elected as a Communist deputy in 1948 and remained one until his death. A figure of the right wing of that political family, he played an important role in promoting Eurocommunism.

62. Cited in Fiori, *Gramsci, Togliatti, Stalin*, 9–10.

Chapter Eight

1. After the PCdI was outlawed by the Fascist regime, it maintained a clandestine network in Italy and created a center for its leadership in France.

2. Gramsci to Tatiana Schucht, August 26, 1927, in Gramsci, *Lettere dal carcere, 1926–1937* (Turin: Einaudi, 1965), 109.

3. Gramsci to Tatiana Schucht, March 26, 1927, *Letters from Prison*, ed. Frank Rosengarten, trans. Raymond Rosenthal, 2 vols. (New York: Columbia University Press, 1994), 1:87 (hereafter *LFP*).

4. One of the main anti-Fascist political parties.

5. Aldo Natoli, *Antigone e il prigioniero* (Turin: Einaudi, 1994).

6. A religious order founded in the seventeenth century with the goal of educating young people.

7. Antonio Gramsci to Carlo Gramsci, August 13, 1928, in *Lettere dal carcere*, 205.

8. This was the case with Vito Semerano, whom Domenico Zucàro met with during his inquiry into Gramsci's last years.

9. Antonio Gramsci, *Istanza del detenuto Antonio Gramsci, n° 7047 a S. E. Novelli, direttore generale delle case di prevenzione e pena*, June 27, 1933, cited

in Ruggero Giacomini, *Il Giudice e il prigioniero: Il carcere di Antonio Gramsci* (Rome: Castelvecchi, 2014), 214–15.

10. Domenico Zucàro, who met him after World War II, describes the vitriol of a man who, expressing sudden amnesia, cared much more about his comfort and his income than he did about the Hippocratic oath.

11. Tatiana Schucht to Piero Sraffa, July 9, 1933, cited in Gianni Francioni, "Un labyrinthe de papier (introduction à la philologie gramscienne)," https://journals.openedition.org/laboratoireitalien/1053, n. 50.

12. Gramsci to Tatiana Schucht, February 20, 1933, *LFP*, 2:272.

13. Angelo Rossi and Giuseppe Vacca, *Gramsci tra Mussolini e Stalin* (Rome: Fazi, 2007), 20.

14. This notion of an organic intellectual, which should not be reduced to the idea of intellectuals educated by and for the PCdI, is mainly theorized in notebook 4 (May 1930–September 1932). Gramsci prepared a course for his party's school, a course that was published in 1930 in *Stato Operaio*, the theoretical review of the PCdI.

15. Account from the Communist prisoner Mario Garuglieri, cited by Giacomini, *Il Giudice e il prigioniero*, 277.

16. Angelo D'Orsi, *Gramsci. Una nuova biografia* (Milan: Feltrinelli, 2018), 313.

17. Cited in Giacomini, *Il Giudice e il prigioniero*, 224.

18. See Paolo Spriano, *Gramsci: The Prison Years* (London: Lawrence and Wishart, 1979), 71. For the full quote in Italian, see Giuseppe Vacca, *Vita e pensieri di Antonio Gramsci* (Turin: Einaudi, 2014), 131.

19. If Gramsci attributed this criminal gesture to communist prisoners, Pertini thinks it wasn't the case. It's also important to remember the role that was probably played by OVRA agitators.

20. To this day, Ceresa's memo has not been found in the Comintern archives. The account reported here is from Ercole Piacentini, another prisoner in Turi during the time Gramsci was incarcerated there. The account is from a letter that Piacentini wrote to Umberto Cardia on November 23, 1988, cited in Vacca, *Vita e pensieri de Antonio Gramsci*, 134.

21. Gramsci to Tatiana Schucht, July 13, 1931, *LFP*, 2:45.

22. This phrase, in German in Gramsci's text, is an explicit reference to Goethe's poem that bears this title.

23. Gramsci to Tatiana Schucht, March 19, 1927, *LFP*, 1:83–84.

24. Gramsci didn't follow this plan to the letter, even if he did cover each of these four themes in his *Prison Notebooks*.

25. A decree issued in autumn 1932, more or less enforced, made it obligatory to have a guard present for a conversation between two prisoners to take place.

26. Julien Benda was not opposed to intellectuals being activists on the one condition that they respected what was just and true. On the Gramscian reading of Benda, see notebook 3, §2 (May–October 1930).

27. This debate principally centers on the dating of notebook 14. In favor of the first theory, see Francioni, "Un labyrinthe de papier," n. 66, and in favor of the second, Giorgio Fabre, *Lo scambio. Come Gramsci non fu liberato* (Palermo: Sellerio Editore, 2015), 374–93.

28. See our bibliography of Gramsci's works.

29. The results of this dating work can be found in Giuseppe Cospito, "L'Edizione nazionale dei Quaderni del carcere," in the appendix to the article, https://journals.openedition.org/laboratoireitalien/1049. We refer to this dating when we cite quotations from the *Prison Notebooks*.

30. Francioni, "Un labyrinthe de papier," paragraphs 62, 70.

31. Ibid., paragraph 71.

32. Ibid., note 10.

33. Franco Lo Piparo, *I due carceri di Gramsci: La prigione fascista e il labirinto comunista* (Rome: Donzelli, 2012).

34. Cited in Vacca, *Vita e pensieri de Antonio Gramsci*, 324.

35. Fabio Frosini, "Le travail caché du prisonnier entre 'littérature' et 'politique.' Quelques réflexions sur les 'sources' des Cahiers de prison d'Antonio Gramsci," https://journals.openedition.org/laboratoireitalien/1064.

36. By coded language, we don't mean a cipher, but rather allusive language that reveals hidden meanings.

37. "We are summarizing this episode in broad strokes here. When Dante, guided by Virgil, moves through the tombs of heretics, he sees two 'compatriots' rising up, Farinata Uberti, leader of the Ghibellines and a political adversary, and Cavalcante Cavalcanti, the father of his friend Guido. Cavalcante is astonished that his son is not there, and Dante suggests to him that Guido, an epicurean and Guelph, would not know how to accommodate the presence of Virgil, a pre-Christian poet and a partisan of the concept of empire:

> I answered: 'My own powers have not brought me;
> he who awaits me there, leads me through here
> perhaps to one your Guido did disdain.'

> His words, the nature of his punishment—
> these had already let me read his name;
> therefore, my answer was so fully made.

> Then suddenly erect, he cried: 'What's that:
> He "did disdain"? He is not still alive?
> The sweet light does not strike against his eyes?'

A despair to which Farinata would give Dante the key, after having announced to him that he, too, would experience exile: if the dead can see into the future, they have a farsighted perspective on the present." From Robert Paris, *Antonio Gramsci, Cahiers de prison, n. 1 à 5* (Paris: Gallimard, 1996), 642n. [I have used Allen Mandelbaum's English translation of Dante's *Inferno* here. —Trans.]

38. Gramsci to Tatiana Schucht, September 20, 1931, *LFP*, 2:74.

39. Antonio Gramsci, *Prison Notebooks*, trans. Joseph Buttigieg (New York: Columbia University Press, 1996), vol. 2, 247 (notebook 4, §78).

40. On the contribution of Gramscian interpretations of linguistics to Marxist theory, see Giancarlo Schirru, "Linguistique et philosophie de la praxis chez Gramsci," https://journals.openedition.org/laboratoireitalien/1059.

41. Romain Descendre et Jean-Claude Zancarini, "De la traduction à la traductibilité: Un outil d'émancipation théorique," https://journals.openedition .org/laboratoireitalien/1065, paragraph 1.

42. Ibid., paragraph 23.

43. Antonio Gramsci, "*La Stampa* and the Fascists," *L'Ordine Nuovo*, July 24, 1921, in *Pre-prison Writings*, ed. Richard Bellamy, trans. Virginia Cox (Cambridge: Cambridge University Press, 1994), 220.

44. Antonio Gramsci, *Prison Notebooks*, 2:44–45.

45. This analysis is shared by Angelo Tasca, Ignazio Silone, Luigi Salvatorelli, and even Guido Dorso, who all theorized, during the same time period, the coessential link between Fascism and the petite bourgeoisie.

46. Antonio Gramsci, *Prison Notebooks*, 3:107–8.

47. Alessio Gagliardi, "Tra rivoluzione e controrivoluzione. L'interpretazione gramsciana del fascismo," https://journals.openedition.org/laboratoireitalien /1062, paragraph 25. "According to Gramsci, a totalitarian politics existed either when power was assumed after a revolution by the force of the workers, and he naturally was referring to the USSR; or in the opposite case, the case of Fascism, when the State is conquered by a political force that wants to block the success of the revolution, putting in place a reactionary politics."

48. Vincenzo Cuoco, *Historical Essay on the Neapolitan Revolution of 1799*, trans. David Gibbons (Toronto: University of Toronto Press, 2014), 108.

49. Gagliardi, "Tra rivoluzione e controrivoluzione," paragraph 42.

50. On corporatism, see S. Cassese, *L'Italie, le fascisme et l'État. Continuités et paradoxes* (Paris: Éditions rue d'Ulm, 2014) as well as the excellent preface by Éric Vial.

51. Gramsci thought that the absence of agrarian reform and the weakness of Italy's industrialization constituted serious obstacles to this transformation.

52. A war of maneuver from August to September 1914, then from March to November 1918, a war of position from November 1914 to March 1918.

53. George Hoare and Nathan Sperber, *An Introduction to Antonio Gramsci* (London: Bloomsbury, 2016), 56.

54. Vacca, *Vita e pensieri de Antonio Gramsci*, 169.

55. Ibid., 175.

Epilogue

1. Cited in Claudio Natoli, "Gramsci in carcere: Le campagne per la liberazione, il partito, l'Internazionale (1932–1933)," *Studi storici* 2 (1995): 310. All the phrases in brackets are ours. The same is true for the other expressions in brackets translating the symptoms affecting Gramsci into contemporary language.

2. Gramsci to Tatiana Schucht, August 29, 1932, cited in Giuseppe Fiori, *Antonio Gramsci: Life of a Revolutionary*, trans. Tom Nairn (New York: Verso, 1990), 268.

3. Cited in Natoli, "Gramsci in carcere," 341.

4. Cited in ibid., 342.

5. Filippo Saporito seemed little disposed toward compassion for Gramsci. Taking advantage of his arrival in the Turi prison, he examined a few of Gramsci's *Notebooks*, from which Saporito drew the following opinion: "incoherent concepts," "nebulousness," "nonsense." Cited in Gianni Francioni, "Un labyrinthe de papier (introduction à la philologie gramscienne)," https://journals .openedition.org/laboratoireitalien/1053, paragraph 20.

6. Cited in Vico Faggi, ed., *Sandro Pertini: Sei condanne, due evasion* (Milan: Mondadori, 1974), 192.

7. Angelo Rossi and Giuseppe Vacca, *Gramsci tra Mussolini e Stalin* (Rome: Fazi, 2007), 163.

8. Gramsci to Tatiana Schucht, September 19, 1932, *Letters from Prison*, ed. Frank Rosengarten, trans. Raymond Rosenthal, 2 vols. (New York: Columbia University Press, 1994), 2:212 (hereafter *LFP*).

9. Angelo Sraffa to Piero Sraffa, May 29, 1933, cited in Paolo Spriano, *Antonio Gramsci and the Party: The Prison Years*, trans. John Fraser (London: Lawrence and Wishart, 1979), 175–76.

10. Gramsci to Tatiana Schucht, May 16, 1933, *LFP*, 2:295.

11. "Gramsci en danger de mort," *L'Humanité*, May 9, 1933; "Gramsci ne pourra survivre longtemps dans les conditions actuelles! déclare le professeur Arcangeli," *L'Humanité*, May 11, 1933.

12. Palmiro Togliatti to Piero Sraffa, May 24, 1933, cited in Spriano, *Antonio Gramsci and the Party*, 173.

13. While he was working for the Comintern in Bulgaria, Dimitrov (1882–1949) was accused of complicity in the Reichstag fire. He was arrested on March 9, 1933. During his trial, he defended himself with such skill that he was acquitted. He acquired so much global renown on this occasion that he became

General Secretary of the Comintern in 1934. He remained in that post until the dissolution of that organization in 1943.

14. See his letters to Tatiana Schucht from September 3 and October 29, 1933.

15. Gramsci to Julia Gramsci-Schucht, January 25, 1936, *LFP*, 2:354.

16. See Giorgio Fabre, *Lo scambio. Come Gramsci non fu liberato* (Palermo: Sellerio, 2015).

17. The story, according to which he would have had to distract a guard while a comrade surreptitiously slipped the notebooks into Gramsci's trunks, is quite dramatic but seems unlikely.

18. Giovanni Germanetto had interceded at the first congress of Soviet writers, which was held in Moscow from August 17 to September 1, 1934, inviting the assembled to continue the struggle to liberate incarcerated revolutionaries, including Gramsci. It was on this occasion that he had solicited Romain Rolland to write an article in Gramsci's favor; see below.

19. Cited in Mauro Canali, *Il tradimento. Gramsci, Togliatti e la verità negata* (Venice: Marsilio, 2013), 158.

20. It has been exceptionally studied by Claudio Natoli, "Le campagne per la liberazione di Gramsci, il PCD'I e l'Internazionale (1934)," in *Studi storici* 1 (1999): 77–156.

21. François Furet, *Le passé d'une illusion. Essai sur l'idée communiste au XXe siècle* (Paris: Laffont, 1995), 357.

22. Massimo Mastrogregori, *I due prigionieri. Gramsci e Moro e la storia del Novecento italiano* (Genoa: Marietti, 2008). This comparison has been criticized by Ruggero Giacomini, *Il Giudice e il prigioniero* (Rome: Castelvecchi, 2014), 191.

23. Romain Rolland: "The Nibelungesque extravagance of fires, pyres of books, orgies of torments and massacres, has dulled the patina of the heroes of bludgeons and castor oil." "Pour ceux qui meurent dans les prisons de Mussolini: Antonio Gramsci" (September 1934), in *Quinze ans de combat (1919–1934)* (Paris: Éditions Rieder, 1935), 221.

24. "We are not people for whom the German murders will erase Matteotti." Ibid., 222.

25. The *confino di polizia* meant a stricter surveillance by the authorities than simple exile (*confino*).

26. Gramsci to Mussolini, "Request of the prisoner Antonio Gramsci, now held under surveillance in Dr. Cusumano's clinic at Formia," cited in Spriano, *Antonio Gramsci and the Party*, 177.

27. Cited in Canali, *Il tradimento*, 156 n. 61.

28. List reported in Giacomini, *Il Giudice e il prigioniero*, 241.

29. Angelo D'Orsi, *Gramsci. Una nuova biografia* (Milan: Feltrinelli, 2017), 355.

30. Account from Piero Sraffa (May 1973) reported by Maria-Antoinetta Macciocchi, *Pour Gramsci* (Paris: Le Seuil, 1974), 287.

31. Tatiana Schucht to Teresina Gramsci, May 18, 1936, cited in Franco Lo Piparo, *I due carceri di Gramsci: La prigione fascista e il labirinto comunista* (Rome: Donzelli, 2012).

32. Ibid., 63.

33. From 1946 on, April 25 became the date of Italy's national holiday. During this day of celebration, the Italians commemorate the Liberation and the end of the Occupation of Italy by the Nazis and their Fascist allies. This date was chosen because on April 25, 1945, the cities of Turin, Milan, and Genoa were liberated by the partisans.

34. Tatiana Schucht to Giulia Schucht, May 12, 1937, cited in Domenico Zucàro, *Vita del carcere di Antonio Gramsci* (Milan-Rome: Edizioni *Avanti!*, 1954), 101.

35. Though it makes sense to remove the preposterous theory of an assassination perpetrated by the Soviets or by Togliatti (what would have been the motive for such an action? how could it have been realized while the clinic was permanently guarded by a dozen police officers?), the theory of poisoning has recently come back into fashion via Ruggero Giacomini (see his work *Il Giudice e il prigioniero*, 263–70). He puts forward several arguments, particularly that Antonio Gramsci's family members always believed he had been poisoned—hence his vomiting—and that the Fascists had never hesitated to physically eliminate their opponents—the Rosselli brothers were killed a few weeks after Gramsci's death, on June 19, 1937, by La Cagoule on the orders of Mussolini at Bagnoles-de-l'Orne. A moving ceremony was held on June 7, 2017, in front of the monument erected to their memory on the same place where the cowards executed them. Nonetheless, the vast majority of historians believe that Gramsci died from the results of a stroke.

36. We're grateful to Mauro Canali for having asked these questions, which are far from anecdotal.

Translator's Note
and Acknowledgments

I am grateful to the scholars who took the time to read full or partial drafts of this translation, particularly Alice Kaplan, Michael Denning, Nadia Urbinati, and Dolores Hayden. Walid Bouchakour provided excellent research assistance despite library closures, sourcing quotations during a pandemic. This text has greatly benefited from Dylan Joseph Montanari's editorial eye and his translations of the original Italian quotations when no English translation was available.

The world of Gramsci scholarship is multilingual, and I have done my best to refer to and cite texts in their original language when an English version does not exist. In a very few cases, I have adjusted the existing English translations of quotations for readability or accuracy. There were also a few cases where, rather than substituting the Italian versions, I kept the author's French-language sources because they represented the archival work of a French scholar, and the materials are not yet available in English.

Because of the evolving nature of party nomenclature, I have tried to refer to organizations, parties, and institutions with the names they had at the time of the events the author describes. For example, Petrograd became Saint Petersburg, but the city is referred to by both names in the text, depending on the time period. The same is true for the iterations of the Russian Communist Party's name. Whenever possible, I've used the existing English translations for theoretical concepts in Marxism and in Gramsci's work, though there is by no means a total consensus.

Last, I am grateful to have had the opportunity to work on this project and to appreciate that, among many other things, Gramsci was also a translator and cared deeply about the transmission of ideas across linguistic borders.

Index

Matteotti, Giacomo (*cont.*)
147–51, 285n24, 292n24; role in
PSU, 118
maximalists, 70–71, 78, 83, 106–7,
129–30, 156. See also *rigidi*
Mazzini, Giuseppe, 17, 28, 169, 210
Melani, Corrado, 191
Mensheviks, 77, 155
Mersù, Gustavo, 149
Mezzogiorno, 3, 6, 13, 20–21, 36–40,
142–44, 153, 158, 167
Milza, Pierre, 151
miner's strike in Buggerru, 18, 20–21
Misiano, Francesco, 109
Missiroli, Mario, 73
Modigliani, Giuseppe-Emanuele, 62,
107, 276n32
Mondo, Il, 143, 170, 272n1
Montagnana, Mario, 113
Montecitorio, 152, 157, 159, 183–84
MOPR (international red aid), 72,
213–14, 243–44, 246, 249
Morgari, Oddino, 76
Moro, Aldo, 249
Münzenberg, Willi, 249–50
Mussolini, Benito: attempted assassinations of, 182, 246; Fascist repression by, 149, 162, 165, 182–84, 235, 247, 293n35; Gramsci, interactions with, 63, 157–59, 169, 177, 202–4, 211, 215, 218, 225, 240, 245, 248–52; rise to power, 110, 119, 130, 140, 150–54, 280n6; role in PSI, 40, 47–z50, 68

Natoli, Aldo, 207–8
Natoli, Claudio, 244
Natta, Alessandro, 286n42
Nenni, Pietro, 129, 166, 278n19
New Economic Policy, 111, 117, 127,
170
Niceforo, Alfredo, 20
Nicholas II (tsar), 76

Nitti, Francesco Saverio, 277n46
Novelli, Giovanni, 216, 239–40, 242, 246

occupation of the factories, 98–102
October Revolution, 73–75, 161
Olivetti, Camillo, 94
Ordine Nuovo, L': articles by Gramsci
in, 62, 84–89, 100, 105, 138; establishment of, 83–85; ideological
positions of, 77, 81, 91–98, 107, 114,
139, 140–42; PCdI and, 101, 108,
112, 161; staff of, 44, 57, 102, 107,
135; third run of, 135
Orlando, Vittorio Emanuele, 279n35
OVRA (Fascist political police), 189, 196, 199, 214, 225,
246–48, 252, 288n19

Pacelli, Eugenio, 201
Pact of Friendship, 244
Panié, Felice, 39
Papini, Giovanni, 61
Paris, Robert, 87, 289n37
parliamentary immunity, 136, 154, 181–84
Parmegiani, Giovanni, 215
Parodi, Giovanni, 98
Partito Nazionale Fascista. See PNF
Passarge family, 181
Pastore, Annibale, 23, 32, 34, 38, 272n4
Pastore, Ottavio, 32, 39, 56, 62, 82, 108,
135, 271n21, 278n14
PCdI: Comintern and, 117–22, 131, 204;
formation of, 50, 96, 100–101, 104,
107; Gramsci in prison and, 205–11,
213–14, 220–22, 240–46, 250, 254;
Gramsci's role in, 108–14, 132–35,
138–44, 149–59, 167, 200; leadership
of, 102, 145, 184, 193, 199; operation
of, 108, 136, 159–64, 168–69; polemics within, 127–31, 146–49, 171–77;
underground existence of, 192, 228
Péguy, Charles, 51

Pertini, Alessandro (Sandro), 219, 221, 240

Piacentini, Ercole, 288n20

Piazza Carlina, xvi, 24, 108

Pirandello, Luigi, 60, 223

Pius IX (pope), 34, 37

Pius XI (pope), 202, 204

Platone, Felice, 82, 226

PNF, 104, 109, 150–51, 168, 183, 280n6, 285n24

Pons, Silvio, 207, 285n34

Popolo d'Italia, Il, 48, 50

popular fronts policy, 249

Potemkin, Vladimir, 248

Prampolini, Camillo, 45

Prezzolini, Giuseppe, 61

Prison Notebooks (Gramsci): ideas in, 13, 27, 36, 45, 58, 74, 102, 128, 169, 176, 186, 231–35, 254; legacy of, 205, 256; style of, 228–31; writing of, 139, 208, 210–11, 220, 223–28

PSI: formation of, 6; Gramsci's role in, 57, 68–73, 81, 91, 161; intransigent wing of, 40, 70, 72; leadership of, 47–48, 82, 95, 101; reformist wing of, 37, 65, 70; schisms within, 96–98, 103–7; Turin section of, 39, 68, 73, 82, 91, 98; unionist wing of, 21; WWI and, 48–56, 63, 65

Puccinelli, Angelo, 211

Puccinelli, Vittorio, 241, 251–52, 255

Quisisana clinic, 252–56

Rabezzana, Petro, 109

Radek, Karl, 105, 111–12, 118, 127, 129, 148

Rákosi, Mátyás, 106, 119, 128

Ransome, Arthur, 77

Rapone, Leonardo, 75

Rappoport, Charles, 90

Rassegna Communista, 108

Ravazzoli, Paolo, 163–64

Ravera, Camilla, 163–64, 213

RCP, 155, 161–66, 169–76, 283n41

RCP(b), 120, 125, 127, 129, 131, 147–48

Red Peasant International. *See* Krestintern (Red Peasant International)

Red Week, 47

Repossi, Luigi, 154

Resta, Giuseppe, 216

"Revolution against 'Capital,' The" (Gramsci), 73, 78, 80, 89, 96

revolutionary syndicalism, 42, 89, 92

Riboldi, Ezio, 184, 189, 279n27

rigidi, 68, 109

Rigola, Rinaldo, 70

Robinson Crusoe (Defoe), 16

Rocco, Alfredo, 157, 243, 282n34

Rolland, Romain, 67, 245, 249–50, 292n18

Romani, Dante, 189, 191

Rosner, Alfred, 90

Rosselli, Carlo, 140, 166, 250, 293n35

Rosselli, Nello, 250, 293n35

Rossi, Angelo, 217

Russian Communist Party. *See* RCP

Russian Revolution, 57, 73, 75–76, 80

Salandra, Antonio, 38, 47, 151, 158, 232, 279n35, 282n30

Salvatorelli, Luigi, 290n45

Salvemini, Gaetano, 17, 31, 33, 36, 39–40, 50, 62, 167, 271n21

Sanna, Carlo, 190

Sanna, Giovanni, 108, 167

San Vittore judicial prison, 187–89, 191, 193, 200–201, 209–13, 215, 223, 237

Saporiti, Alessandro, 195

Saporito, Filippo, 239, 291n5

Sardo, Giuseppe, 194

Sbaffi, Emanuele, 255

Schucht, Apollon, 120–22

Schucht, Eugenia, 119–23, 126, 246

"Workers' Democracy" (Gramsci), 84, 86, 88, 93, 96, 100

World War I, 6, 19, 30, 35–36, 43, 55, 58, 63–65, 82, 98, 104, 186, 190, 235, 273n22

World War II, xvii, 82, 149, 214

Zamboni, Anteo, 182

Zamenhof, L. L., 231

Zanardelli, Giuseppe, 36

Zancarini, Jean-Claude, 230

Zasulich, Vera, 79

Zimmerwald Conference, 68

Zini, Zino, 109, 137

Zinoviev, Grigori, 90, 105–6, 117–19, 128–31, 146–48, 155–56, 164, 169–74

Zucàro, Domenico, 188–89, 191, 194, 288n10